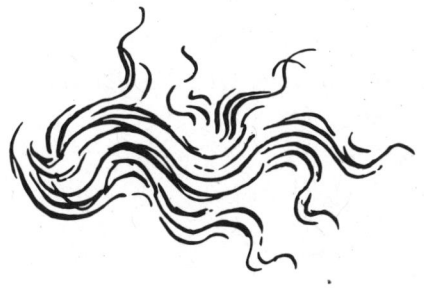

TABLE OF CONTENTS

- 6   ANITA SHAPIRA
  Statehood and the Jews

- 31   OKSANA FOROSTYNA
  Another Country

- 58   CHRISTIAN LORENTZEN
  In Dreams Begin Responsibilities: A Memoir

- 74   ROBERT B. PIPPIN
  The Clarifying Obscurity of Robert Bresson

- 104   ALAN JENKINS
  Four Poems in Memory of Marie Colvin, 1956–2012:
  A Night Sail
  Smoke
  Poster Girl
  Siren's Song

- 116   JAMES McAULEY
  Memory's Cellar

- 142   KENDA MUTONGI
  Living by the Roundabout

- 157   JACK GOLDSMITH
  The Supreme Court Wars: America and Israel

- 178   MORTEN HØI JENSEN
  The Good European

200 CHAIM NACHMAN BIALIK
God Has Not Shown Me

203 WILLIAM DERESIEWICZ
The Quality To Be Tragic

221 ADRIAN NATHAN WEST
The World as an Institute

246 ANNA BALLAN
Forever Taking Leave

283 MIRON BIAŁOSZEWSKI
Gray Eminences of Rapture
This Apartment Can Be Inspired
My Jacobs of Weariness
Self-Verified
Nights of Inseparation

290 HELEN VENDLER
Artless Art

310 CELESTE MARCUS
The Shape of a Question

329 LEON WIESELTIER
The Rise of Narrative and The Fall of Persuasion

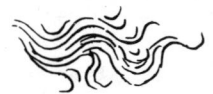

FALL 2023
VOLUME 4, NUMBER 1

EDITOR
LEON WIESELTIER

MANAGING EDITOR
CELESTE MARCUS

PUBLISHER
BILL REICHBLUM

JOURNAL DESIGN
WILLIAM VAN RODEN

WEB DESIGN
BRICK FACTORY

EDITORIAL ASSISTANT
DARIUS RUBIN

Liberties is a publication of the Liberties Journal Foundation, a nonpartisan 501(c)(3) organization based in Washington, D.C. devoted to educating the general public about the history, current trends, and possibilities of culture and politics. The Foundation seeks to inform today's cultural and political leaders, deepen the understanding of citizens, and inspire the next generation to participate in the democratic process and public service.

FOUNDATION BOARD
ALFRED H. MOSES, *Chair*
PETER BASS
BILL REICHBLUM

Engage
To learn more please go to libertiesjournal.com

Subscribe
To subscribe or with any questions about your subscription, please go to libertiesjournal.com

ISBN 979-8-9854302-2-6
ISSN 2692-3904

EDITORIAL OFFICES
1101 30th Street NW, Suite 310
Washington, DC 20007

DIGITAL
@READLIBERTIES
LIBERTIESJOURNAL.COM

Liberties

ANITA SHAPIRA

Statehood and the Jews

The State of Israel recently celebrated its seventy-fifth year of existence. If someone had told us way back in 1948 that the country would count nearly ten million people as its citizens, eight million of them Jews; that it would lead the world in technological innovation; that it would be a regional superpower — we would have told them to keep dreaming. Of the countries founded in the era of decolonization, Israel has been one of the most successful, in spite of the intractable Israeli-Palestinian conflict. But in the past year, barely the blink of an eye in the state's existence, the Israeli government and its prime minister Benjamin Netanyahu have been trampling and traducing the hard-won achievements of numerous governments. They are undermining the economy and scaring off foreign investors, leading to a devaluation of the currency and to global financial institutions losing confidence in Israel, a country which until recently had been considered a pillar of stability and good governance in a part of the world famous for instability and poor governance. Worst of all, they are generating a profound rift, a terrifying chasm, within Israeli society, the likes of which we have never witnessed before.

There is something magical, in Jewish history, about the number seventy-five: the two independent Jewish kingdoms that existed in the Land of Israel in antiquity each lasted about that long. Both were conquered by powerful empires that ruled the region. From the east came the Mesopotamians, Assyria and Babylonia, and then from the west came Rome. The Israelite commonwealth and then the kingdom of Judea refused to make peace with foreign rule, so they revolted to restore their independence. The Jewish population typically split into two large camps, the peacemakers and the warmongers. Those spoiling for a fight usually carried the day. A traditional Jewish prayer states that "we have been exiled from our land on account of our sins." This encapsulates a truth even for the non-religious: internecine fights between moderates and extremists are usually won by the latter, who invite imperial wrath upon them both. A lack of political shrewdness, an inability to maneuver between great powers, and a tendency to value extreme positions are what led to our great national tragedies in the past. The Jewish propensity to duel over trivialities, to defy authority, and to schismatize — we have a veritable gift for schism — brought about the downfall of the Jewish kingdoms of the First and Second Temple eras.

The Zionist movement was ambivalent about the Jewish revolts of antiquity. On the one hand, an emergent national movement needed heroes who embodied a refusal to accommodate themselves any longer to circumstances. On the other hand, Zionism was rational and pragmatic in its pursuit of realizing the impossible — the establishment of a modern Jewish polity in the Land of Israel — by shrewdly taking advantage of current realities rather than working to deny them or overturn them. Zionism existed in tension with itself: it aspired to change everything about Jewish existence, from language, culture, and daily living to the collective self-image and the image projected to non-Jews, while uneasily working within the political status quo, with those in power, first the Turks and then the British, to achieve its goals. This tension was an expression of the longing for national pride and Jewish resurgence coupled with the sober recognition that the world cannot be changed overnight even in an historical emergency, and that in the meantime one must locate fissures and opportunities in the present state of affairs to exploit in order to make the Zionist dream a reality.

Rabbi Yohanan ben Zakkai, in the first century BCE, who abandoned Jerusalem when it was under Roman siege to found a yeshiva in the coastal town of Yavneh, was spurned by Zionist myth as a weakling who was resigned to reality and capitulated to the strong. Instead the Zionists turned Masada into an emblem of strength and fortitude. Shimon Bar Kokhba and his rabbinic patron Rabbi Akiva, who declared him the long-awaited Messiah, were idolized by Zionists. Recall, though, that Judaism itself might have been defeated with Jerusalem if Rabbi Yohanan had not dissociated it from the holy city and made it portable, and that the courageous garrison of Masada died by mass suicide, and that the Bar

Kokhba revolt half a century later resulted in destruction and carnage on a far more massive scale than occurred during the original Judean revolt. Moreover, Rabbi Akiva did not have a monopoly on the identification of the Messiah, but dissenting voices, like those of most moderates, were lost in the clamor of the extremists.

One can admire the courage and the freedom struggles of zealots over the generations, but the significant historical fact is that the survival of the Jewish people was owed not to them but to their opponents. Masada became an integral Zionist symbol of strength only in the twentieth century; for two thousand years the tale of mass self-immolation languished in obscurity and Jewish culture was more or less indifferent to it. From its very inception, then, Zionism has been split between the admiration of defiance and self-sacrifice and the recognition of the need to work within the confines of reality by means of *realpolitik*.

Modern Zionism was founded as a secular cause by intellectuals and activists who had a broad European education and had been exposed to the nationalist currents blowing through Europe in the nineteenth century. The Zionist ideal of returning to the land of the Patriarchs, however, is not at all modern. It is deeply rooted in Jewish tradition, which is fundamentally religious. There has always been a dissonance within Zionism between the secular nationalist project of self-liberation, anchored in the modern world and the unique problems that it poses for Jews, and Judaism, which serves as the oldest justification for such a movement of return and restoration. As we will see below, some fundamentals of Israeli culture originated in the Jewish religion and were reconfigured by the secular movement, but their religious source was not forgotten.

Jewish history has had its fair share of messianic moments, in which the derogatorily named "false Messiahs" fomented uprisings that expressed the aspiration of an exiled, downtrodden people to reverse its fortunes. While Torah-observant Jews disavowed these attempts to "force the end," which is forbidden by the rabbis in the Talmud, the Zionist movement was satisfied to claim these failed attempts as its unlucky precursors. The flame burning for redemption had never sputtered out, even if the fires that flared now and then amounted to no more than a passing excitement. Zionists knew they had to be careful with this flame, because the hottest part was fueled by an eschatological fervor and could quickly consume everything. They had to channel it in a controlled burn, to inflame passions and excite practical activism without inviting catastrophe. The messianic ardor was reduced to as low a flame as possible without extinguishing it.

The old antisemitism had maligned the Jew as an unassimilable foreign body in the heart of the nation. Emancipation and the granting of equal rights to European Jewry were predicated on the Jews identifying themselves with the modern nation in which they lived. The majority of Jews in Western and Central Europe accepted this invitation to some measure of self-erasure and adopted the majority culture and way of life as their own. When a new antisemitism reared its head in the final quarter of the nineteenth century, it did not target the old Jew, the ultimate Other who could not be (and refused to be) incorporated in the larger society, but the new Jew who did as he was told, who spoke the language and partook of the culture and wanted nothing more than to be a patriot. The new hatred zeroed in on an ineradicable, essential difference: race.

The Jew was derided as a parasite feeding off the gracious

and vigorous host nation, for he could not create a country of his own. He offered nothing in return for sapping the strength of the host country because he would not work the land or take dirty jobs, and he used every artifice conceivable to avoid military service. He positioned himself in the middle class and selected an occupation that made use of his education, financial savviness, or cultural production (although his art was deemed distorted and "degenerate" and not an authentic expression of the folk or nation). The Jew, in the characterization of modern anti-Semites, was enfeebled and would take no risks. He did not set out past the frontier to discover new lands or to bring civilization and prosperity to the wilderness. The Jew was far too preoccupied with his money.

These stereotypes perturbed Theodor Herzl and like-minded Jewish intellectuals, especially when Jewish surnames were featured prominently in headlines about global financial scandals. Their most fervent desire was to restore Jewish pride, and Zionism was the means to do so. It would transform the image of the Jew from a confidence man and a free rider into a self-sufficient state-builder and a tamer of wastelands. This Jew would win the respect of non-Jews. Jewish socialists, especially the Russian *narodniks* whose motto was "going to the people," brought to Zionist ideology a deep yearning to build the land with one's own hands. The Jew would not establish his state on the backs of others, like the British and French colonialists who abused their local subjects. No, he would build it himself, with his own work, first and foremost by cultivating the land. In the early twentieth century, the new arrivals in the land treated tilling the earth with an almost religious reverence and idealized agricultural settlement as the makings of a utopia. Now the Jews would be like every other people and autonomously fill out the entire social and economic spectrum, thereby creating a model society.

In the land of Israel, Jews gave the lie to the antisemitic caricature of the Jewish leech. Jews worked the soil, built a society, and took up arms with bravery. They displayed creativity and persistence, exceptional talent and sacrifice, showing the world a new kind of Jew, the intellectual and the worker wrapped in one. But could he (and she) found a state that would endure? Well, seventy-five years have passed since Israel's creation, and it has weathered many crises. Yet how many years will it live beyond this birthday? About ten years ago I attended a lunch at the faculty club of Columbia University with Professor Rashid Khalidi, the noted Palestinian scholar. After exchanging pleasantries, he said to me: "You are like the Crusaders. In the end, you will disappear from Palestine. It is only a matter of time." Is that what will become of the Jewish state? The Arab wars to rid the land of its Jews certainly have not succeeded. What, then, is the current threat to the Jewish state?

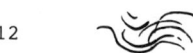

When the establishment of a Jewish state was in the works, Jews had to undertake massive projects and ventures, the likes of which they had not been involved in for two millennia. For the first time in a very long time, they had to constitute organs of government with genuine political power, forge the character of an independent polity, establish a judicial system, conduct diplomacy, establish an army. It was wartime, and discussions about the nature of the government of the state-to-be and the relationship between its legislative, executive, and judicial branches were thin. The institutions of the *yishuv*, or the Jewish community in Palestine prior to statehood, were run democratically, and this administrative framework was carried over to the newborn country, without anyone pausing to question it. Immediately, however, the truly novel question of the state's relationship to religion was raised. Previously, in exile under kings and lesser potentates, Jews sometimes had been granted autonomy, and those in charge of their affairs, the communal elders or notables, had run the community within a socio-religious framework. In the modern period, by contrast, the grip of the collective on the individual weakened, and Jewish rule, when it existed, followed the same general trend.

A new question was on the table. What would be the character of the country? What value system and what body of law would it follow? In 1947, most of the *yishuv* was secular, but they had been raised in religiously observant homes. A single generation separated them from religion. Accordingly, they adopted the trappings of Judaism and reworked them into national symbols. The calendar would naturally be the Jewish one with its holidays and festivals. Rituals marking the transitions from cradle to grave typically assumed the traditional form: circumcision, bar mitzvah, betrothal and marriage under a *huppah*, burial according to Jewish rites. The festivals took on a new cast: Passover became the rite of spring and the celebration of freedom; Pentecost, or Shavuot, the holiday of the first fruits (which, by Biblical command, were brought to the Temple on this festival); Tabernacles, or Sukkot, came to commemorate the stockpiling and enjoyment of the harvest; Hanukkah commemorated the national victory over the Greeks and the establishment of the Hasmonean dynasty in a Jewish kingdom. They reinvented traditions that they imbibed with their mothers' milk so that they would accord with modern sensibilities and the new national spirit. In public, religious freedom was the rule: one could keep the *mitzvot* or not, as one pleased. In the 1920s, there was huge debate over women's suffrage, which the Haredim, the ultra-Orthodox, strongly opposed, but the religious ultras were fighting a losing battle and had to come to grips with the full participation of women in political life.

Secularism was on the rise as religion was everywhere in decline. The Haredim were a small and weak minority in the land. Before World War II, they were vehemently opposed to Zionism. On the cusp of the state's creation, they scrambled to find a way to join the Jewish collective. Ben-Gurion wanted to present a united Jewish front to the United Nations General Assembly when the partition of Palestine would be decided. For that reason, he signed an agreement upholding the status quo, which granted Orthodox Jewry control over life-cycle events determining personal status, namely, marriage and divorce. (This essentially ratified an arrangement that dated back to Ottoman rule, under which the Jews were defined as a religious community known as a *millet*, and which was later confirmed by the British.) Agudath Israel, the rabbinical organization that represented the ultra-Orthodox, a community that had been nearly wiped out in the Holocaust, was permitted to choose four hundred scholars who would devote themselves to Torah study and thereby be exempted from the draft. At a time when religion was on the wane, Ben-Gurion and his colleagues considered the Haredim a vestige of the past that would eventually disappear.

When, in 1948, Israel was founded, representatives of the religious parties signed its Declaration of Independence. God is not mentioned in this founding document, but towards the end there is a reference to belief in "the Rock of Israel," which can be construed as a reference to God or to the Jewish people. The declaration speaks of the State of Israel as the state of the Jewish people, but it also explicitly establishes the equality of all citizens and enshrines freedom of religion, gender, culture, and language. Today the protest movements increasingly view the Declaration as the potential basis for an Israeli constitution. The nation's first elections were held in the autumn of 1949 and the new parliament was supposed to draw up a constitution. This never happened, because the notion of the equality of Jews and non-Jews before the law met with opposition from religious constituents, even at this early stage. Ben-Gurion chose not to open that can of worms in a country that had just taken its first breaths, which led to the glacially slow passing of "basic laws," laws about rights that together would come to constitute a corpus equivalent to a constitution. Was this a historic mistake? If circumstances had been different, might a constitution have been written?

The British Mandate left the State of Israel its legal system, which, *mutatis mutandis*, served as the foundation of the judiciary. The vast majority of Israelis did not hail from democratic countries, so the principles of equality before the law and the supremacy of the law were alien to them. They were more used to obedience to the law than to defending the rights of the individual or fighting for equality. The Israeli legal system came into its own through trial and error. Thus the right-wing judge Benjamin Halevy could declare, after Israeli security forces claimed to be just following orders when, in 1956, they massacred Arab citizens in Qafr Kassim due to a curfew violation, that one may not obey a direct order that seems dubious or excessive or troubling, and that one who does unquestioningly obey such an order cannot escape punishment by bumping responsibility up the chain of command. To take another example: when, in 1953, the Communist newspaper *Kol HaAm* published a relatively minor criticism of the government, Ben-Gurion ordered it shuttered. This led the Supreme Court to decide that freedom of expression trumps an executive order, and the paper was back in business. (This was the first judicial ruling that cited the enumeration of rights in the Declaration of Independence as legally binding.) One can see, then, that the decisions of judges and the Supreme Court became precedents that nudged the Jewish state onto the path of liberalism. This was not orchestrated from above, with the Israeli leadership meeting and deciding on the details of the judicial system or the exact separation of powers between the branches of government, in the way that the Constitution of the United States or the many constitutions of France were conceived. Israel was more like England, in which practice and precedent substituted for an elaborate document.

With the founding of the state, the Israel Defense Force was given a monopoly over military personnel and matériel. When, in June 1948, only weeks after the state had been declared, a ship called the *Altalena* anchored off the coast of Tel Aviv carrying arms for the Irgun, a paramilitary group headed by Menachem Begin that refused to accept the authority of the army of the new state, Ben-Gurion ordered the ship sunk. This act has assumed an almost mythological import for the Israeli right, which deems it unforgivable. But it was the sinking of the ship that eliminated the possibility of politically affiliated armed groups and militias and established the authority of the central government in the young state. The subsequent dismantling of the Palmach, an elite military unit of the Haganah, the forerunner of the Israeli army, which was allied with the left, further hammered in the fact that there would be only one military with a single structure of command. While Begin recognized the *fait accompli*, other splinter groups plotted for another reality, in which the regime in charge would look quite different. The underground movements of the 1950s were a holdover from the past, but what was new was their messianic ideology and their dream of a theocracy.

The same first decade of statehood saw a mass influx of immigrants that shifted the makeup of Israeli society. Most of them were from Arab countries and did not experience the hardships of the war or the suffering that Holocaust survivors did. The new state's efforts in bringing them to Israel were extraordinary, and the immigrants expected the Jewish state to welcome them with open arms. One can imagine their surprise when they encountered a foreign culture, unfamiliar languages, and the squalid conditions of the transit camps for new immigrants. The gulf between expectation and reality became a breeding ground for bitterness and resentment, which stubbornly persisted even when life improved. The horrible experience was transmitted as a kind of transgenerational trauma. Whenever it has seemed like the last embers of discontent might finally die out, some politician comes along to pour gasoline all over them and strike the match to keep the fire alive.

The most dramatic turning point in Israeli history occurred in the aftermath of the Six Day War. In 1967 Israel defeated its foes so quickly, so decisively, and most of all so unexpectedly, that her citizens were left astonished and breathless, trying to make sense of how a nation under existential threat had suddenly metamorphosed into a regional superpower. For the first time since 1948, Israelis could now traverse the length and breadth of the Land of Israel, from the Golan Heights to the Sinai and from the Mediterranean Sea to the Dead Sea. When, in the immediate aftermath of the victory, Rabbi Shlomo Goren sounded the shofar on the Temple Mount, he reawakened an ancient Jewish sensibility. Rabbi Zvi Yehuda Kook, a radical and mystical nationalist, and his religious Zionist comrades had already deemed the founding of the state to be the beginning of the final redemption, and now it seemed that the process had taken a great leap forward. Could one hear the footfalls of the Messiah? Yehuda Etzion, one of the future leaders of the Jewish Underground, the band of settler vigilantes that carried out terrorist attacks against Palestinians in the West Bank in the early 1980s, was convinced that Jews now needed to plan to bring down the mosques on the Temple Mount and rebuild the Temple. But only a small fringe group thought in such wild terms. Most Israelis were basking in the afterglow of victory. They assumed that they would have to cede all of the recent territorial gains, as had happened after Operation Kadesh in the Sinai in 1956, so they flocked to what were then called "the occupied territories" to tour them while they still had access.

An expression of the spiritual upheaval generated by this new reality was the appearance of the Movement for Greater Israel, which called for holding on to the restored tracts of the ancient Jewish homeland. This movement ignored traditional divides between right and left and religious and secular. It included intellectuals, politicians, and some of Israel's greatest writers, including Nathan Alterman (its driving force), S. Y. Agnon, Moshe Shamir, Haim Gouri, and others. Many opposed this position. The scientist and philosopher Yeshayahu Leibowitz demanded the return of every last inch of conquered territory. Ben-Gurion, then in retirement, initially recommended giving back everything except Jerusalem, and then excepted also the Golan Heights due to its strategic position. The government at the time was a national-unity coalition that enjoyed widespread popular support due to the astounding victory that it delivered, yet its internal disagreement over what to do with the territories heralded its collapse. When, in 1968, religious extremists seized the initiative and stealthily took over a hotel in Hebron to celebrate Passover, the politicians could not agree to evict them. Would Jews expel their brethren who sought to live in the City of the Patriarchs? The government did not initially approve the action, but in other such cases it did. The resettlement of certain areas such as Gush Etzion, near Jerusalem, was legally sanctioned because it reclaimed Jewish settlements that had been conquered by the Arabs in the War of Independence. The confluence of legal and illegal Israeli settlement signaled the presence of barely visible currents that would eventually determine the course of Israeli history.

In 1949, after the armistice of the war of independence, the borders of the state were chiefly confined to the biblical "Land of the Philistines" and "Galilee of the Gentiles." The historical sites of ancient Judaism — eastern Jerusalem, the Temple Mount, Judea and Samaria — belonged to Jordan. They had long ago constituted the realm of David and Solomon, the battleground of Ahab and Elijah. But in 1967 the Jewish people were unexpectedly in control of the lands of the Bible, of the geographical settings of its powerful and foundational stories, which fanned the messianic expectations that Zionist pragmatism was supposed to have suppressed. Religious Zionist rabbis and scholars had given the IDF a warning against entering eastern Jerusalem: if we go in, they said, we cannot leave. Remember that the partition plan proposed at the Zionist Congress in 1937 had generated heated debate, and was accepted amid forceful objections. That early encounter between myth and pragmatism was a sign of things to come.

The years between 1967 and 1973 were marked by a bubbly euphoria and a feeling that the Israeli military could not be bested — but anxiety was continuously simmering under the surface. The War of Attrition — an Egyptian campaign of bombardment and shelling that lasted from 1967 to 1970 — had no end in sight, and terrorists were targeting Israelis at home and abroad. The first settlements were established in the Sinai, in the Gaza Strip, and in the West Bank areas devoid of Arab residents, and they were justified on the practical grounds of security concerns. The government was led by Labor, and it accepted the need for a defensible border, that is, for setting the border as far east as feasible. Public debate raged over the emotional and moral costs of the occupation, as well as its toll in human life, but the government would not budge: there would be no withdrawals without signed peace treaties.

The Yom Kippur War in 1973 deeply rattled Israeli society, overturning an unshakable confidence in the Israeli army that had shaped governmental policy and the Israeli mentality more generally. The existential dread that Jews had lived with throughout history, especially during the Holocaust, returned. Israel emerged from the war as the victor, but a severely bloodied one. The war was a national trauma that is still keenly felt fifty years on. Talks with Egypt were initiated not long after arms were put down. A peace agreement was struck, and Israel began a phased withdrawal from the Sinai.

The country's willingness to pull out of the Sinai gave religious Zionist circles cause for concern. The fact that the Sinai was not part of the historical territory of ancient Israel did not soften the blow. Israel was prepared to return the occupied territories in exchange for peace. Gush Emunim, the settlers movement known as the Bloc of the Faithful, with its base in the yeshiva of Rabbi Kook — founded in Jerusalem by Rabbi Abraham Isaac Kook, the first Ashkenazi chief rabbi, and now the headquarters of his son, the aforementioned Rabbi Zvi Yehuda Kook, the spiritual leader of the settler movement — stepped into the perceived breach. There was a palpable messianism to this movement, despite the initial participation of secular Israelis. Gush Emunim took upon itself to populate with Jews what it insisted on calling Judea and Samaria. So long as the left remained in power, there was political disunity and vociferous disagreement about such settlement, which Gush Emunim took advantage of in 1975 to put down stakes in Kedumim, not far from Nablus. Then, two years later, there occurred the "upheaval," as the election of 1977 is known, with the Likud Party emerging victorious. For the first time, Israel was governed by a coalition headed by the right, and Menachem Begin, the right-wing leader forever in the opposition, was now prime minister.

After the Yom Kippur War, Israeli society had lost faith in the Labor Party's ability to be the dominant party in Israeli politics. People were ready for change. Begin was resolute about advancing peace with the Egyptians, and his greatest achievement was undoubtedly the signing in 1978 of the Camp David accords, which yielded a lasting peace. Yet history does not look so kindly on two other choices that Begin made, which altered the course of Israeli history for the worse. First, he sponsored Gush Emunim and its plans for settling the West Bank. Under his aegis, twelve settlements were built. While the Gush was relatively short-lived, it got the ball rolling, and roll it did. While the Israeli settlements in the Sinai were eventually evacuated in 2005, the settlements in the West

Bank, now called Judea and Samaria, multiplied with the wide backing of the government. (And then of later governments.) Second, Begin brought the Haredi parties into the government on their own terms. These included the cessation of El-Al flights on Shabbat, and, most fatefully, the removal of an upper limit on the number of yeshiva students who may be exempted from military service. These two political moves appear negligible when placed alongside either the spectacular success of peacemaking with Egypt or the dismal failure in the Lebanon War in 1982. In the long term, however, they had an outsized impact relative to the amount of forethought given to them.

What fateful events led us into the present crisis? Could it have been the war in Lebanon, the first war to be waged without a national consensus, which broke down our solidarity? Or was it the murder of Emil Grünzweig, an officer who demonstrated at a Peace Now rally against the government after returning from Lebanon? What could have fed the intense hatred that provoked someone with no personal connection to the Peace Now activists to lob a grenade at them? Yona Avrushmi, the murderer, admitted it plainly enough: it was the barrage of unhinged incitement against the left. Or perhaps it was the retaliation of the Jewish Underground for the murder of Jews in Judea and Samaria? What began as attacks against West Bank mayors, who might have been implicated in inciting terrorists to murder settlers, devolved into attacks against students at the Islamic College in Hebron and attempts to harm innocents on five Arab buses. One of the plots of the Jewish Underground was to destroy the mosques on the Temple Mount. The chief architect of this plan, the aforementioned Yehuda Etzion, never expressed remorse for any of this. And those were not the only massacres of Palestinians committed by settlers and right-wing fanatics. Maybe it was this terrorism for the sake of sowing terror, which blew past every moral barrier as it picked up speed, that brought us to our present-day scorn of liberal values and our boundless nationalistic egoism.

To settle within a population that does not want irredentist neighbors and to force it into an economic symbiosis that has the semblance of peace, or at least of toleration, but which in reality has been foisted upon a hapless population by an occupying power — this is an ongoing source of profound moral corruption, the self-reflection of a society that considers itself master of its domain because of divine promises made thousands of years ago that do not withstand the test of reason. The conceit of "the chosen people" has never before been realized as literally as it has in Judea and Samaria. When a religious minister claims that the Temple Mount is a Jewish possession by virtue of King David having purchased it from Araunah the Jebusite, one may dismiss it as the ravings of one man. But when this same madness serves as the basis for acts of oppression and deception, and divine sanction turns wrong into right, then violence becomes the norm, incitement the language, and corruption the means to a "justified" end.

During the Oslo peace process, the incitement hit fever pitch. The rhetorical viciousness of the Israeli right would be hard to exaggerate. It was only a matter of time before someone decided to translate the violence preached over the megaphone into action. The murder of Yitzhak Rabin, a sitting prime minister, in 1995, was a watershed moment. Or was it? Maybe the point of no return came the year before, when the Kahanist radical Baruch Goldstein gunned down dozens of

Muslim worshippers at the Cave of the Patriarchs in Hebron?

Today the settlements are a fact of life. They do not strike us as abnormal, and we altogether prefer to ignore them. The settlers and the army play a never-ending game of cat and mouse: the former try to expand the borders of Jewish settlements and the latter stop them — while simultaneously protecting them. What will be the denouement? Can the clock be turned back on this, or are we on an irreversible track to establishing a single binational state between the two seas? Such a state would have no right to exist. The Jewish state was not founded to create yet another autonomous Jewish society among non-Jews, but to mark off one small spot on the globe where Jews could have their own independent political entity. Bi-nationalism, or a "one-state solution," is hard enough to sustain in countries where the peoples share the same or similar cultures, religions, and traditions. Can you imagine a small state in which two quarrelling nations are separated by unbridgeable gaps in religion and culture and have been engaged in bloody conflict for over a century? If you stand on the tower at the Tomb of Samuel a few kilometers northeast of Jerusalem and gaze eastwards, you will see a landscape dappled with Arab and Jewish settlements. The former display traditional Arab styles of construction, and the second have tiled roofs, announcing the presence of Jews in areas slated for a Palestinian state. There are about six hundred thousand settlers in Judea and Samaria today. The current government has granted exceptional powers to Bezalel Smotrich, who represents the settlers' interests, and one expects the pace of settlement to quicken and the brutality to increase on both sides.

The Haredim present a problem to the peaceful integration of Israeli society no less severe than the settlers. The Haredi sector encompasses Mizrahim and Ashkenazim, Hasidim and

Mitnagdim (the Lithuanian opponents of Hasidism). Some men work for a living, usually in education, but most do not. They either rely on their wives, who are the breadwinners with higher-income jobs, or subsist on government handouts. As of this writing, the number of Haredim in Israeli society is approaching fourteen percent. Since Haredi families are large, averaging six children, Haredi children will comprise the majority of school-age children within one or two decades. Their rabbinic leaders insist on maintaining impermeable boundaries between their community and everyone else.

The current far-right government incorporates the most extreme elements of religious society, and its idea of generosity is to excuse the Haredim from getting a basic education. In Haredi schools, most of which are autonomously run, the children do not learn the disciplines crucial to living in modern society. The core curriculum, which includes Hebrew, English, and mathematics, is barely taught, so that graduates lack even a rudimentary education and earn less in the workplace. There are entire cities of Haredim that live on the dole, and, predictably, they are terribly poor and their residents are woefully unprepared for life in the twenty-first century. If they decide to join the workforce, they are barred from higher-paying jobs because they lack the necessary skills. Haredim do not serve in the army, and their financial contribution to the country is minimal; their low income translates into little or no taxes, meaning that in essence they are living off their fellow taxpayers.

Once upon a time, the Haredim were a positive and practical-minded force for moderation in government, owing to their concern about "what will the goyim think." Not anymore. The Haredi sector has become bigoted and looks down on anyone who does not engage in their level of

Torah study. Owing to their minimal exposure to the outside world, they believe that their study is national service fully equal to the army service of secular Israelis in delivering the country from danger. Their attitude towards women, gay and transgender people, Arabs, and others is unabashedly phobic and discriminatory. When they are in positions of power, as they are now, they display the insufferable arrogance of a beggar on the throne. Their demographic growth has granted them immense power and they wield that power like a cudgel, all the while ignoring the stark fact that the secular sector bears the lion's share of the country's economic and security burden.

The current crisis is convulsing Israel along the religious-secular fault line, pitting democrats against messianists. For the first time in the history of the state, the government is all cut from the same cloth. The prime minister, who is being prosecuted for corruption, scraped the bottom of the barrel to form this coalition. He came up with fringe extremists, nationalistic and religious hardliners, open admirers of Baruch Goldstein and self-described homophobes, whom no one can restrain. Netanyahu is working frantically to prevent this gaggle of strange bedfellows, elected due to tactical electoral mistakes by the left, disperse and the government fall. His minister of justice has spent the past year trying to pass reforms that would spell the end of the judiciary's independence, subjugating the judicial branch to the executive. This would be accomplished by revising the procedure for judicial appointments, so that the government always maintains a majority on the relevant committee, weakening the power of the attorneys general, and curtailing the Supreme Court. The ulterior motive of the "reforms" is to legitimize corruption, prevent the courts from getting involved in cases of human rights, *de facto* remove the equality of citizens before the law, and give preference to Jews over Arabs in every circumstance. It is against this anti-liberal plan that hundreds of thousands have demonstrated week in and week out for many months. The protesters eschew violence and exemplify civic activism of the highest order.

The Israeli right has been fulminating against the Israeli left with its old virulence. From their rhetoric you would think that they are not the ones in power. When air force pilots declared that, should the judicial reform legislation pass, they would not show up for reserve duty, which they regularly fulfill beyond the call of duty by volunteering on a nearly weekly basis, the propaganda machine immediately accused them of treason. A Haredi minister complained that failure to serve in the reserves because of government policy was a step too far, which was rich, as neither he, nor his children, nor his grandchildren, have ever served a day in the armed forces. Aharon Barak, who served as president of the Supreme Court, an internationally renowned jurist who played a very important role in the discussions that led to the Camp David accords, has been outrageously demonized by the right; the eighty-six-year-old Holocaust survivor has been accused of every possible crime by those thronging outside his modest home, despite the fact that he has been retired for decades. The hateful propaganda and fake news promulgated by the right have taken root due to their political influence over Army Radio and the programming of one television channel. The left has tried to give as good it gets, but the right is more wily and their abuse of political power knows no bounds. They are trying to gain control of higher education and the media. The pool of talented people in government, who are unwilling to serve under superiors with no experience or insight, is slowly draining, as functionaries use their clout to appoint utterly unqualified flunkies.

The protest movement is comprised of many admirable and essential sectors of Israeli society: financial, technological, military, academic. These are the people who keep Israel safe and bring Israel honor and prosperity. When hi-tech workers band together with pilots, when all the former heads of the intelligence agencies (the Mossad and the Shin Bet) are saying the same thing as the ex-presidents of the Bank of Israel, when business school professors and their colleagues in the hard sciences sound the alarm, all in opposition to what we are decorously calling "judicial reform," this consolidated force should be assessed qualitatively, not quantitatively. And it should be respected, and not dismissed in the usual populist way as elitist. The mass demonstrations that have been taking place every single week for more than half a year embody the strength of the people; the younger generation has risen up to fight indefatigably for their future, for the future of their children.

Democracy is not merely majoritarian, and it cannot be reduced to a majority of the voters for the Knesset; it must also take into account the rights of a large minority that pays most of the taxes, puts their lives on the line in long army service, and keeps the country going in every critical respect. The struggle, indeed, is over the very definition of Israeli democracy: is it a majoritarian democracy under which the majority makes the decisions and the minority is stuck with them, or is it a liberal democracy, in which everyone has equal rights and the budget is apportioned equitably? Liberal democracy ensures that the rights of secular Israelis are protected, that the Arab sector receives its just and proportional slice of the pie, that the Haredim do not get special treatment and get away with failing to contribute to the economy, that hospitals are built before yeshivas and settlements.

When Chaim Weizmann held the discussions that would eventually produce the Balfour Declaration, he was asked by Lord Balfour: what does a "Jewish state" mean? The question was animated by a concern voiced by anti-Zionists that a Jewish state would mean a Jewish theocracy. Weizmann responded that the country would be Jewish in the same way that England is English. His reply was shrewdly formulated. Unlike the United States or France, England has no separation of church and state. In fact, the church in England is officially Anglican. The national symbols are markedly British: the monarchy, the flag, the national anthem, the ceremonies. And yet all of England's citizens are equal before the law, and there is no legal discrimination on the basis of religion, language, or race. The enforcement of this equality requires an independent judiciary. Israel has a similar structure, unless the present government succeeds in eliminating it. *That* is the meaning of a "Jewish and democratic state."

Will the protests work? Will we succeed in stopping this disfiguration of Israeli democracy, which was incomparably better and more competent than the twisted governance being pushed by this right-wing government? Until now, Israeli coalitions in governments have avoided ideological homogeneity. Diversity in government expressed a deeply held belief that for a country to endure, its various constituencies must be assigned equal weight. This belief is no longer being upheld. The extremist and messianic actors see this as a ripe opportunity to impose a theocratic and even a fascistic regime.

If the government carries out its plan, the ensuing rift will cause many gifted young Israelis to leave. This outflow will not happen overnight. As the country grows increasingly more religious, more extreme, and more isolated from the West, the next generation will seek out a different future. They love their country — even to the point of giving up their lives for it — and they want to live here; but if their country does not want them, they will not stay. And if tens of thousands of the best and the brightest leave, the IDF will not survive the brain drain. Beyond our borders, moreover, our enemies and their strategists are watching what is unfolding here with bated breath.

The ancient historian Josephus described how the Jewish radicals known as the Zealots burned down the Jews' food stores during the Roman siege of Jerusalem. The analogy with the new Zealots immediately comes to mind. Those who brand the current government as the one that will bring "the destruction of the third Temple" — are they right? Jews are well versed in figuring out how to compromise and they excel in adapting to circumstances so as to attain an objective, but once again we are watching a historical drama on repeat, in which the extremists seize power and are destroying everything that their predecessors painstakingly built. Rashid Khalidi was wrong. We are not the Crusaders, and we have no plans to leave this parcel of land that we hold so dear. But a doubt nags: will we learn from the past? Will we draw the appropriate lessons from our own history? Or will we again find ourselves beating our chests as we intone that "we have been exiled from our land on account of our sins"? Can the Jewish people hold on to a state?

OKSANA FOROSTYNA

Another Country

On June 8, 2022, when the world finally recognized the atrocities of Russian troops on the occupied territories of Ukraine, I proposed an intellectual exercise to my Facebook friends: "Imagine that a couple of years have passed. Russian war crimes are discussed less and less. Perhaps some war criminals have even been jailed. Those who survived try to forget and just live a normal life, while the media have turned their attention to other events. And then we learn that there was a writer of genius among the Russian troops in Bucha or Irpin, in the Chernihiv and Kharkiv regions. And he writes brilliant prose about all that happened there. You know, without pathos, without excuses, a bit disinterestedly; he describes the horrors almost aloofly, but without covering up them up. (He himself, according to what we hear, didn't kill anyone.) His genius is undeniable. His book is widely translated and wins prizes. And in bookstores and in libraries, his prose is shelved under 'Ukraine.' Ukrainians are furious, of course, but not as fervidly as they would have been in 2022. And who is listening to them? Everyone agrees, of course, that what they endured, what traumatized them, was horrible. And everyone agrees that this great prose, with its roots in a great culture, no matter how tragic the circumstances were, will outlive this traumatized generation. It will outlive the survivors because it has such a great culture behind it."

If you think that I was being hysterical in my bleak thought-experiment, I should admit that I did make a mistake: the situation that I imagined came to pass sooner than I expected — it was a matter of only a few months. On August 17, 2022, *The Guardian* published a profile of Pavel Filatiev, a former Russian paratrooper who published his memoirs on his VKontakte social media page and fled the country. *The Guardian* also published an extract of Filatiev's account. He describes the looting of Kherson, and the inhuman conditions that Russian troops endured before invading Ukraine, and how the command to invade "turned us into savages." And while it is unlikely that Filatiev wrote great literary prose, his memoir is reported to have been sold for three hundred thousand euros after he reached France. It was published in English, French, and Spanish. I don't know of any Ukrainian writer or soldier who managed to sell his or her works so well. (My PEN Ukraine colleagues confirm this.)

As in most cases when we in Ukraine discuss Russian and Soviet culture, my Facebook post had addressed two issues, one external and one domestic. The domestic issue was the thorny question of our approach to the cultural legacy of Russia and the Soviet Union. For those few Ukrainian Facebook friends who might not recognize the literary allusion in my dystopian scenario, I added a hint: a photo of the monument to the Bolshevik soldiers of the First Cavalry Budyonny Army near Olesko, about fifty miles from my native city of Lviv. Despite its defeat during the Soviet-Polish war in 1920, the cavalry was glorified and earned a substantial place in the Soviet pantheon. Known as the Red Cavalry, it was founded by Semyon Budyonny and was substantially responsible for the earlier Bolshevik victory in the Russian Civil War. Budyonny later became one of Stalin's closest associates.

The monument was huge and ambitious and technically complicated: an eighty-eight-foot-high sculpture of two riders on the top of a hill that jutted dramatically out of the landscape and rose almost directly above the Ukrainian part of the European E40 route (a major highway labeled "Lviv — Kyiv — Moscow" when it was built). The riders were racing wildly, as if they were about to take flight. Whenever I travelled that road, I felt like I was shrinking before the danger that the colossal cantilevered horse and riders would fall on the road at any moment and crush a car. But this monument does not exist anymore. It was ruined in the early 2000s, when its copper and other metals attracted the attention of ideologically agnostic collectors of scrap metal, and despite its protected status under the Ministry of Culture the local authorities didn't really care about the plunder. In 2015, when Ukraine adopted its "de-Communization" legislation, the rest of the composition was dismantled.

The fate of this statue, and the fate of other Communist monuments, became a focus of public discussion: what to do if a Soviet monument is also a work of art? The case of the First Cavalry Budyonny Army monument was a fine illustration of the problem. Its construction in 1975 was politically driven: in the same year, the nearby Castle of Olesko was finally opened for visitors after decades of abandonment and restoration. Olesko had changed masters many times since the late Middle Ages, but it is famous mostly as the birthplace of the Polish king Jan III Sobieski, the hero of the Battle of Vienna in 1683. In Soviet times, Olesko was the only castle for thousands of miles around that was accessible to tourists; the others were either in ruins or being used as warehouses or hospitals. The official reason for the creation of the great equestrian monument was the fifty-fifth anniversary of the First Cavalry Budyonny Army (and the nearby mass grave of its soldiers who died there in 1920). But it was also designed as an unambiguous message to Olesko's visitors: we will grant you a brief glimpse of your European heritage, but don't you dare forget who the boss is here. I have never seen a grosser visualization of foreign domination than those colossal riders. The monument was a kind of visual rape of the bucolic landscape.

In the writer whom I invented in my Facebook parable I was alluding, of course, to the case of Isaac Babel, the Odessa-born Jewish writer. Babel wrote in Russian, and he is most renowned for his *Red Cavalry* and *Odessa Stories*. The events described in both books take place in Ukraine. Babel was assigned to the Budyonny Cavalry as a war reporter and a political officer. He described his experience with the Bolshevik army in Ukraine in a diary that later became *Red Cavalry*, an overwhelmingly powerful book, describing the brutality of both the Red Army and the White Guard. The book enraged Marshal Semyon Budyonny and Marshal Kliment Voroshylov, but Maxim Gorky backed the book and so it was published. Babel was safe for some time, safe enough to travel to France as part of an official delegation of Soviet writers. He was loyal to the system: in 1937 he supported the Second Moscow Trial in the *Literaturnaya Gazeta*, and the agit-prop style of his text, praising Stalin and the Communist Party, was typical of the Great Purge denunciations and propaganda. For a while, as Stalin's repression of culture grew more furious, Babel tried to lie low, but he was arrested in 1939 and accused of spying, of Trotskyism, and of terrorism. While in jail he informed on other Russian Jewish writers. After a hasty trial in Beria's office he was shot in prison in 1940.

Babel was mesmerized by the Bolshevik terror, and also by the criminal underworld of Odessa. His *Odessa Stories* contributed a great deal to the urban legends of Odessa, and also elevated the "Odessa language" to the heights of literary style. It is hard not to be charmed by the milieu that Babel described with love and empathy, including his most famous creation, the Odessa ganglord Benya Krik, whose real-life prototype, the Robin Hood-like figure Mishka Yaponchik, was both a gangster and a Bolshevik ally, providing them with the support of the Odessa criminal world, an alliance that was quite natural for the Bolsheviks. (Eventually Yaponchik formed his own military unit.) This milieu, so brilliantly romanticized by Babel in his masterpiece, also produced another prominent gangster, once Yaponchik's accomplice and partner — Naftaly Frenkel. Frenkel, who allegedly was born in Haifa in 1883, was arrested in the Soviet Union for smuggling, and as punishment for his economic success he was sentenced to Solovki, the first camp of the Gulag, in 1923. He quickly rose to become a member of the camp administration, and soon chief of construction of the White Sea-Baltic Canal (*Belomorkanal*) project, and the head of the Baikal Amur Mainline camp. Frenkel proposed what we now would call "an alternative business model" for the Gulag: he made it profitable, which eventually provoked a demand for more forced labor, and hence more arrests. Unlike Babel, Frenkel was praised, given many prizes, and died in peace in Moscow at the age of seventy-seven.

It is impossible to deny the magnificence of Babel's literary genius, but I do not see how he can be called a humanist, and I have a hard time regarding him as an innocent victim of Stalinism. It is true that with the ruthless Budyonny Cavalry he was just an observer, but before that he volunteered to serve the Cheka (the Bolshevik secret police) as a translator during interrogations. He praised collectivization, and his obsequiousness toward the Stalinist authorities, though it was sometimes interrupted by lapses into silence and nervous withdrawal from the literary scene, is well documented. The literary genius was also a political trimmer, or worse. His correspondence shows that Babel was aware of the Holodomor, Stalin's genocidal famine in Ukraine. There is nothing admirable about any of this.

I know that in the West many people believe that one's view of a writer or an artist must not be reduced to his or her political history. Moreover, many Ukrainians do not share my hostile feelings toward the Budyonny Cavalry monument. But my reservations are not to be explained away by the stereotype (comfortable for those who disagree with me) of a Western Ukrainian's hostility to Russian and Soviet culture. Though born in Lviv, the biggest Ukrainian-speaking city of the Cold War world, I went to a Russian school, and I had trouble speaking Ukrainian up to my university years. In the turbulent early 1990s, our Russian teacher seemed to be the only one who took her job seriously, and she drilled us with *War and Peace* for two months as if nothing outside the classroom was changing. With Russian as my first language, and after decades of reflection on this question, I began to collect anecdotes about the extent to which my Russian-speaking background affects how people inside and outside Ukraine perceive me.

The question of how to think about Russian culture, and certainly about how a Ukrainian is to think about Russian culture, has of course been sharpened since Russia's invasion of Ukraine. Much has been written about this perplexity since the war began, but the main audience for these debates has been in Europe, the United States, or, more broadly, what is called the West. (The war has reestablished the term, and you no longer need a hundred excuses every time you use it.) When some Ukrainian and Central European voices called for a boycott at least of those Russian artists who openly support the war and Putin's regime, or even for revising Western attitudes toward Russian culture in general, their denunciations were met by a moral panic from some Russians (though some supported the cause) and Europeans. German PEN, for example, concerned about "often deceived and always poorly equipped Russian soldiers who die fighting for Putin's power fantasies and paranoia are also victims of this violation of international law," not to mention the fate of Russian writers, including Pushkin and Dostoevsky and Chekhov, published an imperishable press-release called "The Enemy is Putin, not Pushkin" as early as March 6, 2022.

As if Ukrainians were burning Pushkin and Chekhov. They were not, even after the perpetration of unthinkable cruelties by those "always poorly equipped Russian soldiers." What actually happened was that Ukrainian libraries and universities were burned. Ukrainian writers were killed and injured. Ukrainian books were replaced by Russian books in the occupied territories. Nobody in Ukraine was oppressing

Russian culture. The oppression — the war — went the other way. After the aerial destruction of the theater in Mariupol, its ruins were covered and adorned by huge banners with images of Pushkin and Tolstoy.

I understand that the readers of this journal cherish freedom of speech and self-expression, and so do I. For these good people, the idea of cancelling a culture is most likely anathema, especially in the American context. Yet I expect them also to be honest with themselves: the American idea of freedom of speech has never been absolute, even if it has been an inspiration to the world. Red lines exist, and some of them are now the subject of intense debate in the struggle over correctness and wokeness and the other attempts to limit what can be said.

A similar debate about red lines in Ukrainian culture — having to do with the proper attitude toward Russian culture — has been taking place for a long time. It used to be mainly a domestic debate, but it became global with the Russian aggression of 2022. When, in the first days of the invasion, Ukrainians called for the "cancelling of Russian culture," it meant at a minimum to stop inviting Ukrainians and Russians to Western panels, discussions, and events "to present both sides" and, worse, to demonstrate how culture may "reconcile" us. I share my colleagues' outrage that such attempts at "reconciliation" are patronizing and ignorant, and represent a certain arrogance on the part of the relevant Western institutions. I also share their concerns about using the war in Ukraine as a pretext to give a platform once again to "approved" Russians, and the readiness of too many of Russian emigres to be the corpse at every funeral, the bride at every wedding, the baby at every christening.

At first the cancellation of Russians may seem reasonable: if you are so eager to cancel someone for "microaggression," "triggering," "cultural appropriation," and other expressions that may hurt the feelings of some people, why don't you cancel the real villains, the theorists and practitioners of evil, those who openly call for genocide? If you cannot forgive a university professor a dubious metaphor, how can you tolerate an opera singer openly socializing with warlords and visiting occupied territories just a few miles from an actual concentration camp that has been functioning since 2014? How can you be so oversensitive in one case and so undersensitive in another? These are all justified questions.

And yet as fervently as I support the Ukrainian cause, I believe that cancellation is wrong, and for several reasons. The worst problem with "cancellation" as it is practiced in the West is that, like most political and cultural phenomena in the West, it is concerned mainly with feelings, and it reduces the cause for ostracism to the emotional reaction of people who may have been offended, in this case Ukrainians. Yet this has the situation backwards. Russian culture is not problematic because Ukrainians suffer. Ukrainians suffer because Russian culture is problematic. (Also, explaining anything in terms of "emotional reaction" or "traumatization" is just a passive-aggressive way of telling someone that his or her opinion is worthless. It is arrogance disguised as sympathy.)

Another reason for resisting the temptation to cancel is the context. The advocates of "cancel culture" in the case of post-2022 (or post-2014) Russia assumed that the Ukrainian cause had been translated into some universal language, and that Ukrainian emancipation would be welcomed by other oppressed groups and post-colonial nations. Alas, this has not been the case. Our hopes for solidarity from the so-called Global South have been greatly exaggerated, at least so far. And finally, the wording is strategically problematic: to "cancel" would mean to sweep the problem under the rug, not to confront it and solve it. And even if cancellation succeeds in evading the problem for a while, it is not sustainable: eventually the horrors of the war will become family memories and lines in the history books, and the next generation will uncritically turn to, say, Tatyana Tolstaya, with all the rebellious energy of youth, facing their *Widerspruchsgeist*, the spirit of opposition, barehanded.

That is why I believe we need not a cancelling but a revision, a spirited discussion, a hotwash. By "we" I mean Westerners, not Ukrainians. (We Ukrainians need our own hotwash in the matter of our relationships to Russian culture, but that is another matter.) Why is the justice of the Ukrainian cause — a savage war of conquest was launched against us — not the conventional wisdom in the West, where there are so many chairs in the universities, so many fora, so many media, which could accurately explain, with historical and factual evidence, why the invasion of 2022 happened? Why have we so frequently heard the miserable argument that the Russian war has been against Russia's rational interests from people whose job is precisely to deconstruct and explain Russian irrationality? Surely it is their job to distinguish reason from unreason. With so much about the war still poorly understood, with so many lunatic theories (for example, that the Ukraine war is really an American proxy war against Russia) still abounding, we need criticism and rethinking, not a lazy cancellation: the Russian imperial past and Russia's ever-present imperialistic sentiments have never yet faced the scrutiny they deserve in proportion to Russian representation in academia, media, and arts.

I praise those Russian émigrés who have been capable of reflecting critically on the situation, those with the wisdom and the courage to step back, those who as Russians feel some responsibility (such as the Russian writer Sergey Lebedev, a contributor to this journal). Some of them did whatever they could before they had to leave Russia. Some ended up in prison, such as the Memorial historian Yuri Dmitriev. Some might never return home, and some are in danger even living abroad. But there are so few of them. And while some of my Ukrainian colleagues foolishly believe a boycott should be applied to *any* Russian, their Western opponents believe the equally stupid view that *any* Russian deserves the benefit of the doubt. These Western attempts to appoint a few brave dissidents to be representatives of some substantive part of Russian society are not only delusional, they also disrespect the price that these brave Russians are paying for their stand against the majority, the sacrifices that they are making for the sake of someone else's wishful thinking.

And what about the dead writers, those who can't speak on current matters and are said to be instrumentalized by Putin's regime? The dead writers (and artists and composers) known around the world as Russia's great culture?

Some assume that those trying to insulate this Russian culture from political history, who argue that it has nothing to do with Putin, are advocates of Russia for sentimental ("Russophile") or snobbish reasons. This is a simplification. The president of the European Commission, Ursula von der

Leyen, is hardly pro-Russian, but in August 2022 she accepted an invitation to the opening night performance at La Scala in Milan of *Boris Godunov,* and even suggested that Russian culture and the actions of the Russian government should be completely distinguished from each other. Adam Michnik, the legendary editor of the Polish newspaper *Gazeta Wyborcza* and a former dissident, describes himself as a "true anti-Soviet Russophile." At least he has also proved himself to be a real friend of Ukraine. Yet such examples show that there are people out there who sincerely believe that one can be both: a friend of Ukraine (or Estonia, or Georgia, or any other country attacked by Russia) and "a Russophile," since the "Russo" part of the word extends only to Russian culture and not to Russian politics, to one segment of Russian reality but not to another.

The argument that Russian culture has nothing to do with Putin does not hold up. No culture exists in a political vacuum and no political leader exists in a cultural vacuum. In the case of Russian culture, this connection is even more problematic than in the Western world. Unlike European countries, Russia does not have a tradition of checks and balances in its public life — its political order has always consisted in just a monarch or tyrant and his or her subjects. It never had free universities, or even an independent church that could counterbalance the state as it did in the West. Moreover, Russian culture has been inseparable from the Russian state, even when it has been anti-state. The Russian monarchy and then the Soviet monarchy might shower money, invitations, and privileges on Western intellectuals to promote the loyal artists and to protect their political interests, but the inevitable side-effect was that they promoted Russian culture in general, ironically including rebels and dissidents. I know at least one dissident who acknowledges that he survived KGB persecution because he wrote his poems in Russian: "I lived in Kyiv back then, and of course if I were a Ukrainian writer they would just smash me. That means seven plus five. But since I was a Russian writer, I was an older brother, hence good riddance. So an older brother, so to say, got lucky."

The glamour of Russian culture in the West preceded the glamour of Russian dissident culture, and prepared the ground also for the welcome that was extended to dissidents and defectors. I do not doubt that Brodsky, or Solzhenitsyn, or Baryshnikov viscerally hated the Soviet system, and of course I do not question their integrity. But even having hated the Soviets with all their hearts, they perversely benefited from the efforts that the Soviet Union (and the Russian Empire before it) had put into the promotion of Russian culture. The whole world knows Solzhenitsyn as the heroic author of a great book about the Gulag, but who knows Gustaw Herling-Grudziński, a Pole who wrote his account of the Gulag, *A World Apart,* many years earlier? Even an introduction by Bertrand Russell to the English edition in 1951, and the personal engagement of Albert Camus in support of the book, didn't help it. If you happened to be born in an empire, it was always better to be a metropolitan, not to "live in a distant province, by the ocean." It was better to be Russian.

We must be honest about these things. I wish my Western friends, before asking Ukrainians why they might wish to be rid of Pushkin, would ask themselves why they, the Westerners, care so much. Why do they worry about the legacy of Pushkin and Dostoevsky and Tolstoy and the others, but not about the over five hundred destroyed Ukrainian libraries? Why are they stirred by the names of streets but not by the looted Ukrainian museums? Why are they exercised about Russian writers who died in the nineteenth century but not about the Ukrainian writers and scholars who died last year?

I know some of the answers. First, in the matter of their attitude toward Ukrainian culture, there is the excuse of ignorance. This is perfectly fine as long as you admit it. I know almost nothing about Hungarian writers, and they live next door. Why should anyone be judged for not knowing about Ukrainian writers? The next honest answer would be that deep down you consider Russian culture not only superior to Ukrainian culture, but the only real culture available in this region of the world, and that anyone who rejects, or is even unenthusiastic about, Russian culture is barbarically rejecting culture itself. Here, too, ignorance is at work. I don't know contemporary Hungarian literature (except a few names and a few books), but I do not therefore suspect it to be inferior to, say, contemporary French literature. I am aware of the diversity of my part of the world and of my limited knowledge of it. In other words, I know how much I do not know. But many "enlightened" Western observers have been perfectly comfortable to see my part of the world stereotypically, as a homogeneously "shadowed land of backwardness." Exactly as they saw it in the eighteenth century.

This is the point at which I part company with many of my Ukrainian colleagues in our discussions of Ukrainian culture. Anyone who is aware of the centuries of Russian propaganda and "soft power" — Russians were always very good at this — can hardly assent to the idea that "Russophilia" and the downgrading of Ukrainian culture has been owed to the perfect beauty, the intrinsic superiority, of Russian culture. I do not mean to say, obviously, that Russian culture is lacking in beauty. I mean to say, rather, that the field was rigged. And this has been a problem not only for Ukraine, but also for the region that we used to call Central and Eastern Europe. The "Ukrainian cause" is larger than Ukraine. The historical background for this predicament was exquisitely laid out by the American historian Larry Wolff in 1994 in *Inventing Eastern Europe: The Map of Civilization on the Mind of the Enlightenment*, a book that deserves to be re-read in these awful days. (It was from Wolff's book that I borrowed the "shadowed land of backwardness" above.)

Though Russia has taken pains to shape the Western view of Russia, especially in Central and Eastern Europe, the crucial part of the job was done not by the authorities of this era but centuries ago, by the Russian Tsarinas of the eighteenth centuries — by Elizabeth, the daughter of Peter the Great who hired Voltaire to compose a history of Peter's reign, and of course by Catherine the Great. Voltaire was in correspondence with Elizabeth's favorite, the courtier and minister Ivan Shuvalov, who founded many of the central cultural institutions of the state. Shuvalov, particularly in his travels through Europe, did a lot of what today would be called shameless PR for Elizabeth's successor, the Russian empress Catherine II. Wolff's book provides rich material from the correspondence between Catherine and Voltaire, as well as other Western European accounts of what would later become Eastern Europe — the product of the eighteenth century's "diplomacy, cartography, and philosophy [that] operated in a triangular relation of mutual endorsement, reinforcement, and justification." Even taking into consideration the eighteenth-century context, Voltaire's servility — not only to Catherine II, but also to Frederick II of Prussia — is embarrassing. Wolff reminds us that "Voltaire's *History of Charles XII*, the philosophical foundation for the construction of Eastern Europe, was plainly an account of military conquest" and that its "agenda of international relations shaped the invention of Eastern Europe according to fantasies of influence and domination."

It was about power from the beginning. And so it continued: the free-thinking intellectuals Voltaire and Diderot rubbing shoulders with the political and imperial winners, normalizing the vision of the world that served the interests of the monarchs. These relationships are the foundation of the modern tradition of Russophilia and Russian supremacy. Or, to put it bluntly, these Enlightenment mandarins (and others) were given a free hand to disseminate lies about both Russia and unfortunate countries such as Poland, where the Russian army was sent "to establish tolerance," as Voltaire outrageously described it.

In his appeal to the Poles, Voltaire (who had never been to Poland or anywhere east of Berlin) mentioned Diderot's library, which Catherine had purchased and advised Polish "friends" to learn how to read "and then someone will buy libraries for you." Never mind that in 1768, when the pliable Voltaire was writing, there already was a large public library in Warsaw, one of the first and few in Europe back then. It was looted by Russian troops in 1794, when "establishing tolerance" cost the lives of twenty thousand Polish soldiers and citizens, including women and children. Whatever survived of the great library's almost four hundred thousand items was brought to St. Petersburg and within a year became the Imperial Public Library. Not everything that constitutes the illusion of the "great European culture" on the banks of the Neva was bought; much of it was stolen.

Though the partitions of Poland are distant history now, the habit of calling it "provincial" is still with us. And prejudices about Central and Eastern Europe also contributed to this notion of Russia as the origin of everything

Liberties

great: artists and musicians from the conquered lands were re-described as Russian and thus became "great" and no longer provincial, and "provincial" writers switched to Russian to be accepted and, hopefully, counted as "great." Fortunately, there was another view and another party. An opposite "ideological pole," as Wolff defines it, challenged the subordinate conception of Eastern Europe that prevails until today. It was inaugurated by Rousseau, who had also never been there. While Voltaire corresponded with monarchs, approving of despotism "displaced to a reassuring distance," Rousseau addressed the Polish nation, acknowledging its agency. What they had in common, however, was the assumption that they knew better than the nations in question.

These competing visions survived many more dramatic changes of the map of Europe, numerous wars, and some revolutions. Voltaire's heirs still believe in the "spheres of influence" theory of Russia's unquestioned predominance in the region. They consider themselves authorized to give away huge parts of the continent to an "enlightened" despot for modernization or "peacekeeping," or to decide whether this or that nation really needs NATO membership. Rousseau's intellectual legacy, by contrast, secured Central and Eastern Europe its friends and supporters, but too often these friends and supporters struggle to trust local expertise, which is — surprise! — in many cases better.

The second reason why we need to consider critically the cultural premises of the present debate is the ambiguity of Western "Russophilia" in its literal meaning. For the "philia" is in fact about the West itself, not the actual Russia.

These narcissistic optics are the downside of the perennial Western search for an alternative to itself. It is hard to accept that the system you live in, liberal democracy, is the only game in town — that what you have been given is all there is, or even all there should be. One may feel trapped, claustrophobic even. The restless energies of youth may feel thwarted. Coming from a time and a place where the West represented something ultimately good, something to strive for, I had it easier: growing up in the Soviet Union, in its rotten and disgusting realities, there was quite a clear path from bad to good, a path illuminated by hope. But for those who were already there, in the promised land of liberal democracy? If you accept the fact that you already live on the right side of history, but still see all its flaws and all its wrongs, where is the hope for you? Those deluded Eastern Europeans, naïve as puppies, the ones who revere the democratic West and aspire to belong to it, don't see how unjust the Western world is, but you, you see. (This is immediately followed by adrenaline shots of Kissinger-like cynicism.) And you need an alternative, a dispensation more exciting than merely fixing the flaws of the existing system. "Truth comes from the north," as Voltaire put it. You need another country.

This way of thinking has been an inherent feature of Western intellectual history. Remember all those laments, all these books and articles, about "the decline of the West," the endless stream of dystopias, the guilt about every success? I would even suggest that this mode of thinking defines what it means to be a Westerner. Whatever its conclusions, the questions are all the same: What did *we* do wrong? What was *our* mistake? The idea that something in the world may happen without our input, independent of Western influence, is too hard, or too insulting, to digest. Westerners are often criticized for taking credit for all the good in the world, but they also tend to take credit for all the evil. This habit of mind is exactly what made Western countries safe, rich, and preferable for living: the restless anxiety and the race for self-improvement. Yet it is also what makes them largely incapable of understanding evil beyond the Western realm. This stubborn dodging may be confused with political correctness, but it is hard to draw the line between actual PC and the inability to recognize the agency of others at their worst.

The other great attraction of Russian culture for Westerners is that it flatters their vanity about their own profundity. In the modern era, thoughtful Westerners have liked to portray themselves as open to paradoxes and abysses, as rebellious, iconoclastic. As is well known, Russian culture is abundantly stocked with abysses. Nothing makes one feel deeper than a few pages of Dostoevsky. And finally a much more banal context must be considered. We prefer to talk about ideas, not about money; we like words, not numbers. But it was money that brought those mesmerizing Russians to you — that made it possible for Turgenev to hang out with Henry James, and Nabokov to polish his talent in Oxford and Switzerland; that guaranteed the appearance of all those articles about Russian tycoons and their socialite art-scene wives, and the whole media "eco-system" around them, in the *New Yorker* and elsewhere. Money is the main reason you know about Russian culture and its greatness. And not just the monarchy's money, or the Bolsheviks' money. It's not even money in the plain sense of the word: there is also the virtual money transformed into personal, social, and thus cultural capital, the "money" of the prominent promoters of Russian culture throughout the twentieth century, Vladimir Nabokov or Isaiah Berlin or Alexander Liberman or Alexey Brodovitch.

Though most of them were not exactly Russian, almost all of them were well-off and brought up by Russian institutions or in Russian culture. And later they conferred their prestige upon the reputation of that culture. Their milieu was rather cosmopolitan and so was their worldview, and they projected this attractive image onto Russia and Russian culture as they represented it. Due to the isolation of the Soviet Union, these bright personalities were able to confer a certain glamour upon the image of a Russia that no longer existed.

And if one does still more soul-searching, the next honest answer about the Western insistence upon the political innocence of Russian culture will be this: it solves a certain problem. The romance of Russian culture is a safe way to stand for tradition without standing for *Western* tradition, a safe way to stand for culture without standing for *Western* culture. Defending a British monument suggests an old-fart right-wing approval of imperialism, but defending a Russian monument leaves an impression of open-mindedness and even of a progressive inclination. Russophilia is a clever way to canalize imperial or reactionary-nostalgic sentiments: after all, these sentiments are not for a Western empire, are they?

Yet a different distinction, an important distinction, among the imperialisms must be made. The Western countries that had empires, or rather their intellectuals, particularly British and French, vigorously criticized and deconstructed their colonial legacies, and admitted the sins of colonialism, and worked diligently to become more sensitive to the consequences of their overseas dominion, to the difficult situations of their former colonies. Some say that the Western critique of Western imperialism did not go far enough; others contend that the guilt discourse of the West is overdone, and crippling; but the telling fact is that Western introspection about imperialism exists and forms a significant part of Western intellectual life. It is there. Few Russian intellectuals, by contrast, have performed the same service about Russian imperialism. The oppression and extermination of the indigenous people of Siberia, the savage persecutions of Ukrainians, Belarusians, Lithuanians, Poles, Jews, and their own Russian people after all, the encouragement of pogroms by the Tsar's family, the slavery, the cultural appropriation — almost none of these atrocious subjects entered the mainstream of Russian academic discourse. And while the British monarchy is abhorred as mean and illegitimate at all levels of Western culture, high to low, from scholarship to *The Crown*, the Russian imperial past is left more or less unquestioned, when it is not heaped with *Nicholas and Alexandra*-type romanticism.

Obviously the heritage of Russian art and music and literature is immensely rich. My point, rather, is that (to paraphrase Walter Benjamin) every document of Russian civilization is also a document of Russian barbarism. To be indifferent to all these shadows in this time of Russian aggression is especially egregious. It isn't hard to refute the shallow Russophilia of those who imagine Russia as a realm of *Anna Karenina* characters. It is much harder to confront those contemporary worshippers of Russian culture whom I deeply respect. The Polish postwar writer Marek Głasko once remarked, having in mind Ukrainians and Poles, Eastern and Central Europeans, that we will not be properly understood in France until there are Russian tanks in the suburbs of Paris. But not even such a scenario, and may it never come to pass, would convince those Russophiles who have experienced Russian cruelty and still admire Russian culture.

In the summer of 1920, when Isaac Babel joined the Budyonny cavalry's offensive, a young Polish writer and artist named Józef Czapski, an earnest pacifist, joined the Krechowiecki First Cavalry Regiment to fight against the Bolsheviks. That summer they were trapped about twenty miles east of Olesko Castle, and Czapski barely saved his injured brother's life.

Czapski and his comrades were not exactly birds of a feather: he was born into a noble Polish family and grew up in St. Petersburg, and his adolescence was highly influenced by Russian literature. "In the shadow of Tolstoy, Dostoevsky, and revolution," he recalled, "Poland felt kind of parochial compared with titanic, cruel, extreme, and genius-rich Russia." Czapski discovered himself as a Pole only in 1919, a year before he was conscripted to defend his country in its struggle to recover its statehood: his national feeling changed "like a thunderbolt," and he realized that his "inferiority complex towards Russia was induced only by the fear of [Russian] dominance of *polanenszczyzna* [the romanticized national image of Poland]."

But Czapski's fascination with Russia was not the result only of his extensive reading of Tolstoy and the personal influence of the famed Russian writer Dmitri Merezhkovsky. Owing to his exalted social origins, his circle in St. Petersburg in the turbulent revolutionary years consisted mostly of the highest ranks of the Russian government. He lived with his uncle, Baron Aleksander Meyendorff, who was for a while a vice-marshal of the Russian Duma, and his family had a connection to Pyotr Stolypin, the Russian nationalist politician and reformer. (He was assassinated in 1911.) In 1917, Czapski discussed the February Revolution with his uncle's milieu, "an international circle to a certain degree, where English or French was spoken." Georgy Chicherin, Lenin's friend and commissar for foreign affairs, was a relative, too. In other words, Czapski first observed Russian realities from on high.

But it was not long before his vantage point changed dramatically. When Germany and the Soviet Union (an alliance with its own history of being scanted in the West) invaded Poland in 1939, Czapski was a reserve officer. A month after the invasion he was a prisoner of war, along with four thousand Polish officers deported by the Soviets to Starobilsk in eastern Ukraine. (Starobilsk has been close to the frontline since 2014 and was occupied by Russia in 2022.) Czapski was one of only seventy-eight survivors of the camp at Starobilsk. In his memoirs *Memories of Starobielsk* and *Unhuman Land*, Czapski described his experience of the camp, and also of another Soviet camp for Polish POWs, Gryazovets, as well as his release in 1941 and his subsequent journey with General Anders' Free Polish Army from northern Russia to Uzbekistan, Iran, Iraq, Palestine, Egypt, Italy, and postwar Europe. In 1940 Anders tasked Czapski with locating the whereabouts of missing Polish officers, about eight thousand of them, who had fought Hitler and ended up in Soviet captivity. Eventually Czapski would learn that the missing officers were killed by the NKVD with Stalin's approval, most of them in Katyn, Russia. (In England at roughly the same time Churchill ordered a quiet British inquiry into the mass executions — quiet for the sake of "Allied solidarity" — and it, too, concluded that the Soviets were culpable.) After the war the Katyn massacre become a matter of some controversy. In 1952 Czapski testified before the United States Congress about it, and a special committee of the House's report assigned responsibility for the atrocity to the Soviets, but in the years of the Cold War the discussion of the massacre was mostly suppressed in the United States and Europe so as not to offend the Soviets. It was only when the

NKVD archives were opened in the 1990s that Russian authorities admitted to the killings of twenty thousand Poles (and others) in Katyn.

Memories of Starobielsk and *Unhuman Land* are heartbreaking reading, with a troubled history of publication in English. (The French translation in 1949 was not warmly welcomed, to put it mildly.) I read Czapski's memoirs in a Ukrainian translation before the Russian invasion, and back then it resonated in a special way because many of Czapski's camp fellows were doctors, lawyers, and academics from Lviv, my hometown. These people, dying of typhus and diarrhea in lice-filled barracks, once walked the same streets as I now do, and might have stood in the same pews in my church; and their families, too, were deported by Russians, in their case to the Gulag. Over two hundred thousand Poles, Ukrainians, and Jews were deported from Western Ukraine to Russia and Kazakhstan in the two years between 1939 and 1941 alone. Knowing what is happening to Ukrainian war prisoners at the very moment that I write this, and to the forcibly deported Ukrainian families and the kidnapped children, I just don't have the stomach to reread Czapski's books in full. At the same time, the difficulties that Czapski and his colleagues had with British censorship, the Allies' ugly fascination with Stalin, the Western reluctance to hear the truth about Soviets, the anti-Polish sentiments: all this reminds me of how much luckier, if you'll pardon the expression, Ukrainians are today. Present-day technologies will at least provide us with a shield against oblivion and furnish the unequivocal evidence of present-day Russian atrocities. The memory hole will not win again.

In Poland, Czapski is frequently referred as an icon. He is iconic for me too, someone I greatly admire, a great-souled man. I understand his Russian sentiments, but I take them with a pinch of salt. When, in his in his essays and interviews, Czapski's regularly pays homage to the greatness of Russian literature, the piety creates a certain dissonance with his otherwise scrupulous and abstemious voice, with his extraordinary sensitivity to the complexities of history, almost in the way that Babel's awful denunciations in the *Literaturnaya Gazeta* contrast with his subtle prose. I also find it hard to ignore the fragmentation of his vision: while he is observantly aware of his own relatively privileged status in Tashkent, and delicately points to the luxury of Stalin's protégé Alexei Tolstoy's life there, Czapski barely dwells on the privileged status of Alexei Tolstoy's guest in Tashkent, the Russian poet Anna Akhmatova, whom he met there in 1942 and admired ever since. For Czapski, as well as for the world outside the Soviet Union, Akhmatova was a nonconformist and even a rebellious poet. She certainly showed great courage: her husband was shot by the Bolsheviks in 1921 and her son was arrested in 1938 (and again in 1949). But in his book Czapski at least records a rather delicate question: "What was this woman doing, the mother of a convict, in the house of the regime's most devoted writer?" It is an excellent question. He notes without judging that she was praised by Stalin. In 1942, Stalin even sent a special plane on his personal orders to evacuate her from besieged Leningrad, as the city suffered its terrible famine. From Leningrad she went to Christopol, and from Christopol to the safer haven of Tashkent, where she remained until 1944, when she returned to the ruins of Leningrad.

This Tashkent episode may be the most peaceful part of *Inhuman Land*. Still, Czapski did not get the whole picture. Ukrainian poets who were not less talented than Akhmatova — to be honest, I prefer some of them to Akhmatova's melodramatic tone — did not even have the privilege of their own graves, let alone a special plane. In 1937 they were shot in Sandarmokh, in Karelia, with thousands of other prisoners of Soviet camps. Six thousand two hundred and forty-one victims of this massacre have been identified, among them the Ukrainian writers Mykola Kulish, Mykola Zerov, Valerian Pidmohylny, and Marko Vorony, the Ukrainian theater director Les Kurbas, and numerous Ukrainian scholars, teachers, and editors. The toll for Ukrainian intellectuals was so high that the entire generation is now referred to as the "Executed Renaissance." Czapski could not have known about this atrocity back in 1942, but he would learn about it later, after having settled down in Maisons-Laffitte in Paris, the seat of the Polish émigré journal *Kultura*. It was *Kultura* that would publish *The Executed Renaissance Anthology* in 1959.

Czapski's later essays about Russian writers show that this knowledge did not change his standpoint or his tone in evaluating things Russian. Must the love of culture really be so blinding? Yet we must give him credit for artistic intuition: never judging, he wrote in his diary about his second meeting with Akhmatova in 1965, this time in a Paris hotel, that "I think involuntarily of the eighteenth-century idealized portraits of Russian empresses." In that comment he was revealing more than he realized. After all that Czapski had endured, no one can accuse him of being insensitive. A man has a right to his blind spots; we all have them. Even people who have seen the worst have blind spots. But why are these old cultural hierarchies still accepted uncritically, and placed beyond the reach of moral and historical complication?

I doubt that a call for the reassessment of one's cultural hierarchies in the light of Russian crimes in Ukraine will be very popular, but it is past due. The projection of Western likes and dislikes, of Western needs and fantasies, upon Russia must be challenged by the cold realities of contemporary history. And not only upon Russia but also upon Ukraine, Poland, Central Europe, and any place foreign enough to serve as "another country." Perhaps one day a Russian writer will have the guts to "look back at the red towers of your native Sodom," in the words of Akhmatova's poem, to look back without resentment or extenuation at the inhuman land and its people drunk with hatred and violence and a hellish obedience. I believe that Russian literature may produce a great novel on this subject in the future, maybe its greatest novel of all. And I believe that it will be an endlessly sad novel, a tale about extreme human failure, full of sorrow and loneliness, shame and alienation. That is a novel I will be eager to read.

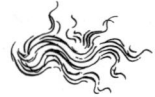

CHRISTIAN LORENTZEN

In Dreams Begin Responsibilities: A Memoir

We knew we were already too late. Too late to be modernists, too late to be reds, too late to turn against Stalin, too late to fight the Nazis, too late to be red-baited, too late to join the anti-communist left, too late to take money from the CIA for our magazines. We were too late to be Cold Warriors and too late to bother trying to ban the bomb — the situation was in hand, we were told. We were too late for cheap rent. We came after Stonewall and, most of us, after the worst of the AIDS crisis. The famous zones of bohemian social life were expired: we never stepped foot in the real Cedar Tavern, or the Factory, or the Bunker, or Max's Kansas City, or the Mudd Club, or Studio 54.

We weren't too late for the Downtown Art Scene Gold Rush, which seems to be permanent, if permanently tainted, because money has to come from somewhere. We weren't too late to go to CBGB's, but we were too late to see Television there; we instead saw bands that sounded like Television because the first thing we learned about when we were children was recycling. We were all recyclers. A term available for recycling at the time of our arrival was *hipster*, so that's what they called us and what some of us called each other or even ourselves, especially when we were bemoaning our artistic or intellectual bankruptcy, which is not exactly the subject of this essay.

We were hipsters but we weren't "White Negroes," which is not a phrase we would use, no matter how many of us were reading Norman Mailer. We were deracinated. We Were postcolonial. We were "diverse," or so it was said. Most of us, it should be admitted, went to Fancy Colleges. If you went to a Fancy College in the late 1990s, you might have been handed something that looked like a magazine called *Diversity & Distinction*. It was the institution's propaganda for us, about us. It wasn't untrue, but we distrusted advertisements, even advertisements for ourselves. It was called Meritocracy and you had to believe in it a little bit because otherwise you wouldn't be there. Otherwise there was no way you belonged, unless it was the wrong kind of belonging, the old kind, the kind you could just pay for. We might have been diverse but we were all good at filling in the right little circles with our pencils, and we loved studying, whatever love means in this context. Maybe we loved reading or maybe winning was what we loved. The campus experience for undergraduates of the late 1990s was a quiet one. The culture wars of the late 1980s and early 1990s had subsided and were spoken of in the past tense by survivors. Political correctness was dormant. There were hardly any drugs. We had irony and hip hop. We were moving from grunge to twee. If you spent early mornings chalking the pavements of the Fancy College Yard against the bombings in the Balkans it was a lonely operation — there might be two of you. And maybe the Kosovars did need us to save them. Maybe your grandmother was Albanian. Chalk is easily washed away by rain.

A strange thing that happened at the end of Fancy College was that many of us signed up to be recruited by investment banks and were hired by them at what were rumored to be very high salaries. Was this always the point? Didn't they write their theses about Habermas? Is that why they cut their hair last year? It didn't matter to us—we would forget them — because we wanted to be Writers and Intellectuals. The summer after we graduated there appeared a double issue of *The City Dweller Magazine* with the slogan THE FUTURE OF AMERICAN FICTION, along with the first lines of twenty short stories, emblazoned across the sky on its cover. The sky was part of a cartoon drawing of a hunched man in tattered clothes looking out at the horizon from the sands of an alluring and otherwise vacant beach. (The sky writing was apparently this coastal hobo's beach read.) Within the issue were the stories — one of them a classic — but, more important, there were photographs of the writers, all of whom were not yet over the age of forty (let's not press this issue). They were pictured as if socializing together against glamorous backdrops — in Brooklyn across the East River (or was it Jersey and the Hudson?) from a blurry Manhattan skyline; on the back of a flatbed truck speeding past some trees perhaps to the Hamptons, or past the vista of a bridge perhaps to the Catskills — and they seemed happy. They seemed to be friends. It might have been a reunion of extras from the pilot of *Friends*, a show we never watched. Literary life was convivial.

Liberties

Some of these figures of the Future we already knew from author photos on the jackets of books we would bring with us to the City. There was Our Hero, and there was Our Hero's Best Friend. (Our Hero would later kill himself and His Best Friend would appear on *Oprah* after grumbling about it.) There was the Dystopian Buddhist. There was The Guy Who Wrote the Novel the Movie *The Ice Storm* Was Based On, as well as The Guy Whose Novels Were Too Weird to Ever Adapt for the Screen, The Guy Who Loved Comic Books, and The Guy Who Wrote the Novel Narrated in the Second Person Plural. (Collectively, these guys were later dubbed The New White Guys by The Mean Gay White Guy.) There was The Guy Who Also Wrote Young Adult Fiction and The Lady Who Would Later Move to Italy. There was The Guy Who Loved Video Games and The Lady from the Tragic Island. There was The Graphomaniac Who Wrote about Sleeping with Prostitutes and Was Sometimes a Lady Herself. Also present: The Guy Who Taught at Iowa, The Hackey-Sack Guy, Two Ladies Whose Books We Never Read. Not present: The Guy We've Still Never Otherwise Heard Of, The Guy Who Opened for DeLillo at the 92nd Street Y, The Edgy Lady, and The Guy Who Gave Us Permission to Do a Lot of Ecstasy One Summer by Writing a Cover Story about It for *The Magazine That Came with the Sunday Newspaper.*

The point is anointment. The point is casual glamor (which is not glamor at all; only The Lady Who Came from England the Next Summer had that). The point is diversity & distinction. The point is: *These were writers*, and, as we would learn from *Trashy Weekly*, where we would have to fix commas in order to pay rent, *they were just like us*. The point is we may have shown up too late to be Modernists or Postmodernists or Dirty Realists or members of the New York School or writers of New Narrative, but we weren't too late for Publicity. We weren't too late to be Famous. We held onto this artifact for more than a decade. Some of us still possess it. Some of us qualified for it the next time they made The List. At least six of us (depending on who's doing the counting) made it the second time around. *The City Dweller* doesn't bother with The List anymore. Too many lists going around. The field is diluted. And most lists these days — you don't want to be on them.

We arrived the month after the millennium turned and signed a lease in Brooklyn, except those of us who came earlier and moved to Manhattan or Queens or those of us came later after the end of Decadence. A few of us had grown up in the city or gone to school here. We talked about starting our own magazines. In the meantime, we had to get jobs. Many jobs were on offer to do things you never dreamed of doing and could not describe, but it was advertised that they came with stock options and equity. How could such things be bad? Not wanting them amounted to not wanting money, not wanting a house, not wanting a future for the children we didn't have yet. Luckily soon enough the stock market crashed and we no longer had to think about those options because they had been discredited, no matter how many times the chimera of mysteriously easy digital wealth would return, eventually literally under the name "crypto." In America the size of the con is always swelling.

Many of the other jobs were not very good. Many of the good jobs did not pay because they were not real jobs; they were internships and were temporary, but could lead to the good jobs that paid, or could lead you straight into being a writer. Maybe you could deliver drugs, launder your money, and fly away to write stories for magazines, as one of us did. But most of us did things like fix commas and check facts at *Trashy Weekly*. The office was convivial. We might toss around a Nerf football. We might sneak a cigarette behind a closed glass door. We might light the Boss' cigarette as he strode among the cubicles — he still retained that privilege. Nobody really wanted to be there, even the Boss, who was being paid well; he wanted to move on to the next better paying job at *Athletics with Photos*, which he soon did. After all, he had edited *High-End Dude Magazine* and was known to be close friends with Hunter Thompson and George Plimpton. How many covers would he run about movie stars losing weight or the soon-to-be-forgotten winner of this week's reality game show? The nights the issues closed, there was free sushi and a free limousine home — or to the club if we preferred. (Nell's was still open that year.) The jobs were vacuous and tedious and centered our lives around finding faults in copy and captions — "display type is the most important thing," we were told — about the careers and love lives of actors, actresses, and singers we had mostly never heard of because we stopped watching television in 1994 in order to become Intellectuals.

It was not the work of Intellectuals. Yet we read about Intellectuals who had done this sort of work, and it seemed, if equally worthless, somehow more worthy. Elizabeth Hardwick read and rewrote dime-store romances for pulp publishers. Henry Miller wrote pornography and was paid by the page. Yet some writers had come to town and gotten decent jobs immediately. Henry Luce hired Dwight Macdonald and James Agee to report for *Fortune*. They both hated the magazine but it got them somewhere. Macdonald testified that the job taught him how to organize his material by putting all the stuff about the same thing in the same place, and then he started *politics*. Agee took an assignment to go to Dust Bowl Appalachia with Walker Evans and the result was *Let Us Now Praise Famous Men*. The Boss, no matter how cool he was, wasn't going to give you an assignment that would result in something like that — say, *Let Us Now Praise Famous Survivor Contestants*. Nor was the Boss' Boss, who, though legendary, seemed like a philistine up close. Yet some of us started getting decent jobs and you saw them at parties.

There was an election, and some of us who didn't vote for Al Gore voted for Ralph Nader. It didn't matter because the only votes that ended up counting that year after a long tedious news cycle about how paper was punched in Florida were those of the Supreme Court justices. Given that we worked in irrelevant jobs and were subjected constantly to phony incentives, casting a protest vote seemed natural. Soon the World Trade Center and the Pentagon were attacked. Luckily our friends who had summer jobs in the towers had left them eleven days earlier to go to graduate school. Some of us weren't so lucky. Some of us volunteered to shovel out the rubble. Some of us moved out of the city in fear, and we would hardly ever hear from them again.

The fun was over, but we were still young, so it couldn't really be over. We observed the responses of our elders, the Intellectuals we admired or at least were meant to admire. Some of them spoke of the events in the vocabulary of Lifestyle, the carnage smelling like "smoked mozzarella." Some of them had their grief consoled by the idea that their own Spanish Civil War had now arrived. Some of them debated the meanings of courage and cowardice. Some of them claimed that irony was dead, but we knew it was still alive in our hearts. We were in no position to voice a response of our own because the Internet was insufficiently advanced at the time and we had yet to form our own relationships with printing presses beyond our comma-fixing. That would soon change.

Our own irrelevance was confirmed when we joined at least a hundred thousand others and millions worldwide to protest the war not yet launched in the vicinity of the United Nations three years after we had signed our first lease in Brooklyn. At the office during your internship at *Patrician Pacifist Monthly* you watched the Secretary of State's presentation to the UN about the deadly aluminum tubes. It was unconvincing. On the same television a few weeks later, working late for free, you watched the bombing begin. You learned not to trust *The Newspaper*. The protests accomplished nothing in terms of halting the invasion and were not meaningfully sustained, though they would erupt now and again, as when the president's party held its convention on Seventh Avenue in Manhattan, and some of us were arrested. This time all of us voted for Kerry, but he lost. We had no control over the country, which belonged to Ohio. By this time you had a real job, and certainly not a well-paid one, down Seventh Avenue from the arena at *Obsolete Bimonthly Cold War Organ*.

    The Boss had worked at the magazine since the 1950s and run it since the 1960s, after the actual Menshevik who had controlled it for decades, and had at times taken actual money from the CIA, died. The Boss had learned journalism covering Broadway for his Fancy College's student paper after the war, and you imagined he was the model for Tony Curtis in *Sweet Smell of Success,* except with almost crippling integrity. He hired you because the only thing you said during your job interview was that you were reading *To the Finland Station.* The Boss' attitude toward you was one of suspicion, because the two most famous journalists of your generation were famous for getting fired from their jobs because they made up their stories.

In Dreams Begin Responsibilities: A Memoir

One of them also seemed to have a drug problem. Luckily, the only writing you were allowed to do was book reviews, and you could always demonstrate you had read the whole book by displaying a tattered galley. Most of your tasks consisted of rewriting the copy of the magazine's most geriatric contributors. Their arguments were sound because they had spent a lifetime thinking about the Civil Rights Movement or the Cuban Missile Crisis or the Triangle Shirtwaist Fire, even if they hadn't quite been present for the last one. But their prose needed work — it could be fragmentary, for one thing — because some of them had passed the age of ninety and were residing in nursing homes. You regarded their efforts with respect and the chance to work on their copy and be published beside them as a lucky thing, even if hardly anybody read the magazine, because there were few subscribers whose constant requests for cancellation were ignored, and no web presence to speak of. You should have fixed up a website, but you suspected the Boss couldn't handle it. Dollars to donuts, the Boss often said, a token and your degree in Ancient Greek will get you a ride home on the subway.

Intellectual modesty was one of the Boss' values and the reason he killed pieces once in a while: they asserted too much and too harshly. It didn't make a difference to the non-contributors because the fees were low (referred to not as fees but as "tangible tokens of our appreciation") and the pieces could be placed in magazines people actually read. One day the Boss was very excited about a piece he had coming in from an acquaintance who had managed to travel to Cuba, a notoriously hard place to obtain copy from if you edited a historically anti-communist magazine that barely paid its writers. But there was disappointment all around when the piece turned out to be a travelogue about shopping amid the island's plentiful bargains. Something you respected about the Boss was that he had no interest in Lifestyle, a subject increasingly prevalent among formerly strictly Intellectual magazines. It was a discovery of the preceding generation: writers could be well compensated by intellectualizing such salad ingredients as cilantro or avocado or by writing a profile of a Chef that cast him as an Artist. *The City Dweller* was more and more filled with such articles, so you stopped reading it cover to cover.

On Seventh Avenue the use of Linotype machines was frequently recalled aloud, and our desktop computers too were referred to as "machines." Pica rulers were in circulation among the staff of three. One of your tasks was to cut out pictures of politicians, authors, and actors from the newspaper, in case they might one day be of use to the magazine's poorly compensated and sometimes not credited illustrators. These clippings were kept in a bank of filing cabinets and sorted alphabetically. It was good to have something to do besides editing because you were told you edited "too fast." Yet you often reached the point you had done all you could or should do, at which point you would sit at your desk pretending to edit but instead reading *Daily Counterintuitive Online Magazine* or *Daily Outraged Complacent Liberal Online Magazine*. All of us with desk jobs did this, yet it must have been something new. How did one waste time at one's desk before the Internet? If you just sat there reading the paper edition of *Distinguished Journal of Book Reviews*, as you often had during your downtime at *Trashy Weekly*, The Boss and his secretary would notice. Your weekly paycheck was handwritten and amounted to less than half a month's rent, so you took a night job fixing commas at *Archaic Neocon Daily*. Once the editors ran a piece saying Saddam Hussein's WMDs had been found because somebody from Damascus came to the office and told them the stockpile was hidden in Syria. Now there was a newspaper you really couldn't trust.

And then came the blogs. You didn't know anybody who died in the towers or anybody fighting in the war (the one guy from the Fancy College you knew who had been in the ROTC was stationed in Japan arranging for the transport of weapons systems), but you knew people who started blogs. If distinctions between High and Low had been collapsing for decades, now they were gone entirely. Going viral was the new option. You tried it at your desk one afternoon and succeeded. You were clever enough to survive if you were ever fired from *Obsolete Bimonthly Cold War Organ* or it shut down. Since you suspected that you were paid largely from proceeds of review copies sold to the Strand, the latter seemed an imminent possibility, and soon enough it came to pass. But by this time your friends had started their own magazine, *Ground 0*, and they were publishing you, if only because you helped them with proofreading and showed them how to put together a table of contents. You learned that the best way to go viral by writing, say, a movie review was to be harsh and call attention to yourself, especially in the opening. This was the style of the Internet. So much for the Boss' credo of intellectual modesty.

The editors of *Ground 0* did not encourage this vice, which was all your own, an endemic viral infection. They were very good at cutting the boring parts of pieces, the obligatory tics you had learned from the Boss, who was always saying, "Put a billboard on it so the reader knows where you're going." *Ground 0* was marked from its origins by a left-liberal political outlook, against American wars of choice if unconvinced of its capacity to deter them; by a skeptical attitude toward the emerging online ecosphere, though under no delusions that it could be halted or anything other than acquiesced to for practical purposes; by an outsider-insider relationship to the academy, defensive on the subject of theory but not professionally beholden to whatever its current standing happened to be; by an emphasis on the present that embraced explorations of recent traditions but eschewed a ubiquitous literary necrophilia; and by a commitment to examine its contributors' conditions of intellectual production. None of this was exactly new — hardly anything ever is, we were learning — but the difference was that we were the ones doing it. Recent new lit mags had taken their aesthetic and ethos from an imaginary nineteenth century or the time of Mencken. Ours came from the New York Intellectuals of the mid-twentieth century, for better or worse. Recycling was still the first lesson we had ever learned.

It was an intellectual style born of an awareness of, a complicity with, a resistance to, or a saturation in Meritocracy, Publicity, Futility, Lifestyle, and the Internet. There was to be less irony than there had been in the 1990s, but we wouldn't be humorless. Theory might inform the arguments, but they would be plainspoken and without jargon. The writerly I would be deployed within narrative terrain, but we knew the New Journalism had already had its day and the point was not confession, of which there would soon be a not entirely unrelated deluge. Clouded by intervening events, our memories now perhaps overemphasize a sense of futility. One editor at the time remarked something along these lines: if Saddam Hussein and his friends could take over a whole country when he was in his early thirties, surely a bunch of us can start a magazine. It should also be noted that the magazine printed posters with slogans including "UTOPIA IN OUR TIME." Pessimism may have been part of the mentality but it was suppressed in the intellectual style. We were trying to do something, after all.

In Dreams Begin Responsibilities: A Memoir

We were trying to contribute something to the culture that had the shape of what we wanted the culture to be. We were also trying to write books, or get book deals, or get jobs. In the meantime, we threw parties. Among attendees of the parties there were still high levels of frustration. Too many of us were still fixing commas or checking facts, even if they were being paid well to do so at someplace like *The Classy Magazine*. It was all taking too long. We were starting to get old and we hadn't saved any money. Meanwhile the bloggers were out there just saying whatever they wanted, shaking off their hangovers with liberal doses of Adderall and picking whose writings got linked to. And they didn't even bother with fact checkers or comma fixers. Some of them were starting to get paid, and not badly. We knew this because we all went to the same bars. What they did seemed, if not hard exactly, at least very tiring. It was difficult to write books and get book deals if you fixed commas by day (and perhaps also by night) and spent the rest of the time at bars or magazine parties or literary readings. It was time to stop going out so much and start producing.

Some of the things we produced fell broadly into three categories: 1) the anti-lifestyle essay; 2) the nonfiction literary adventure; 3) autofiction. What these genres had in common was that they were personality-based and required a stylistic flair. Ultimately, the two elements, being historically conflated anyway, were hard to separate. Of one writer, you would later hear an older esteemed editor remark, "So is she just going to do personality pieces from now on?" What these writings tended to say was: I am very perceptive of the current state of things and I am against them, not just the state but even the things themselves. Or: I have been on a journey far away, to a place where the past still lives, among people with living knowledge of the past, and one thing I can tell you is that history has a happy ending and that happy ending is me. Or: I have participated in the spirit of the times and adjusted my consciousness to it exquisitely in order to produce the work of art you are reading, none of which is necessarily true.

We invented Mumblecore. We invented Flash Mobs. We invented Poptimism. From *Ground 0* and its neighboring generational precincts many now distinguished careers were launched. Some of us wrote these books and some of us reviewed them and we concluded that many of them weren't bad. Of course, it wasn't just us. People were writing stuff like this in other countries, such as Scandinavia. The Norwegians, they were just like us, except with a superior welfare state and a scarier history of intimacy with their formerly Nazi neighbors. Knocks about this writing included that it was narcissistic; that some of it was whimsical and unserious; that it lacked ideological commitment even if it voiced political avowals; that opposition to Lifestyle required being in thrall to Lifestyle by making it your subject, even in a negative capacity; or, worst of all, that they were blogs on paper. One zone where idealists and nihilists find common ground is narcissism. We will always remember the Bush administration as the happiest days of our lives.

Then the Younger People came and they were different than we were. They were more uptight, for one thing, even if they had so many tattoos. They came of age around Obama's election and so had a sense of political hope, even if he would ultimately disappoint them. Their political consciousness had been raised collectively by Occupy Wall Street in a way that ours at that age had not been by the anti-globalization protests, which hadn't happened everywhere but only in certain places we had never visited, such as Seattle. They were more entrenched in the academy and more affiliated with its unions (and also more likely to write book reviews that sounded like term papers, which we considered deadly). They unionized some of the magazines where they went to work. These achievements were salutary. The Younger People also arrived with the advent of social media, which allowed aspiring writers to obtain something that seemed like Fame, and Fame for being something like a Writer, before they had written, or in a meaningful way published, anything longer than a few sentences. Being older, we had difficulty telling if the effects of this novel form of notoriety were beneficial, because confidence building, or grotesque, because of the genesis of perverse incentives. Call it a mixed bag. It did not belong to us.

This essay, which is almost over, is not about the Younger People and certainly not about their oedipal struggle with the Older Generation. We were the generation in between and they allowed us to discover our own irrelevance for a second time, by outnumbering us and dominating "the discourse," a word we only used to use in school. The major difference between us and them is that we knew that we had come too late to live through the 1930s, and they believed they were reliving the 1930s, right down to the manifestation of actual Nazi-like opponents. They had seen what we'd been doing and they had learned from us, but they had learned even more from the bloggers, some of whom had become famous and rich by writing and could take credit for a genuine political impact, a shifting of the boundaries of the more and more tenuous liberal consensus. The Younger People were not around for the homophobia of the 1980s, they saw the regime of gay marriage as the natural state of things, and they believed that there's no reason why liberation should not be complete for all.

Liberties

We worked with the Younger People and we still do. We edited them and now they edit us, at times imposing their term-paper ethos, drearily. The protest movements brought forth pamphlets and gazettes born of intergenerational collaborations, but soon enough the Younger People had their own things. Their magazines are marked by a clearer sense of political mission, including actual goals that might be achieved through elections. They have more of an insider's relationship to the academy because they believe that that belongs to them too, just like everything else. They are critical of Meritocracy because its injustices are obvious, and anything with those has to go. They are not resistant to Lifestyle and its intellectualization because they intellectualize everything, even previously unspeakable disorders of the intestines. Yuck!

What of us now, with our new alienations, our obsolete vanities, our petty unfulfilled apolitical careerism? Some of us have had children and are too busy to worry about it. Some of us have even made raising children our subject, to mixed commercial results. Most of us have tried to keep our heads down and out of the way of the constant crossfire of the culture war, but others dove right in. A few, as you always suspected some might, even became reactionary, "reactionary" not in the old war-mongering way but rather in the new culture war-mongering way. We are no longer coherent socially. The weddings are in the past and the divorces have been piling up for years. The people you used to hate, now you're happy if you see them at a party. We have been scattered to the winds. There are still books you want to write. It's not too late for that until you die.

In Dreams Begin Responsibilities: A Memoir

ROBERT B. PIPPIN

The Clarifying Obscurity of Robert Bresson

What a film demands from a viewer varies a great deal. Often not much is demanded. Keeping the characters straight, remembering what has happened, and following the plot are usually enough for much commercial cinema to "work," to make sense and entertain. We easily accept the illusion that we are watching a fictional cinematic world in which we are not present or detectable, and we allow ourselves to imagine that we are watching, unobserved, what simply happens in that world. We can occasionally notice that an actor is doing a fine job or that a director has edited a sequence in a confusing way, but if that happens too frequently something is going wrong.

Liberties

Things are going well when we are absorbed in the depicted world, not attending to the world as filmed; that is, when we attend to the filmed *world*, not to the *film world*, the world of the actors, the sets, the music, the directorial decisions.

Some cinema addresses its viewer in a different way, though. Something brings us up short when viewing it alters our immediately absorbed attentiveness and seems to demand a regimen of reflective attentiveness. We can still be absorptively engaged in the filmed world; a level of concern, interest in what is happening, tense expectation, still engage us — but in parallel, and, if done successfully, in a way that does not interfere with the normal reaction. We are puzzled that we are looking for several seconds at an empty staircase or an open door or an empty meadow, that the camera lingers on a scene several seconds after a character has departed it, that between one scene and a later one a temporal slice has gone missing and we are not shown events that have happened that we would expect to have seen. We are puzzled that characters speak in a somewhat flat tone, or with minimal affect; that unusually long periods of silence occur; that our attention is drawn to various sounds in scenes, sounds that would not be salient in the normal filmed fictional world; that our angle of vision into the world is highly unusual; that characters' faces are blank when we would expect great expressiveness. And as just noted, this is what can be risky. If not done well, we end up mainly noting a film's self-consciousness about its own artifice and self-conception. If we begin attending too much to the world-on-film, then the fictional world itself ceases to grip our attention and we suspect an artistic or "artsy" pretension that has itself as its own object. This distracts us. And it destroys the sense of genuineness and credibility that a film can, uniquely among the arts, create. It can be the directorial version of the actor's classic

The Clarifying Obscurity of Robert Bresson

absorption-destroying mistake: looking into the camera.

Yet an implicit rejection of a viewer's conventional expectations about movies and movie watching, or our sense, by contrast, that the film is demanding something unusual from us, need not destroy the cinematic credibility of the movie world. The films of Robert Bresson (1901–1999) are frequently said to be "demanding" and "difficult," and in that way often "bring us up short" in the way described above. But the films themselves, in all their unconventionality, are so powerful that it is hard to imagine not being moved, anxious, sad, absorbed and invested in the experience of watching what Bresson has made. (It is hard for me to imagine it, at any rate; I realize that some viewers report being bored or baffled.)

Over a forty-year career, Bresson made thirteen filmed fictional narratives that he claims are not even movies or films at all. They are, instead, "cinematographs." He insisted on this because he was dissatisfied with the fact that movies have failed to make full use of the medium-specific capacities of motion picture photography and have instead rested content with being "filmed theater." His contention is that such a compromise with theatrical conventions has resulted in aesthetic representations that are themselves theatrical, or must inevitably be experienced as staged, and therefore not credible in their presentation of a human world and in some sense false, untrue both to what cinema can do and untrue to what should be cinema's goal: truth itself, truthfully illuminating the human world as lived. Bresson's experiment is to show that the world-on-film can be both the world-as-it-can-be-uniquely-available-to-film and yet, by virtue of cinema's unique capacities, also present fundamental dimensions of the world as such, in its truth, "how it really is" in various psychological, social, and even metaphysical dimensions.

Bresson has a great deal of confidence that a camera can disclose something true about being human that cannot be disclosed otherwise. Truth as something disclosed rather than asserted is immediately controversial: most philosophers would insist that only propositions can be bearers of truth. That restriction would seem extreme, though. It seems quite reasonable when someone says that she suddenly "saw" something about a person's character, given an action that the latter just performed. If the philosopher says that what could be true in what she saw can only be the proposition that expresses what she saw, and that proposition could only be said to be true if we can state clearly its truth conditions and whether they have been fulfilled, then two things seem to be going wrong. First of all, it might not be possible to state determinately in propositional form just what it is she saw, even though she can be rightly convinced that the person is now disclosed as not as she had thought, that is, as someone who would do *that*. And the truth conditions just take us back to the experience of what she saw, and that is an interpretive issue, not an empirical one. We accept the possibility of disclosed truth as a relatively common feature of ordinary life, without accepting the strict determinacy and propositional restrictions.

Moreover, the issue to be discussed in the following — being oriented in a world, understood as a horizon of possible meaningfulness — is not an object that is given to discursive articulation. It can only be known as indirectly disclosed (for reasons to be discussed shortly), subject to the ambiguities of interpretive complexity, and so it seems quite natural to say that Bresson is trying "to show us something true cinematically." He clearly understands his project that way and so he accepts the implications of such a claim about disclosive truth: "One recognizes the true by its efficacy, its power," he observed in *Notes on the Cinematograph*. (Bresson was an articulate, widely read intellectual who gave a number of interviews over the course of his career, and in many of them he was quite forthcoming about why he made his cinematographs as he did, and, like all serious artists, considerably less forthcoming about the "meaning" of his films. In 1975 he published *Notes on the Cinematograph*, a collection of notes and aphorisms that he had been compiling over the years, in which he touched on all the distinctive formal features that have come to be associated with his films.)

This all means, though, that in order to avoid the directorial "mistake" noted above — the fallacy of filmed theater — Bresson had to work to develop a style that has been rightly described as "austere," "rigorous," "pure," "minimalist," "bare," all in a way that does not distract from but even enhances the primary mode of a viewer's receptivity: our "emotional" responsiveness. His success in this attempt would mean that we are still engaged in, deeply emotionally involved in, gripped by, the world filmed, even while the film itself invites a different sort of absorbed attention, one inspired by a different sort of ambition, the highest level of aesthetic ambition: again, truth. We need then to understand the distinctiveness of the "cinematograph" and what it could mean for such a vehicle to be the bearer of truth, to be even a mode of philosophy.

The first step in understanding Bresson's ambition is to understand that deliberately refusing to invite conventional cinematic absorption in a movie world is motivated by more than a commitment to aesthetic concerns, to cinematic purity, to formal and medium-specific rigorousness. It has to do with a range of radical philosophical commitments. (None of this means that the films are vehicles for the expression of those views. The films *are* the views.) I offer this as a corrective to the widespread view that the seriousness, even the solemnity, of Bresson's films must reflect his views about a "transcendent" dimension of human life, a religious sensibility that is honest about profound human sinfulness (even depravity) as well as its possible redemption in moments of grace, understood as a divine gift.

Bresson did make four films about characters who avow religious commitments, *Angels of Sin* (1943), *Diary of a Country Priest* (1951), *The Trial of Joan of Arc* (1962) and *Lancelot du Lac* (1974). Aside from that unusual focus (films about religious life and experience are relatively rare), the influence of the initial reception of *Diary of a Country Priest*, especially by Catholic critics at the *Cahiers du Cinéma*, such as Andre Bazin, Amédeée Ayfre, Henri Angel, and Roger Leehardt (all of whom wrote for the Catholic journal *Esprit*), in the influential book by Paul Schrader, *The Transcendental Style in Film*, which appeared in 1972, and in Susan Sontag's essay "Spiritual Style in the Films of Robert Bresson" in 1964, helped to establish the view, still quite widespread, that Bresson was not only a religious, but a Catholic, and even a Jansenist, filmmaker, and that the films are vehicles for the expression of his religious commitments. It should be obvious, however, that making films about characters with religious commitments is not the same as being a "religious filmmaker," and I want to present an alternate interpretation of Bresson's enterprise by attending to his most famous and most beautiful film, *Au hasard Balthazar*, from 1966. (The title translates as "Balthazar at random" or "Balthazar by chance"; Balthazar in a world of randomness and chance.)

This is not to say that many elements of his films cannot be interpreted in a Jansenist way, especially given Bresson's references (not all of which are positive) to Pascal — in accord with the Augustinian idea that with man's fall our natures became irremediably corrupt and predestined, that there is no way by our own efforts or by what the Jesuits called "mental discipline" to avoid sin, and that only divine grace makes it possible to resist sin. The Jansenists take their bearings from such passages as I John 2:16: "For all that is in the world is the concupiscence of the flesh and the concupiscence of the eyes, and the pride of life, which is not of the Father but of this world." In the face of such inevitable depravity, the *curé*'s final proclamation seems the only response: "All is grace." And Bresson is clearly interested in the situation of a religious sensibility in a world where there is next to no social resonance for the expression of such commitments, especially characters such as the *curé*.

Yet it is important to note that all of the supposedly Jansenist themes in Bresson's films need have no religious meaning. We have little control over own fate, although not no control (as we see in *A Man Escaped*); chance events, shifts in what had seemed important but suddenly can seem insignificant, can drastically alter a life; what Kant called the "serpent of self-love" makes virtuous conduct almost impossible; owing to self-deceit, self-knowledge and therefore intentional self-transformation are rare. Those are not religious ideas. The notion that "all things conceal a mystery" can mean no more than that we cannot discursively account for, or make rationally intelligible, the source of significance, the hierarchies of matterings, in the historical world into which we find ourselves simply thrown.

Bresson's ideal of cinematic absorption, and with that his ideal of cinematic truth, is based on philosophical views about the nature of worldly absorption. The films call attention to our ways of being responsive to sources of meaningfulness in a life in a particular historical world. (For the most part, with the exception of *Les Dames du Bois de Bologne*, *The Trial of*

Joan of Arc, and *Lancelot du Lac*, it is our world, the contemporary world, rural and urban life typified by the French village and the city of Paris.) By meaningfulness, I mean the ways in which individuals purposively direct their lives on the basis of what has come to matter to them, and this on the assumption that something mattering, experienced as significant, is distinct from, and may even conflict with, conscious beliefs about what ought to matter, and distinct also from consciously desiring ends. Mattering in this sense is fundamental, original, primary; we "find ourselves" treating something as significant. Our engagement with anything in the world already assumes the emergence of what is salient in significance and what is negligible, and this experience does not depend on any views we might hold about what is or should be of significance. (Something can matter to us that we think ought not to matter, or we can believe something ought to matter to us but know that it actually doesn't matter, even if we take action to secure it.)

Framing the issue this way also allows us to see the possibility of the failure of meaningfulness or mattering. What had seemed so significant for so long can come to seem, in ways we do not seem to control, insignificant. Moreover, the sources of meaningfulness in a cinematic world, both for the characters in the filmed world and for the film world, are inseparable from the question of the possibility of sources of meaningfulness in a historical world in general. We tend to think of meaningfulness as radically individual, that what might matter to one farmer in a small village need not matter to another, nor to a young student in Paris. But such individual inflections of meaning are inflections of a common historical world, the shared historical world of the second half of the twentieth century. And this notion of a world, as used by Heidegger, or of a form of life, as used by Wittgenstein, this horizon of possible meaningfulness, is not itself available as any sort of object in the world. It is available only in worldly compartments, doings, and projects, where "available" is clearly in the "can be shown but not said" category. (What matters can be said, but the source of possible mattering is always already presupposed.) Bresson believes that it is uniquely, if also indirectly and elliptically, available to the camera. The same inseparability of individual matterings and world-historical possibilities is true when trying to understand the failure of meaningfulness, which is the main theme of Bresson's later films, beginning with *Au hasard Balthazar*.

Let me first summarize the unique cinematic properties of a Bresson cinematograph, and its philosophical dimensions. By far his most well-known directorial decision, beginning with his casting of Claude Laydu in *Diary of a Country Priest*, was to avoid professional actors and to cast unknowns as his major characters, nonprofessionals whom he would never use again in any other roles. (Laydu came to Paris to study acting in 1948, but he was only twenty when he was introduced to Bresson by the filmmaker Jacques Becker and had almost no experience and no film work. He agreed to Bresson's request to live for some weeks in a monastery, but not to discontinue his acting career. Several other unknowns in later films also had careers as actors, although Bresson preferred it when they did not.) His summary account of this was that these unknowns were to be understood not as actors but as "models," in the sense that one would speak of a painter using models for his work. Bresson explains his decision by expressing skepticism that film actors can succeed in doing what they are asked to do. "The actor:

'It's not me you are seeing and hearing, but *the other man.*' But being unable to be wholly *the other,* he is not that other." (I will be quoting from *Notes on the Cinematograph*.) This is because "a cinema film reproduces the reality of the actor, at the same time as that of the man he is being." Bresson clearly believes it is impossible to submerge the former into the latter; no matter how talented the actor, we always see the pretense.

By contrast, what would it mean to instruct a model not to "act"? Bresson's answers to this question more and more disclose an intertwining of aesthetic and philosophical commitments, just as we would expect. A view about what is necessary in order to avoid falseness in the depiction of what human-mindedness and attempts at communication involve, or "are really like," so as to avoid mere seeming and to depict it being as it is, must involve some determinate commitment to *how* it really is, what it in the simplest sense *looks like*. And his report of his instructions to his models makes clear that he has strong views about mindedness itself: "Radically suppress *intentions* in your models." This will result in what can seem an apparent automatism in line delivery and expression. "Nine-tenths of our movements obey habits and automatism. It is anti-nature to subordinate them to will and to thought."

He wants to accomplish this — which he does by "directing" his models about how not to act and by shooting scenes dozens and dozens of times to insure a merely habitual line reading — because of some quite general views that will require attention to the films to understand fully. "Models mechanized externally, internally free. On their faces, nothing willful. '*The constant, the eternal, beneath the accidental.*'" Bresson obviously does not believe that in ordinary life people communicate with each other in what can sometimes seem an affectless, monotonic, robotic way, but he clearly does believe that on camera, the suppression of deliberate or visibly intentional expressiveness, and the use of minimalist voice inflection will allow the camera to record something that the human eye misses in rapid normal interchanges and that is psychologically revealing: aspects of the soul will, in essence, "leak out." This in itself is a modernist strategy with which Bresson, a former painter, would have been quite familiar. Manet's *Olympia* or Cézanne's *Bathers* are both paintings that clearly do not aim at representational verisimilitude, but do try to picture something about beings in a world otherwise missed in ordinary perception. ("On the watch for the most imperceptible, the most inward movements." "Make visible what, without you, might perhaps never have been seen.")

Bresson made these decisions about models and line delivery because he was clearly skeptical that a wide range of meaningful comportment with objects in the world and with others is conceptually self-conscious or at all cognitive, and suspicious as well that actions we perform are rightly understood by references to the intentions that we would self-consciously avow. That is, his suspicion of movie acting reflects a suspicion that why we do what we do is best understood by what intentions we would consciously express when asked why we are so acting, whether because of ignorance, habit, or self-deceit. This may be true in most cases, of course, but the situation is usually much more complicated in critical or decisive situations. (*Au hasard, Balthazar* opens with a reminder of this when the father flatly refuses to buy a donkey for his children and then, in a quick cut to the very next scene, they are taking Balthazar the donkey home.)

"Models who have become automatic ... their relations with objects and persons around them will be *right*, because they will not be *thought*." I suggest that he does not merely mean "will seem right on camera because not acted out." The rightness to which he refers is owed to the avoidance of a superficial view of the role of self-conscious thought in our ordinary familiarity with objects and persons in the world and in our actions. In turn, this implies something much broader: that at the original or primordial level of our experience, simply how things show up as salient in our world, the availability of anything to experience, is first of all a matter of what he calls "impressions and sensations." I think that what he is getting at will require a more perspicacious language than impressions and sensations, which can suggest mere affects causally produced (which is not at all what he means; he is not pleading for empiricism or behaviorism). He is committing himself to something quite controversial: that there is a mode of nondiscursive intelligibility by virtue of which the world and indeed our own being in such a world are originally familiar and meaningful. (Filmed thought is *felt* thought, in other words, but still very much *thought*.)

This is a level of meaningfulness prior to perceptual and conceptual discriminability. Likewise, the camera must try to capture a relation between an agent and her deeds that is not limited to the conscious intentions that the agent would avow. For example, Bresson wants to deny that the effect of his directorial instructions produces *in*expressiveness: "Involuntarily expressive models (not willfully inexpressive ones)." And "no psychology of the kind which discovers only what it can explain." "*When you do not know what you are doing and what you are doing is the best* — that is inspiration." The terms "impressions and sensations" are too limited to capture what the cinematographs achieve, but what he is after is clear enough when he gives this advice about shooting a scene — "Stick exclusively to sensations. No intervention of intelligence which is foreign to these impressions and sensations" — all again, because the intention in shooting this way is to capture how it is, not how it seems.

This amounts to a position on the fundamental basic availability of a meaningful world of objects and others: that it is non-discursively and pre-cognitively available, that elements of a world become originally salient to us in their meaningfulness or mattering, and that we are onto any such meaning by being attuned to it in a way that parallels our unreflective absorption in a filmed world. Ultimately this entails something even more controversial philosophically: that a filmed fictional narrative can disclose something true about the human world, without such a truth being statable in a proposition.

Finally, while Bresson's cinematographs have continuous plots, he does not believe that narrative continuity is the basic way that the films have the disclosive meaningfulness that they possess.

> Cinematographic film, where expression is obtained by relations of images and of sounds, and not by a mimicry done with gestures and intonations of voice (whether actors' or non-actors'). One that does not analyze or explain. That *recomposes*.

As its name implies, Bresson means to compare his method of composition to writing with images, where images are understood not as represented contents so much as acquiring meaning in sequences. (As in the philosophical view known as linguistic holism, where the basic unit of meaning is not the word but the sentence.) "Cinematography: A new way of writing, therefore of feeling."

All this produced in Bresson's work what commentators rightly call a "cinema of montage and rhythm," one that is "primarily poetry and music, the creation of new relationships between things, beings, sounds and images, as in the succession of shots." This notion of a "pure" or completely formal montage as a vehicle of meaning can be taken too far. Bresson's films are not like plotless silent films without intertitles; they are fictional narrative films, with plots, dialogue, and beginnings, middles, and ends. The images, the individual shots, have content, and the link between the shots — that is, the comprehensibility of the sequences — depend heavily on a continuity of sense among these contents, as well as what Bresson is emphasizing by appealing to cinematography: an atmospheric emotional coloring built from montage, the sequence itself. (This goes considerably beyond Lev Kuleshov's famous experiments with montage and its impact upon the interpretation of imagery, since Bresson is assuming that his sequences of images can build to create a non-cognitive attunement to matters of significance and meaningfulness not otherwise available. And it is a reminder that while Sontag is right that form is meaning in Bresson, it goes too far to say that meaning is exclusively form, as in abstraction in painting.)

All of these formal matters bear on the treatment of the existential themes in the films: loneliness, deracination, solitude, the near impossibility of genuine communication, the sources of commitment or the failures of such commitment, and the possibility of radical conversion in a life, but the way they bear on these themes requires a detailed look at the films. And my brief example is the film which many consider his masterpiece, *Au hasard, Balthazar*. Bresson had already been making films for thirty years, and was in his sixties when he made this one.

Au hasard, Balthazar is, in narrative terms, a dual plot film, and as in all dual plot narratives, the two are parallel and linked, each meant to shed light on the meaning of the other. One narrative depicts the fate and suffering of the donkey, Balthazar. Among other associations, Balthazar is traditionally taken to be the name of one of the three magi who visited the newborn Jesus. That status, as a witness, perhaps even as a figure for the director himself, is an important point by ironic contrast. What Balthazar witnesses in this world is not the birth of a god but unremitting depravity and evil. Besides that, another possible source is the story of Lucius in Apuleius' *The Golden Ass*, and the one Bresson cites, the story told by Myshkin in Dostoevsky's *The Idiot*, about how a donkey's braying relieved his depression.

The other story in the film depicts the fate and the sufferings of a village girl, Marie, whom we see as a young girl and as an adolescent. (One signal of the link between the two narratives occurs several times in the film when Marie's father is looking for her and repeatedly calls out her name in a braying way — "Mar*ie*! Mar*ie*!" — that closely echoes the sound we hear from Balthazar several times.) Balthazar is by turns a pet, a beast of burden and farm animal, again a pet of service to Marie's family, a baker's donkey used for deliveries, owned by a drunkard, Arnold, to give rides on tourist tours, a circus animal, Arnold's again, cruelly mistreated by a grain merchant, again Marie's domestic animal, and finally stolen by the most evil character in the film, Gérard, and used to smuggle merchandise across the border with Spain. Marie's fate is likewise miserable. Her childhood romance with the son of the first owners of Balthazar, Jacques, is ruined by her father's bitter and catastrophic dispute with Jacques' family. She enters into a relationship, often confused and conflicted, with the hoodlum and the sadist Gérard. Even more confused and conflicted, and desperate to obtain the money she would need to escape the village, she offers herself one night to the grain merchant before (apparently) changing her mind. An attempted renewal of her bond with Jacques first fails, then appears to succeed as she resolves to face down and break with Gérard and his gang. This does not end well. The gang strips and abuses and probably rapes Marie, and she disappears from the film, likely dying by her own hand. (Throughout the story of Marie, the mindedness of characters is apparently as opaque to them as it is to us; it is nearly impossible to discover intentions, motivations, or any self-reflective moments at all. Her inconstancy and inconsistency are major features in the film.)

Interwoven throughout the main two narratives are several subplots, and these and the two main plots intersect each other so frequently and unexpectedly that it is impossible to follow a continuous narrative line. (Bresson's films are not content-less, but with all the ellipses, the reliance on montage, and the intersecting subplots, they are seriously "de-narrativized.") Much of the editing appears *au hasard*, like chance events, like the drastic way in which the death of the child at the beginning, the sudden appearance of Arnold when Balthazar almost dies, and Arnold's inheritance, impact the lives involved. The original owners of Balthazar and of the vacation home and farm that Marie's father eventually farms for them begin the film in an eerie vignette — the illness and perhaps the death of the youngest child. This sad event is the reason the vacationing family never returns. The scene is a fine illustration of how the minimalization of expressivity can heighten rather than reduce the emotional impact of the images. The absence of any visible reaction to the child's fate concentrates all the emotional power of the scene in the briefest indication of the terrible, limp lifelessness of the child, and then the sudden shock when we, as well as the characters, are suddenly propelled out of this childhood world by the crack of a whip. The scene is also typical of Bresson's frequent use of ellipses. We leap ahead more than a dozen years to when Marie is sixteen.

Another subplot involves Marie's father's ruinous relation with Jacques' family. He changes careers from being a schoolteacher to being a farmer and actually becomes quite successful, so successful that rumors start that he is cheating the owner, who then demands that the father produce the records of the farm's business. "Rumors" only begin to characterize Bresson's treatment of village life as a world of resentment, jealousy, paranoia, conspiracies, and intense mutual surveillance. (The situation is even more extreme in his next and even darker film, *Mouchette*.) The father claims that he is insulted by this lack of trust, refuses to compromise, and ends up ruining his family's life. The film strongly hints that the father has actually cheated the owner. He tells his wife that he cannot produce his receipts because he has not kept them, but we are shown that he has all of them. What seemed like pride turns out to be greed, and as Marie correctly notes, what seems like his righteous indignation is really self-pity.

There is also a strange and one-sided attraction between a middle-aged baker's wife and the nefarious Gérard. The attraction is hardly maternal and is not reciprocated. There is a mysterious murder investigation that we learn little about (we do not discover who was killed, when, where, or how), but both Arnold and Gérard's gang appear to be suspects. Bizarre conversations about "action painting" and agent responsibility occur during one of Arnold's guided tours of the Pyrenees.

Balthazar briefly escapes and is captured by a circus, where he becomes part of a phony "animal genius act," and is recaptured by Arnold. Arnold suddenly inherits a fortune, promptly gets drunk, falls off Balthazar, and dies.

Throughout the two main narratives and these subplots, the film shows us a village in a modernizing transition, from one world to another, and the meaning of the transition is focused on consumer goods and technology, all as figures of later, or post-war, modernity: from donkey carts to automobiles, from ploughs to tractors, the intrusion of modern regulatory bureaucracy into rural farm life, a youth culture now fixated on transistor radios and motorbikes, parties fueled by alcohol and sex, money, and a general environment aptly summarized in perhaps the most basic bourgeois maxim of all by the grain merchant: "I love money and I hate death." This is an explicit theme occasionally in the film. When we first meet Gérard, on his motorbike with his gang, he sardonically praises Marie's father for his donkey: "very modern." Throughout the film, and especially at the end, the only music we hear — non-diagetic music, that is, music heard by the viewers but not by the characters — is the *andante* movement from Schubert's late piano sonata in A major D.959, a moving berceuse or lullaby-like section that seems associated with regret at both Balthazar's and Marie's loss of innocence and first exposure to a world aptly epitomized by that merchant's motto.

Another framing device for the film is its beginning and its end, and this again emphasizes the notion of a world. At the beginning the baby donkey Balthazar is in his world, the animal world, being nursed by his mother, surrounded by sheep whom we barely see, their presence signaled by their tinkling bells. The film begins with him being torn from that world for the amusement of the children, who find him cute and want him as a pet. (The intrusion of one world into another is signaled by that human arm "intruding" into the animal world.) The film ends with Balthazar, after all his suffering in the human world, returning to the comfort of an animal world, dying amid a large flock of sheep and clearly comforted by them. Around the middle of the film, he returns to an animal world in a different way, when he first arrives in the circus and there is a justly famous depiction of some sort of mutual intelligibility among the animals, as if acknowledging to each other that this intersection of worlds is not where they belong, in cages and performing tricks. It is almost as if the circus animals are warning Balthazar to get out while he can.

It is this contrast between worlds that allows features of those worlds that would not otherwise be available to become indirectly accessible. The notion of world in such a claim is on the one hand very familiar — if we refer to the world of *Citizen Kane*, or the world of indigenous peoples, or the world of Balthazar, we know we do not mean merely the totality of encounterable objects — but on the other hand is quite philosophically complicated. World, in this sense, is not all that is the case (contra Wittgenstein's famous dictum). It is a horizon of possible meaningfulness, a historical context that delimits what could matter to human beings at a time, and what could not, which enterprises are possible and which simply would not make sense. As noted, this idea of an always already deeply presupposed horizon of possible contextual significance is not something that could ever be an object in a world, because such a world is a condition for anything showing up meaningfully in experience at all.

A socio-historical account of facts about such a world is possible, but the possible significance or hierarchies of salience in common experience are not facts, and not even consciously held values. The same is true of "Quixote-like" projects; projects that just could not make sense. Everything we encounter in a historical world makes a kind of immediate familiar sense, pre-reflectively. I say immediate and pre-reflective, because this familiarity is not a matter of applying norms, rules, or conventions. The world of possible meaningfulness, by contrast, is itself not so encounterable. This original mode of meaningfulness is not originally a matter of conceptual classification or perceptual discrimination, but a far more direct form of familiarity. We do not first encounter perceptually discriminated objects and then bestow significance. The idea of such a two-step procedure is not phenomenologically credible (any more than a string of sounds is first heard as such and then interpreted as language). Entities and others in our experience show up, are salient, because of their degrees of significance in the practical tasks that a human being engages in, courses of action that are possible and could make sense at a particular time. (Or not.)

For an example, consider an animal world, an issue quite important to Bresson's film. An animal species is, like us, not just visually attentive to everything perceptually present. What emerges as salient — prey, predator, shelter, mate — and what does not, what means nothing to them — highways, power lines, planets — so emerges because of its species form. The suggestion is that how elements of our experience emerge as salient is as well a function of their mattering, but without at all being limited to our biological species form. This all means, as incomplete as such an account is, that when we ask about the human world that the characters inhabit in *Au hasard, Balthazar*, we ask not about what beliefs they have about what matters — given Bresson's obvious doubts about self-deceit and self-opacity, this would be pointless — but about what the camera can show, which emerges as the context of significance that seems to inform and guide the decisions and actions and experiences of the characters, even, paradoxically, if that context is failed meaningfulness, a depiction of absence. How being in such a world bears on possible courses of action is a major issue in all his films. *This is* what Bresson is trying to show us cinematographically.

Let us return to the issue of religion, and to the claim that Bresson is a religious filmmaker, even a Jansenist Catholic, all without any biographical evidence and in the face of his dismissal of the idea. Balthazar, for instance, is sometimes understood to be a kind of Christ figure, silently taking on and witnessing the burden of human depravity, until bearing that burden leads to his (perhaps) sacrificial death. But what these critics insist on as "transcendence" misdescribes the issue of significance discussed here. In Bresson's film, objects are certainly not encountered as mere things or objects of perception, but this distinction does not establish a religious difference. The objects in his film are salient in the way they matter (or do not matter) within a world of possible mattering and in terms of what has come to matter to the persons who encounter them. They bear meaning, and often, as in the lingering shots of stairways and doors, just an intimation of meaning. Sometimes the meaning is aesthetic, as in the beauty of several scenes in his later film *L'Argent*. These are all matters of immanence, not transcendence.

It can look like several Jansenist commitments are evident in the films, if that is what one is looking for: the utter and unreformable sinfulness of human beings, predestination, salvation as a gratuitous and arbitrary gift of grace, never earned. On the one hand, while there is certainly unremitting depravity in many of Bresson's films, he is more sensitive to the attractions of selfishness and resentment in the particular and concrete historical worlds that he is trying to depict. And there is certainly no universal sinfulness and depravity, no original sin, in Bresson's films. Marie is well-meaning, but also confused; her mother is saintly; Jacques is weak and naïve, not sinful; and Arnold is more of a comic character than a villain. Similarly, the fatalism in the film need not be a religious doctrine either, but the consequence of there being very little in the way of concrete alternate possibilities in the depicted world, and "grace," which is only stated as such in *Diary of a Country Priest*, could just as easily be an indication of the unexpected emergence of ways of mattering that could "by chance" (*au hasard*) drastically change or even redeem a boring or wasted life.

In *Balthazar*, the direct allusions to religion seem heavily qualified: quoted, rather than appealed to. The children's baptism of Balthazar in the beginning is likely ironic, a faint suggestion that baptism itself is childish and useless, not to mention that animals are not born in original sin and do not need to be baptized. The early emphasis on the innocence and the happiness of the children — they are as innocent as Balthazar — does not call out for the washing away of any sin. The only "fall" we see is the fall into the profane modern adult world. The single scene in a church serves only to emphasize the superficiality and untrustworthiness of religious practices, since the sadist Gérard is capable of singing like an angel. When Marie's father is dying, the priest who comes to comfort him offers a few lame platitudes which do nothing to comfort the father or be of any use at all to his wife. And when Balthazar appears all kitted-out in religious decorations, likely for the funeral of Marie's father, the impression is clownish, not devout.

All this could still be said to be consistent with the paradoxical "presence of the absence of religiosity," but that absence does not seem to have any real grip in the town, and one would still need to discuss how that failure in particular might bear on the possibilities or lack of them in the world we see. It appears in the film, in so far as it appears at all, the way tradition, family, work, or community appear: as another failed source. While it is possible to see Balthazar as Christ-like in being "too good for this world" and therefore doomed to die, he ends up dying burdened not with the sins of the world but with contraband consumer goods; he resists his role whenever he can, and he dies by accident and in a manner which makes clear that there will be no resurrection.

I have suggested that Bresson's accomplishment is to have discovered a cinematic form that can disclose the meaning, or the failure of meaning, in a person's life by cinematically shifting our attention away from explicit psychological attitudes, away from what characters think about themselves and others (if they ever do — this is rare in this film), and instead by drawing attention to the common historical world that these characters inhabit and the way their conduct is subject to the possibilities allowed by such a world. This is to be understood as a horizon of possible significance, a source of mattering that is not a matter of beliefs or commitments, but a non-discursive orientation from possibilities that might make sense or not. This means that the cinematic depiction of this collective attunement is, at least as Bresson sees it, also largely non-discursive, what Bresson calls "emotional," without the "intervention of intelligence."

Liberties

This is not to say that the characters do not evince attitudes, beliefs, desires, and so forth, but that they rarely seem to be reflective subjects of such attitudes. They are, rather, subject *to* them. Of course, one cannot have a belief or desire without knowing that one does, but such an awareness is normally understood to open up the possibility of asking oneself such things as whether one actually believes what one takes oneself to believe, or why one wants something, or what actually matters to one. Yet the question of why Gérard acts as he does, why Marie's father will not compromise, what the baker's wife wants from Gérard, why Arnold saves Balthazar, why Marie changes her mind about Jacques — this is not a question that is available to the characters.

The cinematic technique expresses a philosophical commitment: a depiction of ordinary life which is characterized by a kind of self-forgetfulness, self-opacity, hierarchies of mattering that are not driven by reflective attitudes about what ought to matter, or even what actually does matters to one, but which rather seem to be inheritances of a common world that narrowly limits what could matter, even if that possibility is foreclosed, failed. Instead of appealing to expressivity, whether in language or even in intonation, facial expressions, and so forth, Bresson portrays what would normally be considered the attitudes and the desires of characters in an "external" way, as if those supposed "inner" states are actual only externally, in the public world that we see. "Movement from the exterior to the interior. (Actors: movement from the interior to the exterior.) The thing that matters is not what they show me but what they hide from me and, above all, what they do not suspect is in them." Most often this is available only in what they do, although any access, for them and for the viewer, to why they do what they do, to their intentions,

The Clarifying Obscurity of Robert Bresson

seems often, especially in critical, life-altering situations, unavailable.

One major disclosure of a character's mindedness is Balthazar himself, who functions not just as a witness but also as a kind of screen on which what is at issue for the characters is projected. In some cases — "scapegoat" cases, we might say — Balthazar is treated as if he were the cause of some character's mistake, failure, or misdeed. The most obvious is a rare instance of humor in the film, when a farmer driving a load of hay pulled by Balthazar drives recklessly, overturns the wagon, and then not only seeks out Balthazar to punish him as if he were at fault, but collects a group of his comrades to hunt down Balthazar, like the village mob out for Frankenstein's monster. Arnold tries to beat Balthazar with a chair in what appears to be his own rage at himself for vowing not to drink and then failing in his resolve. Balthazar is sold by Marie's father out of the same false pride (he thinks owning a donkey makes him look ridiculous) that leads him to destroy his family's lives, without any sense that he knows what he is doing and why. The sight of Balthazar in the snow while Marie and Gérard carry on their assignations, and their indifference to him, their not caring about him, is a measure of the obsessive and self-destructive character of their involvement that is visible to us but not to Marie. The grain merchant's indifference to any moral restraint — one could even say the state of his soul — is "visible" in the sight of Balthazar worked nearly to death, starved and beaten, and then in what appears to be an unmotivated reversal in his narcissism, manifested in his returning Balthazar to Marie's family. Gérard's frustration at his first failed seduction of Marie is projected onto Balthazar as he beats him gratuitously (as Marie, opaque and confused as ever, looks on.)

Liberties

The early garden scene is a different sort of projection, as Balthazar serves as a transitional object for Marie's emerging sexuality. What is striking in the scene is that neither of them seems consciously minded in some determinate way (much like Balthazar, obviously). It is very unlikely that Marie has any knowledge of what she is doing, and the lovers, Marie and Gérard, move toward each other deliberately but not quite intentionally, and then separate the same way. In the last scene, it is as if Gérard is angry and frustrated in what seems a purely reactive rather than determinately motivated way. Balthazar is not conceivably his rival, despite his vulgar fantasies at the beginning of the scene.

Marie adorns Balthazar as if he is a beloved, projecting herself in a fantasy of romance at once childish and provocative (it goes so far as a kiss), and she is clearly aware of the presence of someone else in the garden. We suspect, given her lingering there, that she knows it is Gérard. (As is often the case in Bresson, most famously in *Pickpocket*, hands bear a visual meaning that is at once powerful and also ambiguous.) In the conventional philosophical dichotomy between what I do and what happens to me, where the former is marked out by reflective intentions and the latter by such notions as drives, instincts, evolutionary imperatives, and being causally acted on rather than acting, the scene would probably be characterized by some version of the latter. But the dichotomy does not make room for what we see: someone who does not know why they are doing what they are doing but who is not impelled or driven to do it. Marie is acting deliberately but not knowingly, another indication of Bresson's distrust of reflective consciousness in human affairs.

There is also a prominent emphasis on the obscurity of human motivation in the two most important scenes in the movie: the final "conquest" of Marie by Gérard, with her deeply ambiguous "submission," and her encounter with the grain merchant, where Bresson's ellipses make it impossible to know even what actually happened that night. In the former, Marie's simultaneous attraction and repulsion are conveyed with almost no dialogue, except at the very beginning. Balthazar is again the transitional object — all that Marie has ever loved, all that she knows of love — as Gérard has set him up by the road, hoping to induce Marie to stop as she drives, and she does. And then we have the completion, as it were, of the first scene of "hands" from the garden episode, as she now endures Gérard's touch, allowing the touch even as she weeps at the absence of affection or tenderness. And then finally, in a combination of childish play and an escape game, Marie acts out her confusion, finally ending in an ambiguous posture of what is either willing submission or resigned surrender, or neither, or both. All of which finally ends with Gérard's contrasting certainty about his sadistic victory.

The village life that we see depicted ranges from the transactional and contractual to relations based on ego, vanity, and power, and these appear to be the only sources of meaningful life available in this world, something attested to, and witnessed by, Balthazar in the cruel treatment of him. (Even Marie allows him nearly to freeze to death when keeping her assignations with Gérard.) This is the source of the loneliness and the isolation that seems to envelop Marie and leads her to her most desperate but still conflicted act — her visit to the grain merchant, and an offer to sleep with him for enough money to leave the town — although she seems to withdraw the offer immediately, and then, perhaps, accept it on other terms. Bresson refuses to allow us any confirmation of whether Marie has resolved anything determinate.

The film leaves us with two indelible images that call to mind again the contrast between "worlds" to which the presence of Balthazar throughout the film awakens us. The first image is a silent judgment on the naked reality of modern sources of significance. The second invokes the possibility of a kind of ironic transcendence, not beyond this world into another redemptive one, but an "animal" peace and comfort that looks utopian when compared to what we have.

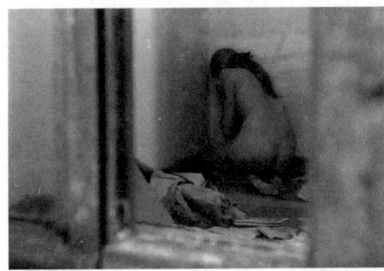
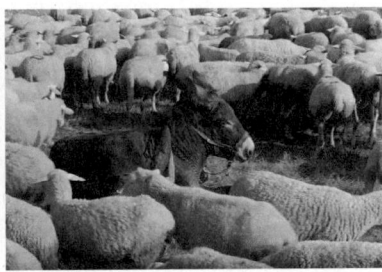

The distance between these two images might suggest that the right judgment to make about Marie's world, with its meager resources of shared significance, is despair. But we know, and we know from the form of the film, that what happened both to Marie and to Balthazar is horrific. And as Shakespeare's Edgar reminds us, "The worst is not/ So long as we can say, 'This is the worst.'"

ALAN JENKINS

Four Poems for Marie Colvin, 1956–2012

Night Sail

I dreamt of sailing *Spray*, grandfather Herrick's
pilot cutter, from its berth in an old black-and-white
on the kitchen wall, past the docks, the cranes and derricks,

not to some sluggish oil-rainbowed bight
with pier and prom, in the lee of Gosport or Goring,
not to the wild side of the Isle of Wight

or even a Winslow Homer Nassau mooring
but a secluded cove, where we'd ride at gentle anchor...
When I woke, you were still snoring

your smoker's snore; I saw the cliff-face of a super-tanker
and, tied up to starboard, someone's super-yacht,
flying the flag of Panama, or Casablanca —

this was before the crash, not
that the crash would have bothered *him* —
motionless behind its oil-rich haze, its hot

sides gleaming and all its tackle trim;
a super-model, fresh from her shoot on the Ile Ste. Marguerite,
her neat mound cupped in a scrap of scrim,

supine on a sun-deck, inviting him eat —
A drink first maybe? You choose...
The air pulsed with the steady thresh and thrum, the beat

of her super-engines, super-screws,
and suddenly someone had drawn a veil, a pall
of grape-dark clouds over the plaque for La Pérouse.

~~~~

Storm-light on the marina, the harbour-wall,
and on the sea beyond. The steady thresh and thrum.
The little pastel boulevards, the palms and all

the quayside bustle and the prosperous hum
of restaurants in that unfashionable resort, the vines
          and olive groves
inland — a sunburst showed me how far I had come

from London, S.E.1 to the purples, mauves
and deep blacks of that bay, the opalescent blues
and blue-greens of a thousand inlets, creeks and coves

— but *Spray* was gone with grandfather Herrick and his muse
and all that I'd held dear was up for sale,
and it wasn't looking good, for me or La Pérouse.

~~~~

You were still snoring. I saw a faded, flapping rust-red sail
and under it, your head propped on sacks of rice
in the bows of a caïque... Here I draw a veil,

a veil of tears and old malt over thinking twice
before coming with you across the wine-dark sea to Zuwara,
for I had drunk the milk of paradise,

I did not keep that appointment in Samarra,
I could only lie awake and listen for your whimpers to subside
to snores or read to you from John Grisham, John O'Hara

or John Donne; I did not see the sewer where they died,
the bloated corpses floating downriver, the villages laid waste,
the heaps of blackened limbs on each roadside;

how the lives of others were degraded and debased
in camps and market squares, in bare-bulbed basement rooms
at police headquarters, how the nameless and effaced

lingered on the air in airless catacombs;
how the first bones to surface from mass graves
were children's bones, how gas from punctured wombs

alerted those who clawed at rubble, or how a man behaves
who finds his wife and daughter, headless, in the street,
how a man sinks to his knees and moans and raves...

~~~~

I would have woken you, inviting you to eat,
if I had sailed with you on that caïque
you took from — where? Not the Ile Ste. Marguerite,

not the Isle of Wight — but the flesh was weak,
or I was, and I made some excuse. The old fear,
of falling short, of being found out, of the yellow streak

that runs through me like the streak on the 'beautiful fusilier,'
caesiao teres, on the yellowtail, or on the gilthead bream,
sparus aurata, that noses through its still-clear

blue-green glaze — further glazed by steam —
on the ancient Persian or Syrian ceramic tile
you picked up in Beirut from a Karim or an Ibrahim

and lugged back for me, that I might sit in style,
in state, under the bathroom shelf
where it sits; that I might look at it and smile

as I think of its weight in your grip, of your contempt for pelf
and perfidy, of your straight dealing and your guts
and have to get a grip on myself

Liberties

when I recall how you forgave my Ifs and Buts
and brought this back for me, thinking of the bream we ate
in that Lebanese place I sit in till it shuts.

~ ~ ~ ~

I sit in and pick at the grilled bream on my plate
and drink the fierce north African rosé, carafe
after carafe, on the evening of our 'date,'

year in year out, imagining the chat, the jokes, the chaff
that could not keep those rockets from their target,
     from the screen-
door of the house you slept in that last night; remembering
     the gaffe

I made the night we met, and the packed shebeen
we met in, crushed up close on benches, and the reek of *kif*,
of Silk Cut and Gitanes, and all the nights between;

remembering how you almost came to grief
so many times, with your 'I guess they don't make men
like they used to,' not in a sudden squall or on a reef

like La Pérouse, but 'in the field,' and how again and again
you'd make light of the risks you took,
  'on the ground,' whether Tamil or Chechen

or Taliban, and how you read me like an open book
when I made my excuses and instead set off —
not on a dhow packed with spices for the *souk*,

not on a fishing smack out of Roscoff
with Tristan Corbière, bound for St. Peter Port,
and not on *Spray*, but on the Eurostar to Paris, *putain, boff.*

~ ~ ~ ~

Then south to that unfashionable resort
where I ate a bream and drank a carafe of the local *gris*,
thinking of the risk you ran when you first caught

Gaddafi's eye, when he came on like the Sheik of Araby
in his desert hide-out, and how your straight-talking
           saw you through;
of that line, *This level reach of blue is not my sea*

and of the storms that broke over you,
the wilder, crueller waves, 'the terror of a child
that is really pure pleasure' — which you experienced as crew,

the *splinters and spars and dripping, salty weeds —*
           and they restyled
as your USP, your 'brand,' those buccaneers
whose bounty you became, though you were undefiled;

of the night I was granted the freedom of Algiers
by some PLO big-wigs you conjured from thin air
in a restaurant in Notting Hill — so I'd have to spend years

not writing my Life of Albert
('Our great *Arab* writer') Camus, as you didn't write
your Life of Arafat; of your struggles with that hair,

its dense cloud of curls, rich-brown, and how night after night
you'd started on the second bottle by the time
I turned up, and the 'cascade of butterflies in shafts of light.'

~~~~

— In Sri Lanka, that was, where they made you mime
Surrender and lie down, and killed you anyway —
or so you thought, from the pain. Another war-crime

(this one cost you your eye)... If we'd sailed from Oyster Bay
to Little Neck, or walked the sands of Zahara
de los Atunes together, or drunk *arak* in Raouché;

if you could have promised, say, a Bedouin tent in the Sahara,
or Leptis Magna, *al-Khums*, Khoms —
but you kept your appointment, not in Samarra,

not in Baghdad or Basra, or among the piers and proms
of the *vieux port*, and not in Tunis, where you were tailed
for two weeks, but in Homs.

~~~~

Half-steam ahead by guess and lead, for the sun is mostly veiled...
Blue and white sails on the river, but one, a faded rust-red,
was not among them — the dinghy that you sailed.

You held the wheel of *Trade Winds*, aka *African Queen*, instead.
You'd invited me so many times to join you for a cruise,
upriver, down; and now that you were dead

you intimated there was 'no way' I could refuse —
your final offer. You laughed your smoker's laugh
when I climbed aboard, as if to say, What have you to lose,

what have you ever had? Moper, mooncalf,
landlubber, pub-haunter...There was dried blood
on the gunwhales, on the coaming, and down one half

of your lovely, laughter-lined face! With the flood
we drifted upstream, through fast-running bends,
past hollow-eyed dark barges sunk in mud,

past the Ship, the Swan. *The luck on which this life depends
(you said), the stats, the stories that we tell, the roar
of incoming, and the sudden death of friends...*

*Here is the slipway where, when you were four,
you watched your mother slip and almost disappear;
the cemetery full of south-west London men 'lost' in the war.*

*But all the things that matter happen far from here.
'England expects,' the signal sent by sat-phone... No more.*
The ferryman was waiting, back at Chiswick Pier.

Smoke

*All autumn, the chafe and jar
of nuclear war*
ROBERT LOWELL, 'FALL 1961'

My father, who'd had
'about as much as he could take'
by '44, and still woke
swearing at flies
and soaked in sweat,

read the *Telegraph*
in dread and disbelief
over his first cigarette,
narrowing his eyes
against the scroll of smoke…

Only half-awake,
dreaming a bitter,
penitential cup
of coffee, we squint
at a screen instead of print,

swipe through
and see plump child-men
jerked by the strings
of Twitter,
their sad posturings

that could turn us to smoke
before we can even laugh.
A father's no shield
for his child — nor
a husband for his wife...

Nothing now is a joke,
nothing is so mad or bad
it cannot happen.
To that 'well-meaning guy'
outside a club in Paddington

who saw her lighting up
and told her she should stop,
Marie just said:
'I promise you,
this isn't how I'll die.'

Poster Girl

You were waiting for me in the Underground.
Larger than life, though less lined or scarred
by it, by shrapnel, vodka, nicotine...

So much more of you than on the screen
I'd stared at all that day, scrolling through
the jumpy phone-footage till I found

you, yes — but faceless, lying under charred
and pock-marked rubble in your dust-caked jeans,
your blue sweater caked with dust.

The S-buckle on your belt, so I knew it was you...
So much more now, and less. I looked hard
at the face, it was the face I loved and took on trust

or took for granted, the sea-green eye alert
for danger, lips parted; and where there'd only been
that shaky picture, pitiful, unjust,

was another you, so clear, and clean,
and alive again, so alive it hurt,
and lost again, in a hiss of doors, a rancid gust.

Siren's Song

Remember when you breezed into the Swan,
The Mermaid or the Dove, and swayed
And swaggered like a buccaneer
Who scented plunder, below decks and above?
Remember how the crew
Sat laughing in the stern, how far gone
The ship's complement of women were?

Remember that sharp stink in the heads,
The rocky beds, the calm as you rowed free
And the path *au bord de la mer* —
A thin brown arm around the cliff?
How you might have made a go of it with her
But instead watched all your gear
Go overboard with your learning and your love?

Will you — same old riff — never learn? —
That you will not find safe moorings here,
Or at Chiswick Eyot, or anywhere;
That you should expect the unexpected turn
Of the tide that leaves you all at sea,
That some mistakes are final, that too late
Is too late, is spindrift, is thin air?

JAMES McAULEY

Memory's Cellar

You enter the cave of horrors in the basement of an Ottoman-era house that is now a small yeshiva just outside the medieval walls of the Old City. On the one hand, there could be no better encapsulation of Jerusalem than this: disjointed histories piled one atop the other like dishes in the sink, all beneath the shade of Aleppo pines. On the other, there is something immediately decrepit about the place. It is wrenchingly nondescript; it looks like extra storage for folding chairs or even for cleaning supplies. Were it not for a Hebrew plaque on the limestone gate outside that reads *Martef HaShoah*, or The Holocaust Cellar, next to an arrow pointing in its direction, you would have no idea where you had arrived. Even now, no notice identifies this rough place as the first Holocaust memorial ever built.

The cellar was inaugurated in 1949 on Mount Zion. It is a monument to the destruction of the Jewish people, yes, but also a monument to the way the destruction was understood in its immediate aftermath by those who had survived, and in the newly established Jewish state. But despite its location, a stone's throw from King David's alleged tomb, the cellar is not, nor was it ever, an august institution that sought to stipulate a collective memory of catastrophe or to impose a narrative interpretation of any kind. No museology or mixed media went into the creation of this dark shrine. It is a site of raw memory, and also a kind of *Wunderkammer* of catastrophe. There are many Holocaust memorials and museums in the world now, but there is no other place quite like this one. To enter it is to confront, without any philosophical or historiographical or aesthetic mediation, in the most startlingly direct way, the unvarnished blinding horror of a vanished moment, before that horror was sanitized into language and meaning. The place is truly terrifying.

The entire space is pitch dark, dank, and smells of mold from years of water dripping on ancient stone. This is a place where survivors brought whatever obscene relics they had salvaged from the camps and had somehow managed to carry to Palestine after the war: lampshades made from Torah scrolls, canisters of zyklon-B, the chemical used in the gas chambers, and bars of soap made from human body oil, all displayed in a candle-lit cave in a prominent glass vitrine with tattered green velvet lining. The soap bars turn out to be fake; there is no evidence that the Nazis ever made soap out of human flesh. But that is entirely beside the point: the soap represents one of the cruelest rumors that circulated in the camps, which these survivors believed to be true — and here, in this cellar, what you come to see is how *they* understood the catastrophe that *they* had endured, what *they* remembered of it and how *they* began to represent those memories with material objects. The mentality that tortured them and sustained them in equal measure is arguably the most important thing on display.

Toward the end of the cellar, to the extent that it has an exposition, is a small niche that resembles an oratory. Here you see ashes — called "martyrs' ashes" — from the concentration camps, brought to Israel in June 1949 in a series of glass jars, painted in blue and white stripes with yellow Stars of David, to mirror the uniform that so many Jews had worn up until their deaths. It is an indescribably desolating feeling to stand there in this putrid cellar, in front of those ashes, and to think of the unnamed bodies whose incinerated remains are blended in these peeling glass vials, to know only how those bodies had died and nothing of how they had lived. In any case, there is no attempt to explain or to tell those stories at Martef HaShoah, which is the source of its power. In the immediate aftermath of the war, these dark rooms were already a commentary on the futility, and even the perversity, of narrative.

These days, the memory of the catastrophe that we now call "the Holocaust" in English or "the Shoah" in Hebrew — as if there is a single word in any language that will capture it — has been spun over the years by governments and memorial institutions in Israel, the United States, Western Europe, and Eastern Europe into respective "lessons" that apparently teach us about this or that: about human rights, about collaboration with evil, about the necessity of Zionism, about the moral failings of bystanders. But these lessons, no matter how true or well-intentioned they may be, when they try to instruct, to caution, or even to inspire, tend to remove us from the actual details of the catastrophe, which is neither parable nor metaphor but quite simply a fact of extreme facticity — a catastrophe in the literal sense of the term — an epochal tragedy that defies facile explanation, a loss with many reasons and causes but above all a loss, devastating, final, incontrovertible. The most crushing horror of the catastrophe is that it happened at all — that facticity; and what, exactly, "it" was. In that sense, the world's first Holocaust memorial is also its most authentic. Here there is no narrative. Here there is only shock and stupefaction, frozen in cold stone.

We do not always get to choose the questions that we ask of the past, or the questions that the past asks of us. But we can ask why those questions are posed in the first place, why they are formulated in the way they are, and perhaps most importantly, what their place in our lives should be. I cannot remember a time when I was not aware of the Holocaust, when its shadow was not somehow a fundamental part of how I understood the world and — as perverse and as sad as this is — of how I understood my own Jewishness. I am Jewish, but I am not descended from survivors. And yet the catastrophe was something of a mediating filter to the entire identity for so many in my generation, the way it was taught to so many of us, the stories we heard as children, the ultimate reason we were told that we had to remain Jewish, as if Judaism was merely a form of resistance and not a thing of depth and beauty that had existed long before — and indeed, long after — those who tried to extinguish it. The first time I read Sartre's *Réflexions sur la question juive*, the postwar treatise in which he asserts with zero humility or shame that the anti-Semite "creates" the Jew, I was deeply unsettled, I think because I saw myself in his formulation, and I did not like what I saw. Was *this*, after all, what Jewish survival was meant to look like, an obsession with reading about the camps, and not, for instance, Yiddish poetry by Avraham Sutzkever and Peretz Markish?

As I got older, I began to question my own questions about the past, questions I had not chosen, but questions that were nevertheless suspect. Why should an event that essentially had nothing to do with me, that certainly does not belong to me, come to occupy so much space at the expense of so much else? Peter Novick and others have shown that at least part of the answer is cultural: in the 1990s, when I grew up, the Holocaust became a public metaphor for any number of things, not least because the murder of millions of Jews in and of itself never seemed reason enough to rivet people's attention. What seemed — and still seems — to concern most people are the meanings that we have assigned to the catastrophe rather than the brute horror of the catastrophe itself, the lessons, and even the platitudes, that we teach our children about it. I have long been struck by the reality of this elision — that even in our morbidly identitarian moment, if one is to speak about this catastrophe, one necessarily has to speak about something else. (A fine example is Ken Burns' recent series on American indifference to Jewish refugees in the late 1930s and 1940s, a film that purports to be a documentary about the Holocaust but is mostly interested in parallels between American immigration policy then and our present-day troubles with immigration at the southern border.)

Maurice Halbwachs, the great French theorist of collective memory, said it best in the essay that introduced the concept. "In each epoch," he wrote in 1925, "memory reconstructs an image of the past that is in accord with the predominant thoughts of the society." So it is today. We arrange for the past, especially the calamitous past, to tell us what we wish to hear. Many of the Holocaust museums that now exist in virtually every large provincial American city basically exhort their visitors to be nicer people. In Dallas, where I grew up, the Holocaust and Human Rights Museum — again, it is rarely enough for any of these museums to be only a Holocaust museum — encourages visitors to be "upstanders" in their daily lives, to step up when they see injustice happening. There is also a "Beyond Tolerance Theater" that teaches viewers about unconscious bias on the playground or in the workplace. In Los Angeles, the Museum of Tolerance, a satellite of the Simon Wiesenthal Center, which recently opened another version of itself in Jerusalem, emphasizes mutual respect in all its forms, and features a permanent exhibition entitled "Finding Our Families, Finding Ourselves," which "showcases the diversity within the personal histories of several noted Americans," including Maya Angelou, Kareem Abdul-Jabbar, and Carlos Santana. The point is that we Americans are all different, and therefore we are all the same. This is one reason why the Holocaust looms so large in contemporary life. It is so *usable*. Approaches such as these indulge, and even depend on, an individual and collective solipsism: the murder of millions of others in faraway lands is relevant only insofar as it is somehow related to me, to us.

That is why I had come back to Israel, a place where I have spent a great deal of time over the course of my life, to see this little cave: this is a relic of the time before collective memory crystallized, before the catastrophe became a fount of moral instruction seemingly open to all. I was interested in its the aftermath from the very beginning, long before the era of platitudes and parables — interested in how, exactly, survivors who emerged from an inexplicable and indescribable hell built a durable memory from the ground up, and also in the sacrifices that had to be made for the sake of that memory, the omissions, the elisions, and the emphases. I took as my starting point a comment by Susan Sontag. "Strictly speaking, there is no such thing as collective memory," she remarked in *Regarding the Pain of Others*. Instead, "what is called collective memory is not a remembering but a stipulating: that *this* is important, and *this* is the story about how it happened." I don't think she was entirely right, in the sense that collective memory is a very real force for many communities, even those who did not experience a cataclysmic event. The mechanisms of collective memory may be mysterious, but the evidence that it works is visible in all our inherited cultures. But Sontag was right to see memory as a construction, as something that was not handed down from on high but actively constructed from below — and sometimes at great personal cost to those who built it. And this is why I had come to Mount Zion: the Holocaust Cellar is above all a chapter in the history of memory in its earliest and most unfiltered stages. To visit here is to return to the source.

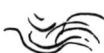

In the beginning — or rather at the end — there was widespread indifference and the constant threat of oblivion. What had happened in Europe between 1933 and 1945 was a catastrophe so immense that its extent could not yet be fathomed, a rupture so profound that it could not yet be named, because naming implies narrative and narrative implies meaning. And who, in the rubble, would have the temerity to pronounce confidently, with the intellectual composure required for the task, on the meaning of what had just happened? Who would dare speak of such a thing? Millions had been murdered everywhere in Europe, gassed in windowless rooms and in the backs of trucks, shot at point blank in wooded ravines, hunted in forests until they lost the strength and finally the will to run. Rich and poor, significant and insignificant, cruel and kind — in certain areas, a whole world was systematically reduced to nothing. The great cities of Yiddishland, an entire civilization between the Danube and the Volga, lay in ruins; smaller towns and shtetls simply disappeared from the map. The great synagogues that had been fixtures of urban landscapes for centuries were desecrated and ransacked and gutted. Jewish homes, even the meager ones, were sequestered, and their contents, even the worthless ones, plundered and thrown into piles — mounds of candlesticks, heaps of inexpensive china. What was the lesson in those piles and piles of teacups in makeshift warehouses? No, this was not a parable. This was an actual calamity of unprecedented scope and brutality, a calamity that in some ways had no religious or historical antecedent even in the experience of a people to whom history had already been merciless.

But along with the utter disbelief, the incomprehension, and the silent awe before the extent of the destruction, there was also a sense among survivors of the encroaching threat of oblivion, the most painful fate of all — one had seen a hellscape, lived to tell the tale, but emerged into a world in which there was no surviving proof of it and no audience eager to believe it or imagine it, all the photographs notwithstanding. Oblivion is the intersection of ignorance and indifference, and oblivion was always a fundamental aim of the Nazi genocide of the Jews, not only the oblivion of the liquidation of the Jewish people, but also the oblivion of *how* they were liquidated — the details of their destruction, the means of their murder. The Jews were simply to disappear, along with any and all traces of their disappearance. Martef HaShoah emerged precisely at this moment, when oblivion was at the door.

In the immediate aftermath of the war, the indifference was instantly palpable. "There was never any mystery about what had happened to Europe's Jews," Tony Judt writes in a remarkable discussion of the subject near the end of *Postwar*. "That an estimated six million of them were put to death during the Second World War was widely accepted within a few months of the war's end." Accepted, but not wrestled with. Few were really interested in the plight of the Jews. In the bloodlands of eastern Europe, antisemitism remained, and Jews who returned home after their liberation from the camps were sometimes met with further pogroms, most notoriously in Kielce, Poland in July 1946. In the west, there was less outright violence but just as much elision. The French newspaper *Le Monde*, for instance, would write, even passionately, of *"survivants des camps"* and even of *"déportés,"* but it would never speak of Jews specifically. What began to matter to growing numbers of survivors was to preserve evidence and testimony, without which all would not only still be lost but also forgotten, which would be akin to losing it all again. As the philosopher Jean-François Lyotard observed, decades later, in *Le Différend*, a treatise that responded to a rising tide of denialism about Auschwitz, the after-effect of precisely this phenomenon:

> It is the nature of a victim not to be able to prove that one has been done a wrong.... The perfect crime does not consist in killing the victim or the witnesses...but rather in obtaining the silence of the witnesses, the deafness of the judges, and the inconsistency (insanity) of the testimony. You neutralize the addressor, the addresses, and the sense of the testimony; then everything is as if there were no referent (no damages).

Liberties

This was why, even as the destruction was still underway, the fight against oblivion had already begun, the struggle to save the documentary evidence. The astonishing story of the Jewish historian Emmanuel Ringelblum and the *Oyneg Shabbos* project in the Warsaw Ghetto is now well known: trapped in the ghetto, he and his group of fellow imprisoned historians risked their lives to preserve every trace they could find that revealed something, anything, about their own destruction. They collected quite a lot — diaries, posters, decrees, and about twenty-five thousand documents that detailed the extermination camps at Treblinka and Chelmno and the ghettos elsewhere in Poland. "It must be recorded with not a single fact omitted," read one of their circulars. "And when the time comes — and it surely will — let the world read and know what the murderers have done." The historical documentation assembled by these historians in extremis was then buried underground in three large milk cans, only two of which have been found. Ringelblum was murdered with his family in March 1944. Only one member of *Oyneg Shabbos* survived — the writer Rachel Auerbach, who later became the head of the testimonies department at Yad Vashem, an institution whose existence was still unimaginable at the end of the war.

Oyneg Shabbos was far from the only such enterprise. The documentary impulse was a form of resistance, and it appeared in Jewish circles across wartime Europe. The writers Vassily Grossman and Ilya Ehrenberg, Soviet soldiers at the time, were in the battalion that liberated Treblinka. Grossman was haunted by the gas chambers that he discovered there, which he struggled to grasp: "What are the pictures now passing before people's glassy dying eyes? Pictures of childhood? Of the happy days of peace? Of the last terrible journey?" But he concluded: "No, what happened in that chamber cannot be imagined." When the two returned home, they set about compiling *The Black Book of Soviet Jewry*, a sprawling five-hundred-page collection of memories from Jewish survivors, interviews with non-Jewish eyewitnesses, and dispatches by the authors themselves — a massive undertaking that was published in Yiddish, not Russian. Soviet censors initially ordered that the contents of the book be changed: they wanted to shift the focus away from Jewish suffering, and they wanted certain passages to be rewritten so as to downplay atrocities committed by Ukrainian civilians against Ukrainian Jews. By 1948, the censors took it one step further: they scrapped the book entirely, destroying even the typefaces used to print it. The attack on *The Black Book* was an opening salvo in Stalin's war against "rootless cosmopolitans," a favorite communist term for Jews, and one of the earliest state-sanctioned attempts after the war to condemn the catastrophe to oblivion.

Much the same was true in Western Europe, far from the slaughterhouses of the east. In occupied France, as early as 1943, Isaac Schneersohn, a rabbi-turned-industrialist from the family of the Lubavitcher rebbes, called a meeting of local Jewish leaders in the small apartment he was renting in Grenoble, then under Italian control. His aim was to document the atrocities that they saw unfolding everywhere around them. "These days, when we evoke the horrible figure of six million victims," Schneersohn later recalled, "the few Jews we ourselves witnessed being deported seem a little less weighty in comparison, even a drop in the ocean. But at the time, when we thought about what they went through, pushed up against cold walls, left in waiting rooms or in train stations, when we contemplated the sheer number of the elderly, of women, of the sick, we were seized with anguish and submerged in sadness." Far from the Warsaw ghetto, he nevertheless responded in exactly the same as Emanuel Ringelblum: what mattered was fighting oblivion until the very end. "No one among us believed he would emerge alive from that oppressive atmosphere where it was literally impossible to breathe....And so I had only one desire: to record all these Nazi crimes so that those who survived could transmit the facts to future generations and record, for history, the memory of the atrocities perpetrated by the Nazis on the Jewish people." Schneersohn did survive, and his makeshift archive became the *Centre de Documentation Juive Contemporaine* (CDJC), the foundation for Paris' *Mémorial de la Shoah*, the first memorial of its kind in Western Europe, dedicated in 1953.

Almost immediately, the question became what to do with all this documentary evidence, hundreds of thousands of linear feet of archival material, diary entries, and typeset testimonies that sought to preserve traces of the inexplicable. In time, each of the names that began to emerge for the calamity was inadequate, because, again, names imply narrative, and each narrative somehow reduced the event into a particular frame that diminished either its horror or its totality, and sometimes both. In Yiddish, some survivors almost immediately began calling the Nazi attempt to liquidate the entire Jewish people a *"khurbn,"* a term that means "destruction" and originally referred to the destruction of the Second Temple by the Romans in approximately 70 CE, the watershed event in early Jewish memory. But the Nazi genocide of the Jews was hardly the same: this time what was destroyed was far more than sacred space — not the "cultic center" of a particular religion but an entire people, many of whom had nothing to do with the religion of their ancestors. By the late 1930s, journalists in Palestine were already using the biblical term *"shoah"* — Hebrew for "catastrophe" — to describe the great darkness that had fallen over the Jews of Europe. "That day is a day of wrath," we read in Zephaniah 1:15, "a day of trouble and distress, a day of *shoah* and desolation, a day of clouds and thick darkness." (The word *shoah* appears in a number of places in the Hebrew Bible, always to denote devastation.) For many at the time, that sense of biblical catastrophe, of primal destruction, encapsulated the Nazi assault. After the Nazis invaded Poland in September 1939, for instance, *Davar*, a great Hebrew daily now defunct, noted that "a terrible *shoah* befell the millions of Jews of Poland, a *shoah* whose scope and sights far exceed anything experienced in recent years." But *shoah* means catastrophe merely in the general sense of disaster, as in natural disaster, as if what happened came from nowhere and had nothing to do with human will.

And then, of course, there was "holocaust," soon to be the most prevalent of all the names and by far the worst of the lot. The word came from the ancient Greek translation of the Hebrew Bible, the roots *holos* and *kostos*, which together meant "totally burnt," completely consumed by the fire, as in an animal offered for ritual sacrifice. "Holocaust" already had a premonitory valence in English: Nathaniel Hawthorne had used the term in 1844 in "Earth's Holocaust," a short story that uncannily anticipated the Nazi book burning at Berlin's Babelplatz in May 1933. It describes a great conflagration of the books of the world: "Thick, heavy folios, containing the labors of lexicographers, commentators, and encylopedists, were flung in, and, falling among the embers with a leaden thump, smoldered away to ashes like rotten wood." In 1933, *Newsweek* had used the term to describe the actual Babelplatz book burning, and in 1943 *The New York Times* did the same to describe the plight of Jewish refugees in Palestine "surviving the Nazi holocaust."

Liberties

But it was Elie Wiesel who was most insistent that "holocaust" be used to describe the catastrophe that he had witnessed. In the 1980s, he explained his reasoning in an appearance at a Chicago synagogue. The term, he said, enshrined the Jewish religious significance of the catastrophe, because it called to mind the *Akedah*, or the binding of Isaac, one of the most harrowing passages in the Bible, when God demands of Abraham that he sacrifice his son. "I call Isaac the first survivor of the Holocaust because he survived the first tragedy," Wiesel said. "Isaac was going to be a burnt offering, a *korban olah* [a type of sacrifice in the Temple that had to be entirely consumed by the fire on the altar], which is really the Holocaust. The word 'holocaust' has a religious connotation. Isaac was meant to be given to God as a sacrifice." But this is precisely the problem with the term. It paints a picture of Jews being led to their deaths like Isaac by Abraham, like lambs to the slaughter, devoid of agency or will, and it also casts the entire event as something ordained by God to purify the world. It confidently presumes a theology. It perversely sacralizes mass murder. And unlike in the story of Isaac's crucible, no angel appeared in the sky to prevent the murder.

Although the Holocaust Cellar appeared amid the emergence of these endless debates, it differed from other early attempts to come to terms with the catastrophe in two ways: it sought to show and not to tell — the articulateness of the place is not discursive but physical; and it was established in the nascent Jewish state, a representation of a world-historical event in a new place whose existence represented another world-historical event. Even now, the cellar is an interplay between destruction and redemption.

The principal architect of Martef HaShoah was Shmuel Zangwill Kahana, the Director General of the new state's Ministry of Religious Affairs, who served in that office for two decades. Kahana was born in Warsaw in 1905 into a family of distinguished rabbis, and he himself received rabbinical ordination from Rabbi Moses Soloveitchik (the son of the renowned Rabbi Haim Soloveitchik and the father of the renowned Rabbi Joseph B. Soloveitchik), as well as a doctorate in Middle Eastern studies from the University of Lieges in Belgium. With his wife and his parents he escaped Poland in 1940 and settled in Palestine. Kahana was a religious Zionist, in his ideology and his party affiliation, for whom the Holocaust — or the *Shoah*, or the *khurbn*, or whatever the catastrophe was to be called — belonged squarely within the long sequence of disasters in Jewish history, from the destruction of the Second Temple in 70 CE to the massacres by the Crusaders in the eleventh and twelfth centuries to the atrocities by the Ukrainians in the seventeenth century to the pogroms in Russia from the 1890s to the 1900s, a teleology of tragedy to which the establishment of the State of Israel was the ultimate rejoinder.

Kahana believed that commemoration should be something of a religious rite, that it should adhere to Jewish religious tradition and its inherited approaches to mourning. This is why the choice of location for the cellar was paramount. "The cellar projects onto Mount Zion," Kahana wrote shortly after the opening. "And Mount Zion in return projects onto the Holocaust cellar." (The road that winds up to the top of Mount Zion is named for him.) A verse in Obadiah declares that "upon Mount Zion shall be deliverance and there shall be holiness." But the choice of Mount Zion had also another significance: it projected onto Mount Moriah, where according to the Biblical account Isaac was bound, further to the east, where the gold-domed mosque now stood, still behind the cease-fire lines and beyond Israeli jurisdiction. That was not just coincidence: for Kahana, as for Wiesel, Isaac was the first survivor. The religious dimension of the cellar is still unavoidable, though it does not interfere with the experience of the place. Nothing could.

As has been hotly debated for decades now, the Jewish community in Palestine, and later the state of Israel, had an impossible relationship with the catastrophe in Europe, when it was unfolding and especially when it was over. In the words of the Israeli journalist Tom Segev, the response during the war was "less than compassionate" and, in the uncertain aftermath "a great silence surrounded the destruction of the Jews." It was only in 1961, with the public trial of Adolf Eichmann, as Segev and others have insisted, that there began "a process of identification with the tragedy of the victims and survivors, a process that continues to this day." But other historians, most notably Anita Shapira, have convincingly complicated this view of Israeli diffidence or indifference, noting that, among other things, Ben Gurion's push for reparations from the German government in the early 1950s, as well as the ferocious pushback against that campaign, led by a young Menachem Begin, showed that Israel's establishment in those early years was not so much "silent" regarding the Holocaust as terrified of its explosiveness. Before the Eichmann trial, after all, there was the Kasztner trial, a major moment in the public consciousness of the new state, when, in 1953, a hotelier named Malkiel Gruenwald, who lost fifty-two relatives in Auschwitz, accused the Hungarian-born journalist and civil servant Rudolf Kasztner of collaborating with the Nazis, and Adolf Eichmann in particular. The government took Kasztner's side, suing Gruenwald for libel. But the courts acquitted Gruenwald and ruled that Kasztner had "sold his soul to the devil." When the government attempted to appeal the case, it collapsed under public outrage. Kastner was assassinated by a group of veterans walking into his Tel Aviv apartment in March 1957. (His granddaughter is now the head of the Labor Party in Israel.) This was not silence; it was trauma.

But if there was not silence, there certainly was stigma. One of the reasons that the bars of soap on display in the cellar are so moving, inauthentic as they may be, is that in Hebrew survivors were often and cruelly called *sabonim*, which means "soapsters." Among the Jews of Palestine, there was often an undisguised contempt for the fact that their European brethren had not defended themselves and had, at least in the eyes of some, allowed a terrible fate to fall on them. How could they have let the Germans turn them into soap? In 1944, *Davar* asked that question in a headline: "Why are the Jews of Hungary not defending themselves?" The Zionist ethos rebelled against the apparent lack of resistance. Likewise, Yitzhak Gruenbaum, a Polish Zionist leader who later became Israel's first Interior Minister, had nothing but disdain for the Jews of Poland who "had not found in their souls the courage" to defend themselves. In his mind, they had preferred "the life of a dog over an honorable death." These condescending Zionists exaggerated, of course: there certainly was Jewish armed resistance in the Nazi inferno. But there was not, nor could there have been, enough.

So many new citizens of the newly minted state had come from Europe and were stranded, as it were, in trauma and stupefaction. No one has written about this better than David Grossman, whose novel, *See Under: LOVE*, published in 1989, follows a young Israeli boy, Momik, the child of two survivors, who tries to exorcise what he calls the Nazi "beast" from his family's life. There is a moving passage early in the novel when Momik tries to get rid of the tattoo on his grandfather's arm. His grandfather is always muttering, locked in a trance, and Momik is convinced that the tattoo is the problem. "The numbers drove him crazy because they weren't written in ink and they couldn't be washed off with water or spit. Momik tried everything to wash grandfather's arm, but the number stayed fixed." Indeed, the numbers could never be washed away.

"The moment it happened it was known here," Yehuda Bauer, the great Israeli historian of the Holocaust, one of the first to study the subject seriously in any language, told me about the catastrophe. It was a late summer afternoon in Jerusalem, and Bauer, now ninety-seven, kindly received me in the small apartment that he keeps in an assisted living facility above an anonymous shopping center next to the Shaare Zedek hospital, not far from Yad Vashem. I brought a box of cookies from the bakery downstairs, and instantly regretted it: Bauer struggles to walk, and insisted on rummaging in his kitchenette for the right plate to serve the cookies. He and his family had left their native Prague on the night the Germans invaded Czechoslovakia, and his father brought the family to Palestine, where he has remained ever since. "We knew about the ghettos," he said. "What was clear was that if the Germans conquered Palestine we wouldn't survive." When he was a Ph.D. student, Bauer told me, there were not yet any scholarly studies of the Holocaust, but he had been influenced by Abba Kovner, the Polish-Jewish writer and partisan leader who had led Nakam, a postwar paramilitary organization devoted to vengeance – to murdering six million Germans in exchange for the six million murdered Jews. Kovner fainted after giving testimony at the Eichmann trial, one of the most memorable moments in that ongoing drama, recorded on live television for all the world to see. "He persuaded me very early that the Holocaust was the most important event in the Jewish twentieth century, and maybe in all of Jewish history," Bauer said. "When I told him I didn't know the languages at the time, that I was scared, he said, 'that's fine—you should be scared.'"

It was clear from the very beginning that some edifice would have to be erected in Israel in commemoration of the catastrophe in Europe, but the government could not decide what form, exactly, that commemoration should take. The question became urgent in June 1949, when the Israeli government received a glass coffin containing thirty-one jars of "martyrs' ashes" from Austria. (Simon Wiesenthal led the group of survivors who brought them to Jerusalem, and their installation in the cellar is regarded as the first public ceremony of Holocaust commemoration in Israel.) But it was the Ministry of Religious Affairs, under Kahana's stewardship, that took charge of this occasion, not any other part of the government. He devised a major public spectacle: a coffin containing the jars lay in state in Tel Aviv, where thousands of people visited it, and it was later transported to Jerusalem by military convoy, wrapped in an Israeli flag. Kahana prepared for the arrival of the martyr's ashes in Jerusalem by soliciting many pieces of Judaica that local survivors had brought from Europe — Torah crowns, incense boxes, menorahs. His aim was clear: the cellar, quickly cleared from a basement in an old Ottoman building, was a response to the Destruction of the Temple, however small. The newspaper *Hatsofeh* put it this way: Kahana's cellar was "a counterpoint to the removal of the articles from the Holy Temple in Jerusalem to Rome." The cellar was nothing less than a retort to the Arch of Titus. The symbolism was complete.

Before the Israeli government decreed, in April 1951, that *Yom Ha'Shoah*, or Holocaust Remembrance Day, would fall on the twenty-seventh day of Nissan, which was the date in the Hebrew calendar when the Warsaw Ghetto uprising was crushed in 1943, Kahana had his own ideas. In 1949, in keeping with his agenda, and his view of the Jewish past, *Martef HaShoah* was officially inaugurated on Tisha b'Av, the ninth day of the month of Av, a religious day of fasting that commemorates the day on which the Babylonians destroyed the First Temple, the Romans destroyed the Second Temple, and many other calamities befell the Jews across the centuries. In this way the Holocaust was fitted into the tragic pattern of Jewish history as enunciated by the great nineteenth-century Jewish historians — Heinrich Graetz, Leopold Zunz, even Simon Dubnow, murdered in Riga in 1941. But no interpretation, not even the lachrymose one, can master what one sees in those dark rooms: what they evoke is beyond a mere chapter in a saga of suffering. I actually thought of Dubnow when I wandered through the cave. *"Yidn, shraybt un farshraybt,"* a number of survivors recall him saying before his murder— Jews, write and record. This is precisely what Martef HaShoah seeks to do, however humbly, however violently.

In the years that followed the establishment of the state, there were frequent attempts to establish the cellar as a site of political inspiration, as the historian Doron Bar has ably documented. Kahana arranged for Tisha B'Av to be commemorated in the cellar every year, with the ashes of murdered European Jews brought to the nearby synagogue at David's tomb. In 1950, the year after the cellar was dedicated, the ceremonies of Israel's Independence Day began on Mount

Zion, and with one of the objects in the cellar — the blowing of a shofar that had been brought from Europe. Kahana was hopeful that all of these events would entrench his vision of what the catastrophe would mean in the eyes of the wider Israeli public. "The commemoration in the Holocaust cellar," he said, "will undoubtedly penetrate wider public circles and bind them to the memory of the Holocaust, as specific dates become accepted. For the time being, we are laying the foundations and making attempts to establish special events. We will see the effects of those actions as time goes by." Those ambitions alienated some, including Bauer. "I was never religious," he told me in Jerusalem, when I asked him what he thought about the cellar. "I was never interested in that sort of thing."

But this was really as far as "narrative" ever got on Mount Zion, at least in relation to Holocaust memory. Regardless of Kahana's intentions, the space that he cleared for his terrible chamber never quite became a museum that sought to depict the catastrophe in religious terms. This was because it became a space for survivors to come and grieve on their own terms, in a time when there was virtually nowhere else for them to go. In the north the kibbutz Lohamei Hagetaot, the Ghetto Fighters' kibbutz, had not yet opened its famed galleries, known as the Ghetto Fighters' House, and neither had Yad Mordechai in the south opened its museum. For a few short years, Martef HaShoah was essentially all there was, and it touched a nerve far beyond what Kahana imagined. People came from everywhere, carrying what they had — memories of lost loved ones, treasures from forgotten towns, objects that somehow testified to the destruction that they had survived. They did not come to Mount Zion to "tell a story" as much as they came to ensure that what they remembered did not vanish along with everything else they had known. During Hanukkah, a number of survivors would assemble in the cellar and light candles in lamps that had been brought from Europe.

In 1953, the fourth year of its existence, a local association of Hungarian survivors decided to establish an archive of sorts in the cellar — a *beit gnazim*, as they called it — that would record the names of the murdered along with any other relevant documents they had. Around the same time, small communities of survivors began to put up plaques with the names of their towns in Europe that the catastrophe had either devastated or eradicated altogether. By 1952, hundreds of these plaques were placed on the walls of the courtyard outside the cellar as well as inside, all over its dark walls. This was why one unnamed survivor told the religious Zionist newspaper *Hatsofeh* in December of that year that the site should be Israel's "traditional monument for the commemoration of the Holocaust," because there were publicly displayed names of "all the lost communities." In fact there was no room, in this small spot, for the names of all the communities, but the place names that are given are deeply affecting. Each one represents countless graves that were never dug. They even look like gravestones.

At the same time, on the other side of the city, there was another Holocaust memorial project devoted to memorials and names, to be called "Yad Vashem" for precisely that reason. Its name derived from Isaiah 56:5: "And to them will I give in my house and within my walls a memorial and a name (*yad vashem*) that shall not be cut off." In August 1953, the Knesset passed the Yad Vashem Law, establishing the Holocaust Martyrs' and Heroes' Remembrance Authority, which was to be Israel's official national memorial to the Holocaust. Debates had raged since even before 1948 about what the place of

Holocaust memory should be in the landscape of the new state, but Ben-Gurion had hesitated until memorials began to crop up all over Europe in the early 1950s. He had been present at the dedication of Isaac Schneersohn's *Mémorial du Martyr Juif Inconnu* in the Marais district of Paris in the summer of 1953, and had returned to Jerusalem adamant that the Jewish State, and nowhere else, be the official home of Holocaust memory. And so the purpose of the newfound memorial project, according to the law passed in the Knesset, "is to gather *in the homeland* material regarding all members of the Jewish people who laid down their lives, who fought and rebelled against the Nazi enemy and its collaborators, and to perpetuate their memory."

Martef Hashoah was a humble cellar outside the Old City, on the eastern side of Jerusalem, which derived its gravitas from its proximity to some of the holiest sites in Judaism and Jewish memory. Yad Vashem, which would not open to the public until 1973, very much derived its legitimacy from its position in the west of the city, the "new" city, on the slopes of Mount Herzl, the hallowed ground of secular Zionism. As it grew in size and stature in the decades after its opening, the newer memorial museum and archive became the place where Israel tells the story of the Holocaust — a sophisticated museological exposition of the European events, in various media, that ends with stunning views of Eretz Yisrael, the rightful home of the Jewish people. Point made. The site is now a massive complex with state-of-the-art technology, in a structure that the architect Moshe Safdie boldly cut through a mountain. This is where Israeli prime ministers bring endless delegations of foreign leaders to understand something about the Jewish, and the Israeli, past. The Zionist lessons of Yad Vashem are plain. IDF soldiers are routinely brought through the museum as part of their training. Rest assured they do not visit the cellar on Mount Zion, or even know that it exists. They can be forgiven, as the site is open by appointment only, and even that is irregular. When I visited most recently, I had to beg for access. It was a stroke of luck that I was allowed in.

How far we have come from the cave on Mount Zion, from its rawness, from its urgency. Today much of Holocaust memory — or much of public Holocaust memory, I should say — is high-minded kitsch. In museums and memorials across the globe, it often seeks to sanitize and moralize in equal measure, to spin the nightmare of Auschwitz into some kind of sermon about the future. Forget, but only for a moment, that the cautionary power of Auschwitz has demonstrably failed: the memory of the past has not stopped or genocides, even in Europe, nor has it impeded antisemitism, which, perhaps especially in the United States, is more than alive and well, and at a time when Holocaust education has never been more mainstream. Beyond all that, Holocaust memory has now become a pixilated performance, and sometimes even a genre of entertainment. This, it would seem, is the future of cautionary memory.

For many memorial institutions, the reigning anxiety is the impending disappearance of the last generation of survivors, women and men who have been living custodians of memory for decades and who have helped the event come alive for generations of schoolchildren and others by means of memoirs, documentaries, and interviews. There is a manifest belief among the leaders of many of these institutions that survivors should simply not be allowed to die like everyone else, that somehow they owe us more of their time and more of their trauma beyond the grave. Hence the bizarre "Dimensions in Testimony" project, an initiative of Steven Spielberg's Shoah Foundation at the University of Southern California in Los Angeles, which has created literal holograms of twenty-five survivors, a technology now available at twelve different Holocaust museums worldwide, from Skokie, Illinois to Sydney, Australia. In the words of the project's promotional materials: "Now and far into the future, museum-goers, students and others can have conversational interactions with these eyewitnesses to history to learn from those who were there."

Holograms! Spielberg was accused of kitsch, and worse, for *Schindler's List*, a film that actually dared to depict victims *inside* a gas chamber. "Dimensions in Testimony" is not nearly as impudent and outrageous as that, but it is cut from the same cloth. I have now seen a number of these spectacles of artificial intelligence in museums in different cities, and it is the "artificial" part of the "intelligence" here that bothers me most. After all, so much of the fight for Holocaust memory was, and remains, a fight for the truth, proving against the violence of denialism that the catastrophe really did happen, that it was not, in fact, a distortion or a hoax. And yet here we are, relying on literal distortion, on a technological hoax, to tell the story.

"Dimensions in Testimony" goes something like this. You sit down in an auditorium of some kind, the lights dim, and all of a sudden a hologram appears, a pixilated reconstruction of a smiling survivor, who is magically alive again, and gives a brief summary of his or her experience, and then takes questions. You can ask the survivor almost anything you want — their favorite color, their favorite food. In fact, that is the point: to make sure people know that these holograms are real people, which they are not. The docent running the show at one museum I visited told the audience that we should make sure to ask the survivor to tell us a joke. Someone even did, and people even laughed. I rubbed my eyes in disbelief. What stupendous disrespect! But this is where Holocaust memory, and collective memory, is headed: insults to decency and insults to intelligence in equal measure. Before you know it, sorrow will be fun.

Martef Hashoah is more or less entirely forgotten in our era of Holocaust holograms. But the cave of horrors bears revisiting, if only to confront anew the stupefaction, the muteness, the shock, the colossal humbling, that it offers. As we progress further and further from the catastrophe itself, that original sense of the smashing of the mind against it is too often forgotten. We think that we can believe that the catastrophe happened — obviously it happened, didn't it? — and we are no longer even all that afraid of it, because we have allowed it to make sense in some strange way, with all the arrogance of theory and hindsight. We are so familiar with it, when we think about it at all. But on Mount Zion familiarity is out of the question. There we are reminded that there is no narrative, no intellectual or religious or emotional framework, that can adequately capture the hopelessness and abjection preserved in these basement rooms, no lesson they can be said to teach. The ashes are the ashes; the soap is the soap.

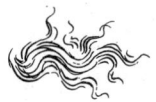

KENDA MUTONGI

Living by the Roundabout

"This is Jane calling from central Kenya. *Sasa*, so, I am in a lesbian relationship, and we are hoping to get married, and I would like to pay bridewealth to my partner's father, but we don't know how to bring this issue up with him because he thinks we are just friends." The voice spills from our taxi's radio, tuned to one of the FM call-in stations that have recently begun to proliferate in Kenya — perhaps *Radio Maisha*, Lifestyle Radio, or Classic 105 Kenya.

It is July 2018, and my daughter Ada and I are seated in the back of the taxi. Ours is one of at least two hundred cars stuck in traffic at a major roundabout on one of Nairobi's main thoroughfares. The four traffic policemen manning the roundabout have let the vehicles in the other three lanes enter and exit the circle twice, but we remain stuck, packed as tightly as kernels on an ear of corn. Three rows of motionless vehicles, as still as a parking lot. All the while we are being assailed by brash vendors, both men and women, selling bottled water, peanuts, bananas, padlocks, tea strainers, and all kinds of plastic merchandise from China or Thailand.

Apparently, it is a common practice for the police to rotate the traffic jam on each of the four roads feeding into the roundabout so that the vendors have captive customers throughout the day. It just happens that it is time for vendors to "eat" from our side of the road. We have been sitting in the traffic for almost ten minutes now, listening to the radio.

"So, are you the husband in the relationship?" The male host of the radio asks with a hint of mockery. Before Jane can answer, another male caller interrupts: "This is interesting. So, you are the husband in the relationship, and you want to pay bridewealth. Instead of wasting money like that, why don't you give it to me, and I will pay bridewealth for my wife?"

"*Sasa*, now," Jane replies bashfully. "You don't understand, but my girlfriend and I are passionately in love, and we have been living together for three years now and we want to get married and make it official."

Ada and I exchange glances. "Make it official," I wonder out loud. "But gay marriages are not legal in Kenya." The government claims that same-sex relations are a foreign transgression and that they pollute Kenyan religious and cultural values. According to the law, the penalty for those found engaging in homosexuality is fourteen years in prison. George, our taxi driver, smiles but does not say anything.

"What?" Another woman caller interjects. "A woman

Living by the Roundabout

wants to marry a woman and pay bridewealth for her? You people are showing bad behavior for the young people. And this is a sin." You can almost see her nose curl and her head shake with disapproval.

"You don't realize this but the love between my girlfriend and me is more passionate than that between a man and a woman," Jane responds.

In the background we hear several phones ringing, but rather than answer them the radio host decides that he is ready to provide a solution: "Take the time and introduce the idea of bridewealth slowly to your girlfriend's father. And depending on how much money and livestock you are willing to offer, he might be amenable to it."

I look at my watch. We have not moved for fifteen minutes. "Why are we not moving?" Ada asks me. I redirect the question to George. "The vendors have paid the police to stop the traffic so they can sell their goods."

Ada still looks a little confused, so I repeat the question. George looks at me and clicks his tongue: "*Si hawa watu wamelipa polisi.*" These people have paid the police to bring the traffic to a halt so they can sell their goods. "*Hawa watu wanatusubua kabisa.*" These people are messing us up. George has a gaunt black face, a face thinned by years of overwork, and when he curses his temples tighten. You can feel his weariness; it sinks into you.

July is the coldest month in Nairobi and all the vendors and policemen are clad in sweaters and coats. A female vendor is wearing a sweatshirt emblazoned with "University of Iowa," which she probably purchased from one of the many used American clothing markets all over Kenya now. The bougainvillea bordering the roundabout looks sad. Gray and dusty. The bright pink and orange flowers of April and May are all gone.

Liberties

July in Nairobi is leaden English weather without the rain.

Bored and thirsty, confined by the vendors and policemen's "entrepreneurial spirit," many of the nearby drivers part with forty or fifty shillings (about fifty cents in American dollars) to buy bottled water, bananas, or peanuts. They might even buy a flashlight in anticipation of a power blackout, or a plastic tea strainer as a gift for their mothers or grandmothers next time they visit the village. Buying trinkets is a pleasant enough way to pass the time, and none of the drivers seem to mind parting with a few shillings. The car next to us is a hulking black Range Rover. When I look over at the driver, I see a prosperous-looking man nestled in the passenger seat passing a hundred-shilling note to the vendor, and the vendor, a man who barely looks to be in his twenties, handing him a blue handkerchief wrapped in plastic.

My daughter leans her head against the window and sighs. I don't blame her; it has been a long day. We have just spent nearly five hours on the congested train from Mombasa to Nairobi and are eager to get to our guesthouse on the western side of the city. Our taxi is still stuck. We haven't moved for twenty minutes.

And then, without warning, the police officers instruct the vendors to clear the road, and wave us through into the roundabout. Still annoyed, George clicks his tongue again, starts the car engine and complains. *"Hawa watu wabaya kabisa"* — these people are terrible. For taxi drivers such as George, making money requires moving fast and getting the first crack at the next passengers. The delay has cost him money.

As soon as the taxi starts moving, George turns up the volume of the radio—he is eager to hear about the next caller's dilemma. Her name is Petronella and she is from the Kisii region of Kenya, and she is calling to bemoan the fact that her husband is useless and has abandoned her and their five children. Because she cannot find him, she has been forced to sleep with other men to make ends meet. Callers respond with the predictable condemnation and support, in equal measure.

I manage to tune out the radio conversations. I have become used to hearing these kinds of call-in complaints all over Nairobi, on FM radios in taxis or matatus, and on radios in beauty shops and while waiting in line at vending kiosks. These call-in conversations have infiltrated daily life, and it occurs to me that they may provide more than just demoralizing gossip. Their insistent focus on pressing social and economic issues have bit by bit turned ordinary citizens into ethnographers of family life, and the radio into a civic forum. But I am too tired now to engage with the various comments on Petronella's dilemma.

We navigate the roundabout, and then quickly pass All Saints Anglican Cathedral, where the rich and famous of Nairobi marry or are mourned as they pass from one life to another. The colonial-style edifice, with its red tiled roof, stone walls, and well-tended gardens, feels out of place next to the tall dilapidated 1980s office buildings on the opposite side of the street. I attended the wedding of a friend's sister there once, a highly elaborate affair with all the traditional trappings. I wonder how the couple is doing now. Have their lives stalled or been obstructed by an unhealthy marriage like that of Petronella?

Thankfully, we are nearing our guesthouse. Ada and I are anxious to get out of the car and away from the noise of the spiraling talk and traffic. Once out of the taxi Ada rolls her eyes, lets out another deep sigh, and asks why people in Nairobi are so captivated by salacious talk shows. "We have this stuff in America too," I remind her. "Remember Jerry

Springer and Jenny Jones? People somehow love these kinds of shows." Then I recall that Ada is only seventeen years old and is probably too young to know who Jerry Springer or Jenny Jones are. The format is new to her. But here in Kenya it cannot be escaped. The number of radio stations have multiplied in the last few years, since the Kenyan government deregulated radio broadcasting and licenses have gotten cheaper (There were over a hundred radio stations in Kenya in 2018 compared to a mere ten in 1999.) Call-in shows are cheap and easy to produce, and many of the seven million people who live in the Nairobi area tune in everyday to hear the latest tales of frustration and woe.

Of course, gayness, let alone gay marriage, is illegal in Kenya. Ada knows this, so she rightly wonders why someone would want to out themselves like that on public radio. I shrug and offer an explanation: the people calling in remain anonymous, and besides, rumor has it that this stuff is just made up. That it is staged. The radio hosts or their producers probably arrange for people to phone in with fabricated stories because they believe listeners will find this stuff interesting — and clearly they do. The appetite for ordeal — of whatever kind — seems insatiable. Even if they are staged, the shows must be striking some nerves since they continue to be highly rated.

I sometimes think, rather cynically, that the callers' dilemmas comfort the audience by assuring them that others are worse off than they are and that their own troubles are not so bad. After all, nearly half of Nairobi's population live in poverty in places such as Mathare or Kibera, crowded together in makeshift dwellings of corrugated iron sheets,

Living by the Roundabout

without electricity or running water. Most of these people did not end up in Nairobi by choice. Roughly one quarter of Nairobi's current population was forced to move into the city due to the increase in population and lack of arable land in the rural areas, and due to falling agricultural commodity prices. The World Bank's and the IMF's economic policies of the late 1980s also exacerbated the problem. The neoliberalism of the day stipulated that the economy be opened to free trade to stimulate economic growth, and so the World Bank and the IMF proceeded to cut aid to the Kenyan government — which inevitably meant a decrease in funding for schools, hospitals, sanitation, general infrastructure, and services for the poor. No doubt the government's general mismanagement of the economy did not help. This kind of thinking was seconded by Dambisa Moyo, the celebrated Zambian-born economist, now Baroness Moyo, who wrote *Dead Aid*, a book that sought to explain that "aid is not working and how there is a better way for Africa." Entrepreneurship was, for her, the better way.

But entrepreneurship meant that young people were obliged to leave the villages and move into cities such as Nairobi or Kisumu to try to earn more shillings. Soon the city streets were teeming with kiosks, shoeshine stands, street hawkers peddling chapatis or roasted maize, fruits of all kinds, newspapers and magazines of all kinds, and nearly anything else that could be turned into ready money. The shoulders of all the major thoroughfares were soon lined with jerry-built *dukas* — small shops made of unhewn timber and roofed with tin or tarps to shelter the scanty merchandise. (Some of the better shops now occupy repurposed shipping containers that at least seem less haphazard.) If you had nothing to sell you could set yourself up as a palm reader or quack doctor.

Adding to the disorder was the growing number of street kids and prostitutes. Uwen Akpan poignantly told their stories in his extraordinary book, *Say You Are One of Them*, in 2008. So did the late writer Binyavanga Wainaina, whose essays on Nairobi describes the painful lives of poor people in the city. It didn't take long to transform the low-income areas of the city into a crowded labyrinth of clogged alleys whose occupants had to dodge dark piles of indeterminate sludge as they meandered their way through sale racks of plastic, tinseled imports. Skirmishes, some of them violent, became inevitable, as each vendor had to protect the little they had and to keep newcomers from encroaching on their paltry plots. Wherever one looked, the struggle to find a livelihood laid siege to the senses. It quickly became evident that the unregulated market managed to solve the problems of only a lucky few, and that there were scarcely any real prospects for most of Nairobi's new arrivals. The economic promises of neoliberal aid turned out to be little more than a conceit believed only by its few beneficiaries.

The precarious situation continues to exist to this day — as I write, Kenyans have spilled into the streets to protest the rising prices, as well as the 1.5% progressive income tax proposed by the government to help build affordable housing. The protests were limited to small pockets in the city, mostly in poorer areas such as Kibera, and they were met with tear gas and water cannons. More than anything, the protests represent a distrust of the government's ability to deliver on its promises, especially promises to help the poor. It is no mystery, then, why the call-in radio shows might provide a scrap of consolation to listeners. They aren't enjoying a sense of *schadenfreude*, exactly, just the reassurance that their suffering is relative, and not absolute. Their lives could be more difficult — if they were gay, for example.

And perhaps this also explains why discussions of gay people have become so conspicuous on the radio, as well as in print and on social media. The media and government officials exploit prejudices against LGBTIQA+ people and make them scapegoats for everything that has gone wrong in Kenya. Objecting to a recent Kenyan Supreme Court ruling that allowed gay people to assemble and advance their agenda through Non-Governmental Organizations (NGOs), an editorial in *TUKO*, a major online news outlet in Kenya, noted: "Homosexuality is biblically evil and culturally distasteful. Period…Sodom and Gomorrah were destroyed because of these kinds of evil thoughts and practices. Kenya is setting herself up for a similar tragedy by entertaining this mediocrity from the West." These kinds of crass appeals to religion and revulsion are, sadly, hardly confined to Kenya.

On the other hand, the radio host in Jane's case appeared to be sympathetic to these issues. He demonstrated a fair amount of patience and persistence when he argued that the caller take her time and introduce the idea of bridewealth slowly, with circumspection. Over time, he suggests, money and cattle might soften even the most stubborn of prejudices, even those of God-fearing fathers. It is even possible that the host is using Jane's case as a subtle form of protest, as an indirect way of normalizing the idea of gay marriages, so that eventually the government will have to acknowledge them, and even change its policies.

It is still the case, however, that LGBTIQA+ issues are discussed almost exclusively on radio talk shows in Kenya and rarely in everyday conversations. Still, these call-in shows might encourage people to talk more openly about these concerns in their living rooms, kitchens, and places of work. Didn't American sitcoms such as *Modern Family* or *Ellen* help make people more at ease with the idea of gay marriage? It occurs to me that the radio hosts are trying to suggest to the larger public that change is possible, even socially acceptable. While discussions of gay marriages are not openly designed to be subversive, it is likely that they are meant to be a subtle form of persuasion which shifts the Overton window just a bit. We can at least hope, in the long run, that all the radio show talk becomes part of a more elaborate social choreography, one that — for now — dances around the presence of homosexuality and that might in good time make even the most unaccepting listen to the music and acknowledge its reality.

When we finally arrive in our room at the guesthouse, Ada flops on the bed, looks at me and observes how interesting it is that in Nairobi having money doesn't always make one's life easier: "I can't believe all those people in Mercedeses and Range Rovers were stuck in the traffic for twenty minutes, completely paralyzed. They were practically held hostage by those poor vendors. Just like us." Of course, they got to sit secure in the comfort of their leather seats and air-conditioning. But this is one reason I love Nairobi. There was an important lesson about class and equality in that clogged but busy roundabout.

Unlike many Western cities where the rich can live easy lives and forget the poor exist, in Nairobi the rich are forced to confront the consequences of poverty as soon as they emerge from their gated compounds. The social and economic difference does not confer an epistemological difference. Once the security guard closes the gate behind them, the well-to-do walk — or more likely drive — on the same streets as the poor. They have no cognitive privilege or protection. All that divides them from the unruly hustle outside is a car window.

"Just look at the roads in this rich neighborhood where we are staying," I say to my daughter. "They are as rough and pitted as those in the poor areas of the city. The wealthy must dodge potholes along with everyone else." While the well-off may be able to hide behind guarded compounds and remain relatively safe, unperturbed and undeprived, they can never completely insulate themselves. It is impossible for them, try as they might, to evade the poor streets, or the poor on the streets. The moment they venture out, they witness all the cheerless vexations of the disadvantaged and the destitute.

"Of course, if the government paid policemen a living wage, they wouldn't feel the need

to take bribes from the vendors," Ada says. I reply: "But what would the vendors do then? They wouldn't be able to make a living. It looks like the system works. In the end, the police get what they want, and the vendors get what they want." Ada doesn't like the sound of this: "That doesn't seem right, mom." "Yes, I know. But that's the way it is in most of the Global South."

The "instrumentalization of disorder" is what the scholars Patrick Chabal and Jean-Pascal Daloz like to call this kind of social arrangement. Their argument has always seemed to me slightly disheartening, particularly since it depends upon a process of profiling the pathological as the norm. It usually starts at the government level, at least according to their influential book, *Africa Works: Disorder as a Political Instrument*, which appeared in 1999. In it, they argue that African political elites have purposely engineered the present state of disorder and corruption on the continent, and that they have done everything in their power to preserve it — because it works for them, especially in their dealings with international institutions. The elites, Chabal and Daloz contend, hope to "maximize their returns on the state of confusion, uncertainty, and sometimes even chaos, which characterizes most African polities." For example, state officials will sometimes fabricate "NGOs" to attract new resources from abroad, so as to unburden themselves of the expensive and politically arduous task of building effective state institutions and bureaucracies. And since African governments are highly patrimonial, officials often use these foreign resources to fulfill their patronage obligations by distributing the largesse to their clients in exchange for political allegiance. The chaos works quite well for them. As long as the disorder and the corruption continue to benefit the elites, the system manages to perpetuate itself. This theory also gives African leaders an aura of agency, making them seem less obviously the hapless victims of outsiders.

But surely, argues Ada, a country cannot run on perpetually contrived disorder, especially if the system only benefits only the elites and their cronies. This is true. So few people profit from trickle-down patronage that this system cannot go on much longer. It works no better than trickle-down economics. It is neither inclusive nor equitable, and very little trickles down from the patrons who are supposed to be looking out for everyone's well-being. The practice is unlikely to create any kind of sustained and stable wealth for most Africans. When government institutions don't work for the majority of people, those people will inevitably employ a variety of strategies to meet their needs—including working around a system that is perceived to be unjust or exploitative. Often it requires passive resistance, and sometimes active sabotage: the needy will employ whatever means necessary to survive. Hidden in these work-arounds is an entire political philosophy. What has emerged on the streets of Nairobi is a kind of civic pragmatism, a host of improvisatory and creative practices that amount to a supplementary accommodation which grants the poor a meager means of survival.

At the roundabout, for instance, the police see themselves as part of the civic community rather than impersonal functionaries in the government apparatus. They see themselves as performing an extra-governmental service or, perhaps, as exercising a supplemental authority that allows them to help the poor. Of course, this kind of unsanctioned authority can have a dark side: it may invite corruption. But at least in this instance the police believe that they are serving and protecting; they do not believe that they are corrupt. And who are we to disagree?

Working with the poor vendors is probably what any good and reasonable person would do, and if the police receive a few shillings or a few mangos to take home, everyone is happy — except perhaps the prosperous commuters in their comfortable cars or taxi drivers such as George, who are taxed for a few moments of their time. Though the actions of the police may be open to doubt, at least fewer of the poor are forsaken. What others — particularly outsiders — may see as instances of everyday corruption are, for the players, a means of keeping the wheels turning, a means of survival. And since much of the law-making process in Kenya and other parts of the Global South is inchoate or reactive, this kind of illicit adaptation allows ordinary citizens such as street vendors to become part of an informal rule-making system with its own guidelines and practices.

Perhaps this embodies a sort of democratic law-making, a different kind of common law. You might even say that, given its continued existence, we can recognize in their society-wide agreement Edmund Burke's idea of the practical wisdom of given arrangements.

So maybe it works better this way, at least for now. Who is to judge? In Cambridge, Massachusetts, where we live, homeless people take advantage of long stoplights at a few of the busier intersections to walk between the rows of cars carrying signs describing their plight, hoping that someone will roll down their window and hand them a few dollars. Meanwhile the occupants in the cars listen to the progressive NPR. The stoplights control the traffic. They are efficient and impassive, and we obey them mechanically. Everything appears orderly, except for the poor and homeless who weave through the rows of traffic hoping for a handout.

They are considered interlopers, whose cardboard petitions announce their lonely disenfranchisement. In other words, observing the law does not necessarily produce better living conditions for the poor, and it certainly does not provide a solution for the unhoused. Throughout Boston, impoverished men and women curl up with their belongings in corners of subway platforms or on moving trains to claim a few hours of warmth. Unlike the other passengers, the unhoused end up going everywhere and nowhere at once. The rich are never forced to interact with them, exceptional for the occasional solicitation. The poor may not be completely out of sight, but they are permanently blurred and kept mostly out of mind.

I do not mean to compare the levels of poverty in Boston or Cambridge to those in Nairobi. They are on a different scale. But in Nairobi, time and again, we witness the informal practice of civic accommodations playing out on the streets and on the radio talk shows. The police manage to compromise with the street vendors so that they are both better off. Everyone knows gay marriages have been outlawed in Kenya, but the radio show hosts knowingly ignore the law (or indirectly participate in the law-making process) by openly discussing the matter and offering counsel. Maybe the discussion will lead to changes in homophobic laws as more listeners are exposed to these stories. Maybe not. But the callers are not silenced. In fact, by virtue of the airtime granted them, they become indirectly legitimized. In time these discussions may contribute to a more open and inclusive form of civic democracy.

What seems to matter in Nairobi — whether on the streets or on the radio — is that people find a way to manage their relations, that they somehow try to find a way to get what they need or get where they are going, regardless of economic or political frustrations. Indeed, much of the "real" business of politics takes place in informal negotiations and in localized settings, usually outside the scope of the government apparatus. This is not to say, of course, that the problems are solved. These are fixes, not solutions. Gay people are still persecuted, the streets remain potholed, the infrastructure still crumbles. The poor certainly remain poor. And yet, through an inventive kind of civic pragmatism, the citizens of Nairobi find a way of "instrumentalizing disorder" in ways that allow them to survive. Somehow, in a roundabout way, people keep trying to get by.

JACK GOLDSMITH

The Supreme Court Wars: America and Israel

One of the many extraordinary powers that the progressive Israeli Supreme Court has given itself is the authority to invalidate a government action based on the Justices' conclusion that the government did not weigh, or properly weigh, all relevant public interest considerations before acting. This "reasonableness" doctrine is an open-ended judicial check to ensure that elected officials and civil servants "respect their fiduciary duties vis-a-vis the public they serve and exercise their powers with a view to advancing the public interest," explain Israeli law professors Amichai Cohen and Yuval Shany, defenders of the doctrine. The Court has invoked the reasonableness doctrine to invalidate numerous government appointments and initiatives.

The right-wing coalition government in Israel, which prevailed in the elections of 2022 by a very slim margin, despises the reasonableness doctrine and other tools that the Court has wielded to neuter the Israeli right's victories at the polls by thwarting their policies in office. On July 24, 2023, the Knesset narrowed (but did not eliminate) the reasonableness doctrine by disallowing the Court and other Israeli judges from applying it to cabinet ministers. "This is the destruction of Israeli democracy," declared Yair Lapid, the leader of Israeli's largest opposition party. Lapid was puffing wildly. The July 24 vote imposed a relatively modest and perhaps circumventable check on the Court that left intact all of its powers over legislation and the vast majority of its powers to review government action.

Lapid's deeper worry is that the government will pass a broader package of judicial reforms that would dramatically diminish the only check on its otherwise boundless power, as the current government has vowed to do. The ultimate stakes in the Israeli judiciary debate are about who controls the future of the State of Israel: the demographically ascendant nationalist and religious groups who currently control the Knesset but who have long been losers in the Court; or the demographically less ascendant secular and progressive groups currently excluded from political power whose interests have long been reflected in and protected by the Court. These stakes explain Lapid's catastrophizing, and why judicial-reform opponents have engaged in massive disruptive protests — including threats by reservists to quit the military and by prominent businesses to leave the country — since the reforms were introduced in January 2023.

Sixty years ago the great legal scholar Alexander Bickel

labeled the question of whether unelected judges can legitimately invalidate laws enacted and enforced by elected officials as the "countermajoritarian difficulty." The Israeli judicial reform movement argues that as practiced by the Israeli Supreme Court, the answer is no. But there are other answers. John Hart Ely claimed that judicial review bolsters democracy when it checks anti-minority biases in the elected branches and supports prerequisites to democracy such as freedom of speech and voting rights. One can see traces of Ely's idea in the opposition to reform, which is premised on a belief that the Israeli Supreme Court is the nation's only bulwark against the government's corruption, its privileging of religious rights, and its diminution of human rights for groups excluded from politics, including Palestinians and Arab Israelis.

The United States has also recently experienced a clash of judicial visions, albeit at a lower temperature and with the political roles flipped. Here the conservative shift in the Supreme Court following President Donald Trump's three appointments — Neil Gorsuch, Brett Kavanaugh, and Amy Barrett — has led many progressives to paint the Court as a threat to democratic values, to try to discredit it, and to propose reforms to limit its authority in the name of democratic control. In April 2021, President Biden appointed a bipartisan commission to analyze these proposals. (I briefly served on the commission.) Its final report later that year was a consensus document without strong recommendations. But it seriously considered many reforms, including expanding the Court's size, imposing term limits or super-majority voting rules, rotating Justices, stripping the Court of jurisdiction to decide certain cases, and empowering Congress to override Supreme Court decisions.

The parallel debates in the United States and Israel seem like they are about the same issue, but vast differences in the histories and the legal and political cultures of the two nations counsel caution in the comparison. And yet these debates considered together have much to teach about the necessary but invariably unsatisfying role of independent courts in a democracy.

Progressive agitation to curtail the power of the U.S. Supreme Court reached a fever pitch in the summer of 2022, when the Court overruled *Roe v. Wade*, expanded gun and religious liberty rights, and made it much harder for the executive branch to redress climate change. The Court had been moving rightward for decades, as Republican presidents since Nixon have appointed fifteen of nineteen Justices. But it had sided with the left on most social issues during this period, and conservatives continued to lose on other issues they cared about as well.

With the term ending in June 2022, the most conservative Court in almost a century finally seemed to have overcome all constraints on effectuating its vision. Groups on the left were enraged over having lost complete control of the Court that did so much of its bidding for so many years going back to the New Deal. Frustrated by Trump's success in appointing three Justices (and in the failure of President Obama's appointment of Merrick Garland), and appalled by the Court's rulings, they began to attack the Court as illegitimate. And they clamored for action to cut back the Court's power by packing it with liberals, impeaching conservatives, and fast-tracking Congress' power to override Court decisions.

It all seemed pretty radical, but none of it was new. Since the beginning of the republic, the Supreme Court interpreted the Constitution's many open-ended provisions to limit state and federal laws and actions. Through such judicial review, the Court has asserted the final say over the nature and the scope of governmental power and the range and content of fundamental rights. At times the Court pressed a progressive vision on the country — for example, from the mid-New Deal through the 1970s, when the Court reordered federal and state power and constrained both with revolutionary new civil and political rights. And at times it pressed a conservative vision on the country — for example, during most of the first four decades of the twentieth century, when it was guided by a stark *laissez-faire* philosophy, and again, increasingly so, in recent decades.

It would be surprising in a democracy if such broad interventions by unelected judges went unchallenged. In the United States, they have not. The Court's outsized power has from the beginning been a topic of fierce contestation accompanied by political efforts to shape and control the Court's decisions. The Constitution gives the Justices life tenure and salary guarantees as a check on these tendencies. But it also contemplates many mechanisms for political pushback on the Court.

Consider the Court's size. The Constitution leaves it to the political branches to decide how many Justices serve on the Court. Several times in the nineteenth century, Congress and the President sought to influence the Court by adding or subtracting seats. During the transition of the presidency from John Adams to Thomas Jefferson in 1801 — a period of bitter partisan polarization not unlike today — the outgoing Federalist Congress reduced the number Supreme Court seats from its original six to five, in part to maintain Federalist dominance of federal judiciary. The outraged incoming Jeffersonians reversed this move. Congress also increased the size of the Court from six to seven in 1807 and from seven to nine in 1837, both times to ensure Supreme Court decisions that favored the party in power.

Congress increased the Court's size from nine to ten in 1863 so that, as the legal scholar Tara Grove put it, "President Lincoln could appoint Justices who favored the Republicans' agenda of combatting slavery and preserving the union." In 1866, soon after Andrew Johnson became president, Congress reduced the Court's future membership to seven because (to borrow the words of the Biden Commission's Final Report) "the Reconstruction Republicans who controlled Congress in the post-Civil War era did not trust Johnson to nominate Justices sympathetic to the reconstruction efforts in the South." On March 4, 1869, the day Ulysses S. Grant became president, fellow Republicans in Congress increased the number back to nine.

The number has stood at nine ever since. In 1937, Franklin D. Roosevelt famously proposed to increase the size of the top bench up to fifteen in an effort to arrest its invalidation of New Deal legislation. Congress did not go along, and many historians believe that Roosevelt lost political momentum in his New Deal reforms as result of this failure. Yet the plan appeared to succeed in one important sense. Soon after the proposal, and long before its rejection, the Court started upholding New Deal laws, though scholars still debate the extent to which the Justices changed course under pressure from Roosevelt's plan. From the late 1950s until Donald Trump's presidency, there appeared to be a firm norm against changing the number of Supreme Court justices even though it would be lawful to do so. But ever since then, the norm's firmness seems to have eroded.

The political branches can also control the Court's agenda by narrowing its power to hear certain cases. The most famous example involved a challenge in 1868 to the constitutionality of congressional Reconstruction. After an oral argument suggested that the Court might declare Reconstruction unconstitutional, and while the Justices were deliberating, Congress passed a law that removed the Court's power to hear the case. The Court promptly dismissed, reasoning that in light of Congress' control of its appellate jurisdiction, "it is quite clear . . . that this court cannot proceed to pronounce judgment in this case." Legal scholars have tried to devise limits on Congress' dominion over the Court's agenda. But the brute fact is that the Constitution by design and in operation gives the political branches of the government enormous control here. It is norms of political restraint, not law, that hold Congress and the president back.

The same is true of the appointment and confirmation process. While these things go in cycles, judicial selection and confirmation have often been very partisan affairs. Presidents have nominated justices based on judicial outlook, policy goals, or rewarding constituencies. Merit, a slippery term in this context, has sometimes mattered, but often not. And the Senate has often not confirmed the president's nominee. As the political scientists Lee Epstein and Jeffrey Segal have shown, the Senate has confirmed fifty-nine percent of Supreme Court nominees under divided government, and ninety percent when the president's party controlled the Senate. As the Court expanded its reach in the twentieth century, interest groups started to play a larger role in the confirmation process. And the norms that used to govern confirmation battles have eroded significantly since the 1980s. Here again, norms and politics are the protectors of judicial independence.

Today it is American progressives — winning in politics but losing in the Court — who urge Supreme Court reform to influence decisions they find illegitimate. Not too long ago, conservatives were in the same position doing the same thing. Republicans responded to the Warren Court with all manner of constitutional and statutory proposals to limit the Court's power. And they were still at it during the Reagan administration. In 1982, a young Justice Department lawyer named John Roberts wrote to the Attorney General in support of the legality of numerous Republican bills that would strip the Court of power over cases involving school prayer, desegregation, and abortion. The following year, the future Chief Justice, then a White House lawyer, wrote about a Senate-proposed constitutional amendment to limit federal judicial tenure. "There is much to be said in favor of changing life tenure to a term of years, *without* possibility of reappointment," Roberts declared, since the "federal judiciary today benefits from an insulation from political pressure even as it usurps the roles of the political branches."

The threats and occasional reality of Court-packing, jurisdiction stripping, confirmation fights, and constitutional amendments are but a few ways that American politics engages with the Supreme Court to control judicial review. Presidential elections, in which the Court has been a central electoral issue, have often led — as in the case of the Trump presidency — to appointments that impact the direction of the Court. Other options lurk in the background, including impeachment and presidential underenforcement of Supreme Court decisions.

The prevalent influence of politics on the Court, and the Court's ultimately fragile independence, protected mainly by norms, supports several general conclusions.

The United States has never solved the countermajoritarian difficulty. Bickel recognized that one of the Court's vital roles is to check the passions of popular democracy in the name of a richer conception of democracy that protects fundamental rights. He simply underscored the inevitable awkwardness of judicial review, especially when, as is always a danger, the unaccountable Court strikes down directives of the elected branches in ways not obviously compelled by the Constitution. The problem is compounded because the proper method for interpreting the Constitution has always been contested and the interpretive tools deployed by the Court have changed over time.

That said, the countermajoritarian difficulty has always been tempered because judicial review has never taken place outside of politics. When the Court has adjudicated matters that go to the core of the national project, and especially when it has taken important matters out of the hands of the people, the people and their representatives have always pushed back. Often, but not always — it depends on the underlying politics — they succeed. Judicial review in the United States exists within politically structured bounds.

These political factors have worked to keep the Court from running too far, for too long, from the basic preferences of the people and their representatives. Sometimes the impact has been stark, as when the Court backed down or tacked in the face of political pressure. 1868 and 1937 are examples of backing down; there are others. But more broadly, as the scholar Michael Klarman has shown, the Court has rarely acted in ways that are significantly and persistently out of touch with majority opinion. Thus, landmark cases on the most salient societal issues of the day — *Dred Scott v. Sandford, Plessy v. Ferguson, Brown v. Board of Education,* and *Obergefell*

v. *Hodges* (the gay-marriage case) — all reflected the beliefs or commitments of at least half and sometimes more of the country. Put another way, as Klarman sometimes has, there is practically no chance the Court would have decided, for example, *Brown* or *Obergefell* ten or fifteen years before it did.

Bickel once observed that the Court "is a leader of opinion, not a mere register of it, but it must lead opinion, not merely impose its own; and the short of it is — it labors under the obligation to succeed." He added that the Court should interpret the Constitution in ways that "will — in time, but in a rather immediate foreseeable future — gain general assent." It is controversial whether this idea can serve as a normative guide to judging. But it is surely a largely accurate descriptive account of when the Court brings serious trouble on itself and the country.

When the Court decided *Roe*, for example, democratic support for abortion was growing and abortion laws were liberalizing. As Ruth Bader Ginsberg maintained, however, the Court went too far too fast in wiping out most state laws on the subject and in disabling state legislators altogether from regulating abortions in the first two trimesters. The result violated Bickel's "general assent" principle. It gave rise to what Ginsburg described in 1992 as "a well-organized and vocal right-to-life movement" that "succeeded" not just "in turning the legislative tide in the opposite direction," but, we now know, in sparking a powerful movement that changed American politics and the direction of the Court.

It is too soon to tell whether the Court's newly aggressive conservative turn has set it on a path that will similarly fail Bickel's test. In the year in which it overruled *Roe*, the Court was noticeably more moderate and gave surprising victories to liberals on voting rights, immigration enforcement, tribal rights, and state control over federal elections. "Along With Conservative Triumphs, Signs of New Caution at Supreme Court," declared the headline in the *New York Times'* annual assessment of the Court. "Perhaps the justices… have faced up to the public's waning confidence and decided to self-adjust," said Epstein, a leading scholar of Supreme Court trends.

This continuous calibration between judicial decision and political reaction mitigates the counter-majoritarian difficulty. The threat and reality of political control constitute, as Charles Black once argued, "the rock on which rests the legitimacy of the judicial work in a democracy." Almost every time the Court exercises judicial review, it does so pursuant to authorizations in jurisdictional statutes that the political branches can withdraw. It thus can be said to have the tacit blessing of the polity for its actions. And the failure of the political branches to limit the Court's jurisdictional power can be seen as an acknowledgment that the Court is acting legitimately even when it issues very controversial decisions. In this sense, the ultimate political control over the work of the Court, and debates about whether its power should be tempered, are, in the round, healthy and justificatory.

The danger, of course, is that politics might spin out of control and destroy the Court, and with it all of the incontrovertible virtues of judicial review in a democracy. The norms of judicial respect and independence that constrain the political branches from going this far have been remarkably firm for a long time, despite persistent anxiety about the Court's work. And while they appear to be weakening — at least if the quantity and the extremity of the fiery rhetoric are measures — they remain widely shared, as President Biden's skepticism about reform makes clear. The American left is apoplectic over the Court, is attacking it viciously, and has engaged in unprecedented protests at the Justices' homes. But it is not yet taking to the streets on anything like the scale in Israel.

Yet it would be foolish not to worry about the Court's place in American government. The Court's public approval is at a modern low, and there is every reason to believe that the anger and protests and efforts at delegitimation by the left will continue and increase. Independent of the conservative path of its decisions, the Justices have diminished their public credibility by failing to craft and respect a comprehensive public ethics code. Internal dissensus on the Court is high, made worse by the unprecedented leak of the *Dobbs* opinion that overruled *Roe*. All of this is happening during a moment when the norms that have propped up institutions are cratering in nearly every other governmental context.

In January 2023, a group of American law professors wrote an open letter to "strongly oppose" the judicial reforms in Israel. The scholars worried that the reforms "will seriously weaken the independence of the judiciary, the separation of powers, and the rule of law" in ways that "would pose a dire risk to freedom of expression, [and] to human and civil rights." A few of the signatories were prominent critics of judicial review in the United States. The same people who wanted to preserve judicial independence in Israel wanted to diminish it in the United States. They believed that judicial review was necessary to protect civil and political rights in Israel, but harmed, or at least was unnecessary to protect, civil and political rights in the United States.

One might view these left-of-center professors as hypocritical in their views about the place of courts in a democracy. But they left themselves wiggle room because the letter stated that "some of us believe that the Israeli Supreme Court has over-reached in important respects and would support a scaling back of its power to review legislation and executive decisions." In any event, there is no contradiction between advocating for diminished judicial independence in the United States and strongly defending it in Israel. Or vice versa. Israel and the United States have very different political and legal systems, with Supreme Courts that scrutinize government action in different ways and with different justifications. Israel has a much greater need for judicial scrutiny of government action than the United States; but unfortunately judicial power in Israel rests on a much more precarious foundation than in the United States.

The Israeli Declaration of Independence of 1948 promised a constitution within the year. But Israel's founder and first prime minister, David Ben-Gurion, opposed the idea. "We chose a parliamentary form of government" in which "the nation decides on the laws, and their representatives implement them," he said to the Knesset's Committee on Constitution, Law, and Justice on July 13, 1949. "I don't think it's possible to delegate authority to the court to decide whether the laws are kosher or not kosher." The promise of the Declaration was never fulfilled. It was agreed that the Knesset would over time enact Basic Laws that, in the end, but not until then, would form a Constitution. But this slow process was never completed.

Thus the new nation had nothing akin to a written Bill of Rights or a Fourteenth Amendment. This was a serious lacuna in a modern democracy, and a fateful one for Israel, which from the beginning was burdened with profound internal divisions about the nature of the state and novel problems of relations with non-Jewish citizens, but which lacked the disciplining and legitimating impact of fundamental law effectuated by judicial review. By contrast, judicial review was widely understood to be entailed from the outset by the U.S. Constitution's conferral on the Supreme Court of "the judicial Power" to interpret federal law, including fundamental law, the Constitution.

In addition to firmly grounding judicial review, the U.S. Constitution and laws impose other institutional restraints on government action. Legislation must be passed by both houses of Congress and signed by the President, and these three institutions are not typically controlled by the same party. Senior executive branch officials outside the White House must be confirmed by the Senate, which often is not controlled by the President's party. There are loads of internal legal and normative constraints on executive action — inspectors general, laws governing agency action, limitations on vacancies appointments, and the like. These constraints are in theory changeable by Congress, but in practice they enjoy wide bipartisan support as a check on an oppositional branch of government; they aren't going anywhere. (Donald Trump is scheming to skirt some of these protections should he be elected in 2024, but doing so is much easier said than done.) And the United States has a federal system with states that counterbalances federal power.

Israel from the outset was in a very different position. It lacked institutional constraints on government action other than the difficulty of forming a governing coalition and a few procedural rules on lawmaking. The Supreme Court early on stitched together additional constraints modeled on English administrative law, and it used various techniques to build a modest human rights regime. But the Court, in decisions in the 1980s and 1990s known as the "judicial revolution," under the leadership of Aharon Barak, did what the Israeli government and Israeli people were unable to do: it gave itself enormously robust powers to constrain the government. "What Barak created out of whole cloth was a degree of judicial power undreamed of even by our most aggressive Supreme Court justices," wrote Judge Richard Posner in 2007. "He puts Marshall, who did less with more, in the shade."

The Israeli Supreme Court rejected justiciability constraints on decision-making that are an important precondition to judicial review by the U.S. Supreme Court. In the United States, only injured parties can sue; in Israel, anyone can. The Court also ramped up the reasonableness doctrine to a place that in practice has no counterpart in the United States or any other legal system. It also, crucially, empowered executive branch lawyers to constrain the government through binding decisions unless and until the Supreme Court rules differently. And the Court rectified the absence of fundamental law by declaring that two "Basic Laws" in 1992 gave the Court grounds to review legislation for consistency with human rights, including rights unenumerated in those Basic Laws, and for consistency with other Basic Laws as well. This was a remarkable development, since the two laws were passed by a small fraction of Knesset members and were not viewed at the time of passage as fundamental law. It was an act of judicial hocus-pocus that, in Barak's words, happened "almost clandestinely."

The appointments process for Justices in Israel and the United States are also notably different. In the United States, it is fully embedded in politics: the president nominates but the Senate must consent. In Israel, it is more distant from politics, and the Court has a big say. Appointments are determined by a nine-member committee that consists of two cabinet ministers, two other Knesset members (including, typically, an opposition member); two lawyers chosen by the relatively progressive Israel Bar Association; and three Supreme Court justices chosen by the Court's president. Since it takes seven votes to appoint a Supreme Court Justice, the Court has effective veto rights on successor justices. (Imagine John Roberts, Clarence Thomas, and Samuel Alito having a power to nix new Supreme Court Justices.)

The Court has wielded its extraordinary powers to push a largely progressive agenda, at least from the perspective of conservative, religious, and nationalist groups who have been gaining political power in recent decades and whose initiatives the Court has regularly frustrated. "These legal beagles have fashioned a system whereby they replicate themselves with impunity and occupy every central intersection of policy-making," writes the *Jerusalem Post* columnist David Weinberg. "These much-too-powerful actors have upset Israeli democracy by usurping powers to themselves never intended by Israel's founders or parliamentarians; powers which extend far beyond those held by the legal system in any other democracy."

This, is a nutshell, is the basis for the extensive judicial reforms introduced in the Knesset in January 2023: eliminating reasonableness review, limiting judicial review of Basic Laws, empowering the Knesset to override certain Supreme Court decisions, and enhancing political influence in the selection of Supreme Court Justices.

The debate in Israel is about preventing a single component of the Israeli government from having practically unchecked power. The left thinks the worrisome branch is the coalition government. The right thinks the worrisome branch is the Court. Both sides have a point.

If the Israeli government were to achieve all the reforms it proposed in January 2023, it would diminish the Court's power significantly. This is a dreadful prospect to many in Israel who fear that the coalition would then implement the ultranationalist and ultrareligious wishes of its extreme parties. The worst-case scenario is much greater religious autonomy for ultraorthodox groups, imposition of religious precepts throughout Israeli law, exclusion of Israeli Arabs altogether from politics, and perhaps even a theocratic Greater Israel that greatly deepens the hardships for the already-degraded Palestinian people — in short, a radically changed Israel.

This will not come to pass. Both the entire package of judicial reforms, and the extremist agenda of some of the coalition parties, lack full coalition support. Still, the "religious coercion, radical inequality, and nationalist aggrandizement" of the extreme right agenda is seen to "represent a version of politics that requires our moral condemnation," as Michael Walzer put it. The mainly secular elite leftish groups in the streets threatening hardball tactics are nominally focused on protecting the Supreme Court, but they are really motivated by abhorrence of the far-right vision, by what it implies for their lives in Israel, and by deep loathing for some of the people and groups that now dominate the Knesset, including Prime Minister Benjamin Netanyahu, whom many believe is pushing judicial reform primarily to gain the authority to halt a corruption prosecution against himself.

The problem is that the protesters' ultimate vision of the Court is just as unattractive as the ultimate vision of the reformers. They claim to seek to protect democracy, as Lapid's reaction to the July vote implies, but their actions seem to indicate that any judicial reform, including the Knesset's diminution of reasonableness, is unacceptable. One argument is that changes to the Court's power require a broader social consensus than a three-vote majority in the Knesset. This argument lacks a basis in Israeli law and forgets that the Court grabbed its enormous power without any social consensus. Yes, fundamental law is often based on what Bruce Ackerman calls a "constitutional moment" of higher super-majority politics. But the power claimed by the Court has no such justification. Entrenching the Court's unilateral assumption of power while disabling the Knesset from enacting (reversible) laws to check the Court — which is basically what the protesters want — is not an argument easily grounded in democratic theory.

This issue is now teed up, since the Supreme Court has agreed to consider in September whether the reasonableness reform is lawful. It will be a defining moment for the Court. If it upholds the reform, it will embolden the Knesset and legitimate the possibility of greater judicial restraint. If it strikes down the reform, it will spectacularly confirm its democratic illegitimacy. For it will basically be saying that a self-proclaimed judicial doctrine to control government action cannot be changed by legislation or without an impossible-to-reach supermajority that is not required even to pass Basic Laws. (It might also reason, more radically, that the Knesset cannot amend a Basic Law, which is how the reform was implemented.). Such a judgment would amount to a declaration that the Court's power is irreversible, and that Israel is in fact a krytocracy, not a democracy. This would mirror the arguments of the street protesters, who lost in the political process and some of whom threaten to abandon Israeli society and institutions unless krytocracy prevails. They may well have the moral high ground, as Walzer says. But arguments for a largely unchecked Court to constrain a largely unchecked government are not arguments for democracy.

There are of course many potential intermediate possibilities between the extreme poles of judicial hegemony and legislative hegemony. Israeli president Isaac Herzog tried hard to forge a compromise in the first half of 2023. He failed, and both sides say that the other negotiated in bad faith. The Court could also try to promote a compromise by affirming the Knesset's authority to temper reasonableness while still proclaiming the Court's authority to assess the validity of other legislation, including Basic Laws. Still, it is doubtful that such a ruling would bring the two political sides together. Israeli society is divided in fundamental ways far beyond the fissures now bedeviling American society. And its judicial system lacks the grounding in politics, and the ability to adjust to changing politics, that has always prevailed in the United States. The Israeli Supreme Court cannot claim democratic legitimacy the way its American counterpart can — from a written Constitution or from authorizing statutes that political actors can shape. And Israel lacks a ready mechanism to alter the political hue of the Court over time.

One consequence of the upheavals in Israel is that if the Court emerges relatively unscathed from the current unpleasantness, it may be able to claim a justification based on the higher politics that we are not witnessing. The unprecedented attacks on the Court, followed by an unprecedented defense, could, if the defense is successful, give the Court a legitimacy it has always lacked. One suspects that some of the opponents of judicial reform, who have chosen extreme tactics, may have this end in mind. Or at least they have nothing to lose in seeking it.

The Supreme Court Wars: America and Israel

The eventual problem for the protesters is demography. Though the current population numbers are far from apocalyptic for the Israeli left, the religious and nationalistic right is growing faster than the secular left, and has been for a while. No judicial power in any society can stand in the face of persistent majority displeasure. What we are witnessing now in the streets of Israel is people who are fighting for time but who may come to realize that in the long run the battle over the Court may already be lost.

One day before the Biden Supreme Court Commission released a draft of its report on October 14, 2021, Secretary of State Anthony Blinken gave a major speech in Ecuador entitled "Making Democracy Deliver for the Americas." Hours before the speech, Ecuadoran president Guillermo Lasso declared a state of emergency to combat drug-trafficking violence. It was an awkward backdrop, but Blinken praised Ecuador's commitment to democracy and the rule of law, and especially the role of courts. The Columbia Law School-educated diplomat was also, it seems pretty clear, speaking to the debate about judicial reform in the United States.

"Consider a country," Blinken said, "where a leader is elected in a free and fair election, and then sets about chipping away slowly but surely at the pillars of democracy" by, among other things, "undermining the independence of the courts." He then asked the audience to "imagine that leader then seeks to use the levers of democracy to pass anti-democratic reforms," including, prominently, "packing courts." He continued: "That's the story of more than one democracy in our hemisphere. And it's one of the ways that democracies can come undone." Blinken added that this was the story of Ecuador a decade earlier, but that these anti-democratic efforts did not succeed in Ecuador because "institutions like the courts... pushed back."

Blinken was restating what has become a core element of American foreign policy: a healthy democracy that protects human rights needs independent courts and judicial review. Blinken articulated that policy in early 2023, when he commented on the judicial reform debate in Israel. The United States and Israel shared values about "core democratic principles and institutions, including respect for human rights, the equal administration of justice for all people, rights of minority groups, the rule of law, a free press, a robust civil society." President Biden and other American officials have been pushing a similar message all year. "The genius of American democracy and Israeli democracy is that they are both built on strong institutions, on checks and balances, on an independent judiciary," he said last February.

Biden's comments elided all of the many differences between the legal systems in the two countries. So, too, did the conservative American columnist Matthew Continetti, who, in a comment typical of the right, claimed that Biden is "condemning Bibi for pursuing the same policy in Israel that the progressive left would like to see pursued in the United States." As these comments imply, preaching the virtues of judicial independence to other countries will become increasingly difficult in light of the American domestic situation, as progressive attacks on the conservative Supreme Court, and calls to diminish its independence, continue to grow.

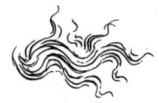

MORTEN HØI JENSEN

The Good European

On the evening of June 7, 1914, police officers were dispatched to break up a crowd of over a thousand people assembled outside the Comedy Theatre on West 41st Street in Manhattan. Hoping for a last-minute ticket, they had been turned away at the doors and were now blocking traffic on Sixth Avenue. Inside the theater, every seat and every inch of standing room was occupied by people eagerly waiting for the evening's program to begin. What had they come to see? Not a performance by Enrico Caruso, the Italian tenor then at the peak of his fame; nor a ragtime revue by Irving Berlin, or a play by George Bernard Shaw. Strange as it sounds to contemporary ears, the many hundreds in attendance had come to be lectured on Shakespeare by the Danish literary critic Georg Brandes, then in his early seventies. As an article in *The New York Times* put it the following day, it was "one of the most remarkable welcomes ever extended to a foreign lecturer."

It ought to have been a crowning moment for a writer once described by Thomas Mann as "the northern Sainte-Beuve" and by Stefan Zweig as "the international master of the history of literature," who was nominated for the Nobel Prize for Literature by Anatole France and hailed as "a good European" by Nietzsche, a writer whose lectures on European literature in Copenhagen introduced Scandinavian readers to realism and naturalism, whose books had been translated into German, English, French, Russian, Polish, Yiddish, and Japanese, and whose biographical study of Shakespeare in 1896 achieved worldwide recognition and was admired by Joyce and Freud. Yet there was a huge cloud over the event in New York.

Brandes' American lecture tour was darkened by concern for the fate of the European continent. For years, for decades, he had been saying what no one wanted to hear: that Europe was on a suicide mission. As early as 1881, he had warned that by the turn of the century "Germany will lie alone, isolated, hated by the neighboring countries: a stronghold of conservatism in Europe [...] protected by all the weapons of murder and defense which science can invent." In 1905 he criticized the Anglo-German naval arms race, particularly the English politicians who openly spoke of an "unavoidable" war with Germany. In 1913 he cautioned against a new generation of French intellectuals, including Charles Péguy and Maurice Barrès, who looked upon war as "a purifying force." (Peguy was killed in action just before the Battle of the Marne.) When the

Archduke Franz Ferdinand and his wife Sophie Chotek were bunglingly assassinated in Sarajevo, Brandes had little doubt about the immediate future. "A wave of misery washes over Europe," he confided to his diary.

For Brandes the war in Europe had profound personal implications. A Jew from a provincial Protestant backwater, his career was indissolubly bound up with the internationalism of the European culture of the second half of nineteenth century. He became one of the great Jewish cosmopolitans. His countless lecture tours brought him to France, England, Italy, Germany, Spain, Portugal, Switzerland, Austria-Hungary, Poland, Finland, Russia, Belgium, the Netherlands, Egypt, Greece, and Scotland. He met and corresponded with Thomas Mann, Henry James, Guy de Maupassant, Rainer Maria Rilke, Arthur Schnitzler, Thomas Hardy, Emile Zola, Theodor Fontane, Edmund Gosse, the brothers Goncourt, Lou Andreas-Salomé, Gerhart Hauptmann, Hugo von Hofmannsthal, Peter Kropotkin, Theodor Herzl, and Benedetto Croce. His essays and articles had appeared in almost every major European newspaper and literary review, many of which he was attached to in some editorial capacity.

The war took it all away. Overnight, literary and intellectual salons in Paris and Berlin, hot with patriotic fever, closed their doors to him. In the new nationalistic Europe, liberal cosmopolitanism, especially that of a Jew, no longer had a home. Brandes was publicly attacked by former friends such as Georges Clemenceau (with whom he had often vacationed in Karlsbad) and the Scottish writer and critic William Archer for refusing to take sides in the war and for supporting Denmark's neutrality. (H. L. Mencken later called him "the only genuine neutral the war has produced.") Disgusted with the belligerence and the chauvinism of Europe's empires, Brandes endeavored to defend the continent's embattled minorities instead. But when he began reporting on the persecution of Jews in Poland, he was denounced by the Polish Author's Union, which denied that any pogroms had ever occurred on Polish soil. Stefan Zweig wrote to congratulate Brandes for his courage, assuring him that "a coming age will recognize those who dared to stand unarmed against the brunt of hostile opinion as the true heroes."

But that age never came. Brandes' life after the war was one of increased illness and growing isolation. Though he lived until 1927, his reputation never regained its pre-war eminence, at least not outside Denmark. Like so many other good things, his international literary standing effectively died with the war. The tributes that poured in on the occasion of his death — from Mann, Hamsun, Kerr, Gosse, Barbusse, and Schnitzler — already seemed to harken back to a vanished world. Perversely, Clemenceau's cruel response was the appropriate one. Upon being informed of Brandes' death, the former French prime minister said, "So he has died! He was right to do so. Only he should have done it sooner. Now that story is forgotten, like so many others."

Georg Morris Cohen Brandes was born in Copenhagen on February 4, 1842. His parents were a part of the Danish capital's vibrant Jewish minority, which had grown steadily since the granting of full civil rights to Danish Jews by royal decree in 1814. Brandes later recalled that he was first made aware of his Jewish identity when a few young boys shouted an unfamiliar slur at him in the street. He asked his mother what it meant:

"What does it mean?" "Jew!" said Mother. "Jews are people." "Nasty people?" "Yes," said Mother, smiling, "sometimes very ugly people, but not always." "Could I see a Jew?" "Yes, very easily," said Mother, lifting me up quickly in front of the large oval mirror above the sofa.

I uttered a shriek, so that Mother hurriedly put me down again, and my horror was such that she regretted not having prepared me.

Brandes was not raised religiously. For him, Judaism was an anachronism associated with old rituals and dietary restrictions. "The poetry of it was a sealed book to me," he wrote. And yet it marked him, in Protestant Denmark, as an outsider and set the stage for a life forged in adversity and opposition.

In school, he was quick to doubt the veracity of his Christian religious instruction, with its wearying emphasis on miracles and rituals. "The demand made by faith, namely, that reason should be fettered, awakened a latent rebellious opposition," he recalled in his memoir. Later, as a precocious, querulous teenager, he discovered Lermontov, Heine, and Byron, writers who imbued him with a sense of what he called "the demonic": "the worship of one's own originality, under the guise of an uncompromising love of liberty." At the University of Copenhagen, where in 1864 he completed a doctorate in aesthetics, he rebelled against the abstract metaphysical and dourly German (read: Hegelian) atmosphere that predominated among his professors, most of whom were trained as theologians. They had hoped to mold the brilliant young student in their own image, but by then it was far too late. Brandes already had his back to them. In 1866 he made his first trip to Paris, where he met and befriended Hippolyte

Taine, whose multi-volume *History of English Literature* became an "antidote" to his university teaching. And though Brandes, characteristically, remained skeptical of the more deterministic aspects of Taine's positivism, the French philosopher welcomed the young Dane into his home and introduced him to friends such as Ernst Renan and the painter Charles Gleyre. For the remainder of his life, he would always have one foot outside Denmark's borders.

Brandes' other transformative encounter at this time was with John Stuart Mill. In 1869 Brandes translated *On the Subjection of Women*, as a result of which Mill decided to look up his young Danish translator. Brandes later recalled meeting the sixty-four-year-old philosopher: "His eyes were bright, and of a deep, dark blue, his nose slender and curved, his brow high and arched, with a strongly marked protuberance over the left eye; he looked as though the labor of thought might have forced its organs to extend in order to make more room." He visited Mill on several occasions at his home in Blackheath in southeast London in 1870. During one of their meetings, Mill confessed that he had never read of a word of Hegel, just as Taine knew little of German poetry and Brandes' university professors knew nothing of English empiricism or French positivism. Surprised by the ignorance that even some of the most eminent minds in Europe seemingly had of one another, Brandes realized that "one could do much good by simply studying, confronting, and understanding these great minds that fail to understand each other." His desire to serve as a kind of European intellectual emissary grew from these early encounters with national obtuseness.

In 1870 Brandes set out on a fifteen-month trip through Europe, traveling to France, England, Italy, and Germany. The awakening that his readings of Taine and Mill catalyzed came to completion through this journey. Everywhere he went he saw the wheels of history turning dramatically: the capture of Rome, the Franco-Prussian War, the Paris Commune. By comparison, Denmark seemed to him backward and parochial, half-asleep in its Biedermeier nostalgia. He resolved to bring his riches home with him, to introduce his own small world to the enormous one into which he thrust himself.

While abroad, Brandes struck up a correspondence with Henrik Ibsen, then living in self-imposed exile in Dresden. Though the Norwegian writer Bjørnstjerne Bjørnson had written to warn Ibsen against Brandes — "there is something wrong with a person who does not have faith in God at his center" — Ibsen took an instant liking to the young Danish firebrand. On his way back to Copenhagen, Brandes paid Ibsen a visit on July 14, 1871, Bastille Day, an appropriate date for an encounter between two minds itching to hasten their own countries into a new era. The two recognized in one another the same hunger, and a kindred loyalty to their respective origins enriched by a curious and quickening cosmopolitanism. When they parted ways that evening, Ibsen called out to Brandes: "You provoke the Danes and I'll provoke the Norwegians!"

Brandes heeded his friend's directive, and speedily. November 3, 1871 marks a turning point in Scandinavian cultural and intellectual history. That evening, in Auditorium 7 at the University of Copenhagen on Vor Frue Plads, Georg Brandes appeared before a large crowd to deliver the first of his lectures on the subject of "Main Currents in Nineteenth Century Literature." For weeks the occasion had been shrouded in rumor and intrigue. Brandes had already courted controversy with his translations of Mill and his newspaper articles attacking the theology of Rasmus Nielsen, Denmark's leading philosopher. (Nielsen figured in Kierkegaard's intellectual development and was for a while his friend.) In a city of just two hundred thousand inhabitants, these things did not go unnoticed.

The audience was a who's-who of Copenhagen's intellectual life: aspiring young writers such as Jens Peter Jacobsen and Holger Drachmann, the politician and bishop D. G. Monrad, Kierkegaard's old punching bag H. L. Martensen, and Carl Christian Hall, the Minister of School and Church Affairs. (Monrad and Hall had both served as prime ministers of Denmark). Brandes, just twenty-eight years old, began his lecture by asking for the audience's forbearance. It was his first time speaking from the pulpit and no doubt his delivery would prove wanting. As far as the substance of his lecture was concerned, however, the audience could take it or leave it. "What may offend you today will not be altered," he declared. "I consider it a duty and an honor to pay tribute to those principles in which I believe: my faith in the right to free inquiry and the ultimate victory of free thought."

Framed as "a comparative study of European literature," Brandes' lectures, which over the course of the next two decades would swell to become a huge six-volume epic, constituted a dramatic account of European literature between the French Revolution and the uprisings of 1848. They were an astonishing display of erudition, evincing an awesome mastery of entire canons and the intellectual dexterity to weave them together into an intelligible whole for an ignorant and unprepared public. Arranged as a portrait gallery of all the major and minor writers of the period, beginning with Rousseau and Chateaubriand and concluding with Heine and Hegel, it is one of the earliest examples of what we now call comparative literature, as well as a precursor to studies such as

Axel's Castle and *To the Finland Station* (Edmund Wilson ranked Brandes alongside Taine, Sainte-Beuve, and Leslie Stephen), and perhaps even to Raymond Aron's *Main Currents in Sociological Thought*. It introduced Scandinavian culture to radical new ideas of positivism, Darwinism, and biblical criticism, while its success abroad can be attributed to the connections that Brandes made between writers and ideas across national and cultural boundaries. Thomas Mann summed up the impact of *Main Currents in Nineteenth-Century Literature* when he called it "the bible for young European intellectuals" and a "classic document in nineteenth century intellectual life."

The immediate reaction to Brandes' opening lecture was one of horror and derision, not least because he mercilessly condemned the cultural and political backwardness of Danish society (personified by many of the members of his audience). "Today, as usual, we are forty years behind the rest of Europe," he complained. Since he believed, rather programmatically, that literature ought to take up the most pressing social and political problems of the day, Danish literature appeared to him sunk in a complacent stupor. Where was the Danish George Sand? The Danish Feuerbach? The Danish Voltaire? In order to contribute to the continued progress of humanity, Danish writers needed to adopt a critical attitude toward the conditions and the institutions of society. They needed to yank themselves free of the chains of their pastoral idealism. Brandes blasphemed against the bard of Danish Romanticism, Adam Oehlenschlæger, for his folklorist tragedies, and against B. S. Ingemann for his historical novels modeled on a genre invented by the "full-blooded Tory" Walter Scott.

Brandes' patriotism manifested in his desire to pull Denmark forward. That impulse was unsurprisingly interpreted as disloyalty by the Danish establishment. To the attending members of Copenhagen's cultural and political elite, Brandes' chastisements were incendiary and insulting — especially coming as they did on the heels of the revolutionary uprisings in Paris and the founding of the Danish chapter of the First International. That Brandes was not a socialist hardly changed the fact that his ideas were perceived as a threat to Danish society in a time of sweeping national anxiety. (Denmark's humiliating defeat to Bismarck's Prussia in the Second Schleswig-Holstein War in 1864, in which a third of the country's territory was lost, had a debilitating impact on the national psyche.) Brandes was accused of immorality, atheism, even treason. D. G. Monrad published a small pamphlet called *Free Thought and Dr. Georg Brandes' Lectures*, in which he castigated the young critic's "revolting" rhetoric. Worst of all, when Carsten Hauch, professor of aesthetics at the University of Copenhagen, died in 1872, Brandes' application for the position was ignored — despite the fact that Hauch had singled him out as his natural successor. (As an added insult, the position would remain vacant for twenty years.) Sensing the despondency of his young friend, Ibsen wrote to encourage Brandes to remain a steadfast soldier in the war of ideas. "A war such as yours should not be waged by a royally appointed civil servant. If they weren't slamming doors in your face it would mean they aren't afraid of you."

Engendering fear may be flattering, but it is also isolating. As Brandes continued his lectures into the new year, the attacks on him intensified in their vindictiveness and their malevolence. The Danish press exposed their own anti-Semitism by portraying him as a freethinking Jew with a lecherous appetite for the daughters of the Copenhagen bourgeoisie. Caricatures in newspapers and magazines accentuated the size of his nose. In 1873, the minor writer H. F. Ewald published *Agathe*, a polemical novel in which the main character, Gustav, has recently returned from Paris filled with ideas of "chaos, the unleashing of our wildest desires, barbarism and refined hedonism in beautiful surroundings." Gustav marries the titular Agathe and takes her with him to Paris only to later abandon her, whereupon she dies of shame and grief. The novel was loosely based on Brandes' relationship with a married woman named Caroline David — a love affair that caught the public's prurient attention when David decided to divorce her husband and leave her family for the younger man. (After her relationship with Brandes, David wound up living in Naples with an Italian silk merchant. She died of tuberculosis in 1878.)

The English writer Edmund Gosse, who twice traveled to Denmark between 1872 and 1874, was first introduced to Brandes around the time of the earliest *Main Currents* lectures and the David scandal. "It was difficult to account for the repulsion and even terror of Georg Brandes which I heard expressed around me whenever his name came up in the course of general conversation," he later recalled. "He belonged to the race of iconoclasts, like Heine before him, like Nietzsche after him, and he was expected to disturb all the convictions of his contemporaries." Gosse often visited Brandes in his apartment on Møntergade in central Copenhagen, where he would read to him from the poetry of Shelley, Wordsworth, and Swinburne. One day Brandes confided to him that he felt it necessary to leave Denmark. "He said to me, as we parted," Gosse wrote, "that if I came back to Copenhagen, one person I should certainly not find, and that would be himself.'

Between 1877 and 1883 Brandes lived in intellectual exile in Berlin, though the culture war that he had instigated, the battle between forces that yearned for a larger cultural horizon and those that were committed to a militant parochialism, continued to be fought in Copenhagen in his absence. For decades intellectual circles in Denmark splintered into anti-Brandes and pro-Brandes factions, sometimes even coming to blows. As late as 1912, a fight broke out during a lecture at the University of Copenhagen when a professor inveighed against the pernicious influence on Danish society of Brandes' "Jewish-liberal materialism." It is hard to imagine the heat that these ideas carried, the fevers that they inspired. (When someone in the audience pulled out a revolver, everyone had the good sense to flee the scene.)

Nor did his absence soften his image at home, where his allies and his enemies continued waging polemical warfare. In Berlin he could at least walk the streets without being recognized. The new German capital was expanding at an explosive rate and offered access to grand museums and well-stocked libraries. At *Zum schwarzen Ferkel* ("The Black Piglet"), a bar on Unter den Linden, he met and conversed with his fellow Scandinavian misfits August Strindberg and Edvard Munch. His books slowly trickled into German translation, he became a regular contributor to the Viennese newspaper *Neue Freie Presse*, and he was even briefly considered for a professorship at the University of Vienna.

But money was tight. Despite his monstrous productivity — during his Berlin years he cobbled together a collection of essays and churned out studies of Benjamin Disraeli, Ferdinand Lasalle, and the Swedish poet Esaias Tegnér — he often found himself in the embarrassing position of having to turn down social invitations because he could not afford the price of a cab. He had married his wife, Henriette, in 1876 and felt that domestic life in Berlin was too expensive. (And perhaps a little awkward: Henriette was the ex-wife of Brandes' friend Adolf Strodtmann, Ibsen's German translator.) Fortunately, thanks to string-pulling by his younger brother Edvard, Brandes was eventually offered a ten-year endowment by a group of anonymous donors on the stipulation that he return to Copenhagen and resume his public lectures at the university. It was an offer he couldn't refuse. As he put it in his farewell address at a dinner at the Hotel Kaiserhof in Berlin: "In Germany I could have no other goal than to make my name more and more known. But in the North are all my tasks. In the North there is a generation of youths whose teacher I must be."

On his return to Copenhagen in 1883, Brandes resumed his role as the chief enforcer of what became known as the Modern Breakthrough, that richly productive period of Scandinavian literary history when writers in Denmark, Norway, and Sweden first embraced realism and naturalism, breaking with their idealistic and Romantic traditions. It was Brandes who gave the movement its name: in 1883 he published *Men of the Modern Breakthrough,* a collection of essays on the new generation of Scandinavian writers. (Though he agitated admirably for the emancipation of women, Brandes remained mostly male-centric in his literary tastes.) The writers to emerge from this movement include Jens Peter Jacobsen, Herman Bang, Knut Hamsun, August Strindberg, Henrik Pontoppidan, Alexander Kielland, Arne Garborg, and Hans Jæger.

All of them, in their way, responded to the challenge and the incitement of Brandes' example. Jacobsen's *Marie Grubbe* was the first realist novel in Scandinavia and earned comparisons to *Madame Bovary* for its frank portrayal of female sexuality. Garborg's debut novel, *A Freethinker*, dramatized the consequences of individual free thought in a morally dogmatic Norwegian society. In *Lucky-Per*, admired by George Lukacs and Thomas Mann, Pontoppidan wrote a sweeping social novel of Denmark in which Brandes himself figures as a minor character. Many of these writers ran afoul of government censors and public morality. Herman Bang, whose novels and stories chronicled the quiet lives of lonely and isolated women, was subjected to a barrage of smear campaigns for his homosexuality. Arne Garborg lost his job as a state auditor following the publication of his novel *Menfolk*. Hans Jæger's novel *The Kristiania Bohemians* was confiscated and the author sentenced to sixty days' imprisonment.

Brandes, perhaps a little predictably, was not always favorably disposed toward the writers whose literary beginnings he encouraged or enabled. He wrote a glowing review of *Marie Grubbe* but never quite reconciled himself to Jacobsen's remarkable second novel, *Niels Lyhne*, finding it too disillusioned and interior, as well as wildly overwritten. In like fashion, he dismissed Hamsun's viscerally powerful *Hunger* as too monotonous after a cursory scanning of the first few chapters. It is probably true, as Hamsun's biographer Ingar Sletten Kolloen has argued, that Brandes was too much of a rationalist at heart; his appetite for concepts and principles circumscribed his imagination. "A radical thinker," Kolloen observes, "Brandes may have raised the banner against God, the priesthood and politicians, but never against reason itself. He had no desire to identify with a literary figure with whom he could not engage intellectually." Edmund Gosse similarly found Brandes' literary tastes to be too narrow. He tried in vain to interest him in Baudelaire, only for Brandes to dismiss him as *un sale monsieur* — a filthy man. Perhaps this limiting rationalism was the price he paid for being capable of consecrating his life to ideas.

And yet, for all his peculiar blind spots and often overtly political approach to literature, Brandes was unquestionably a perceptive critic. He played an instrumental role in fostering the awareness of Dostoevsky beyond the borders of the Russian empire, writing of his use of dialogue that it was "a kind of inquisition, a continued contest between men who seek to wrest their secrets from each other." In 1877 he published the first biographical study of Kierkegaard at a time when the Danish philosopher was little known outside academic circles in Copenhagen. His long and pioneering essays on Ibsen, Strindberg, Flaubert, Turgenev, and Zola contributed to the international renown that these authors all enjoyed in the closing years of the nineteenth century.

The most influential lectures that Brandes ever gave, more influential even than *Main Currents in Nineteeth Century Literature*, took place at the University of Copenhagen in April and March of 1888. Two years previously, a young German philologist had sent Brandes a copy of one of his books by care of his publisher. It was titled *Beyond Good and Evil*. A year later, two more volumes arrived in the mail: *Human, All Too Human* and *On the Genealogy of Morals*. It did not take long for Brandes to grasp that he was in possession of something radically new, something brilliant, something at once profound and disturbing. "A new and original spirit breathes to me from your books," Brandes wrote in his first letter to Nietzsche on November 26, 1887. "I do not yet fully understand what I have read; I cannot always see your intention. But I find much that harmonizes with my own ideas and sympathies, the deprecation of ascetic ideals and the profound disgust with democratic mediocrity, your aristocratic radicalism." Nietzsche responded a week later, gratefully acknowledging that "such a good European and missionary of culture" should now rank among the five or six friends who understood his work. He also endorsed the expression "aristocratic radicalism:" "It is, permit me to say, the cleverest thing I have yet read about myself."

On April 10, 1888, Brandes delivered the world's first lecture on the work of Nietzsche. Since nobody knew who the German thinker was the event was sparsely attended, but word traveled fast and on the occasion of the second lecture the auditorium was completely packed. Following a brief biographical sketch of the author's life, Brandes emphasized Nietzsche's assault on moral prejudice and cultural philistinism. "All of us are now born into a society of cultured philistinism," Brandes said. "It confronts us with prevailing opinions, which we unconsciously adopt." Since we go about our day and find everywhere the same tacit conventions with respect to religion and morality and marriage and family, it is the task of the individual to liberate himself from this cultural mediocrity and seek out "the highest examples of humanity itself." Against the utilitarian notion that we should aim for greater happiness for a greater number of people, Brandes interpreted Nietzsche to mean that the highest significance of human life is achieved instead by "being lived for the rarest and most valuable examples of the human race." In his final lecture, Brandes explained that his principal reason for calling attention to Nietzsche was that Scandinavian literature had "been living quite long enough on the ideas that were put forward and discussed in the last decade" — which is to say, the very ideas Brandes himself had introduced: "a little

Darwinism, a little emancipation of woman, a little morality of happiness, a little freethought, a little worship of democracy, etc." To paraphrase what Martin Amis once said of Christopher Hitchens, one occasionally gets the impression that the only person Brandes thought truly worth arguing with was himself.

Following the conclusion of the second lecture, Brandes reported back to his new German friend that "some three hundred people listened with the greatest attention to my exposition of your works." And as an indication of just how embedded Brandes was in Europe's cultural and intellectual networks, he encouraged Nietzsche to send copies of his books to Bizet's widow in Paris and to the liberal Prince Urusov in Saint Petersburg. He also instructed Nietzsche to acquaint himself with Kierkegaard and boasted that he had won over for him the "mad Swede" Strindberg, with whom he eventually put Nietzsche in touch. When it was published in German in the *Deutsche Rundschau* in 1890, Brandes' "An Essay on the Aristocratic Radicalism of Friedrich Nietzsche" lit the fuse of the German philosopher's explosive influence. "We Germans must never forget," Mann wrote many years later, "the ray of sunlight that shone on Nietzsche's cold loneliness when word of a certain Dr. Georg Brandes' lectures at the University of Copenhagen first spread."

To many observers there was something perplexing about the meeting of these particular minds. Nietzsche, after all, was a merciless critic of the modernity and the rationalism for which Brandes had spent two decades crusading. How did the translator of Mill come to champion the ideas of an avowed enemy of democracy? Once again Brandes found himself bogged down in intellectual battles both at home and abroad. In Denmark, the philosopher Harald Høffding accused him of embracing anti-democratic ideas. In Germany, he was singled out by Max Nordau in his bestselling reactionary screed *Degeneration*, which appeared in 1892, for popularizing the "unhappy lunatic" and his degenerate ravings. Brandes responded in vain that his principles and fundamental beliefs had not been altered in the slightest by his encounter with Nietzsche, that he was long past the age in which it was possible to change one's view of life. But still the attacks continued. As Nietzsche wrote in his last letter to Brandes, "When once you had discovered me, it was easy enough to find me: the difficulty now is to get rid of me." He signed the letter, in the sad and slightly demented tone of his last years, "The Crucified."

The remarkable career of Georg Brandes reflects many of the divisions and the contradictions of the late nineteenth century. By the time of his Nietzsche lectures, his attitude toward Taine's positivism had slackened. "Taine looked upon criticism as applied science," he wrote, "but no methodical research can give us the key to a composite human spirit." His interest in Enlightenment-style emancipation contracted to a narrower focus on individual genius. He now shared with Nietzsche and Ibsen a belief in what we might call the Great Man Theory of Culture: that great art is brought forth only by exceedingly strong-willed individuals. "Nietzsche's value," he wrote, "lies in his being one of these vehicles of culture: a mind which, itself independent, diffuses independence and may become to others a liberating force, such as Schopenhauer was to Nietzsche himself in his younger days." He devoted many of his later years to writing multi-volume biographies of some of Europe's great men: Shakespeare, Goethe, Michelangelo, Voltaire, Caesar, and Homer.

As the scholar William Banks has recently pointed out, these works were noticeably more apolitical than Brandes' earlier writings. "Everything in his literary works of the 1890s," Banks notes, "was pointing away from political engagement." Yet this was not because Brandes himself had become apolitical. On the contrary, he was more engaged than ever with the issues of his day. The shift is better described as a bifurcation of his writing: literature on the one hand, politics on the other. For at the same time that he wrote his massive biographical tomes, Brandes became an outspoken critic of Europe's encroaching nationalism and a defender of oppressed peoples inside and outside the continent.

Around the turn of the century, Brandes began putting his considerable celebrity in the service of the burgeoning international human rights movement. In his essay "Thoughts at the Turn of the Century," he wrote: "The decisive political event we have experienced at the end of the nineteenth century is this: the great powers divide the world among themselves [...] they act with an injurious recklessness, because for the sake of economic advantage they sacrifice not only those peoples whom they conquer by fire and by sword and in all manner of horrors, but further all the small nations within their immediate orbit, which are either absorbed for the sake of national unity or exchanged as bounty or delivered up to brutality." Being an outsider from a small nation on the margins of Europe heightened Brandes' sympathies with the oppressed. In an address in 1904, he said that "it should be known that, despite the small size of our country, men lived here who felt sympathy with all wronged individuals or peoples across the world and who lifted their voices, spoke on their behalf." He continued: "All Poles and Finns, Ruthenians, Georgians, Armenians, should know that freedom and justice lived in Denmark."

It is worth pointing out a few occasions on which Brandes lifted his very prominent voice on behalf of the wronged. Between 1896 and 1906, he wrote twenty-two articles about the Dreyfus affair. In the essays "The Aryan Race" in 1905 and "Race Theories" in 1912, he objected strenuously to modern race "science," writing that "every modern people, like every one of antiquity, is the result of a nearly immeasurable intermixing of tribes." He criticized Kaiser Wilhelm II's so-called "Hun speech" on the occasion of the dispatch of German forces to China to crush the anti-colonial Boxer rebellion, condemning European powers for having "swarmed like birds of prey over China and ripped her to shreds." (In 1923, the Chinese writer Zheng Zhenduo declared that "Brandes does not belong to Denmark, he belongs to the world!") He opposed British and Russian involvement in Persia, at one point even meeting with the Iranian politician Hassan Taqizadeh in Copenhagen to draft an article denouncing czarist policy together. In a celebrated anti-imperial address delivered in Oslo in 1922, he was admirably forthright about the cruelty of conditions in French North Africa, especially in Tunisia and Algeria.

Yet the central calamity of his long life was the First World War. It unraveled the internationalism of fin-de-siècle Europe, destroying the links between nations that Brandes had helped to create. Worse: it killed over fifteen million people in a little over four years. Outraged, Brandes wrote dozens of articles and appeals, collected in *The World at War* (1917) and *The Second Half of the Tragedy: Peace* (1919). But his activism served only to isolate him. For the consummate European, this was a heavy toll. Brandes' very public break with Clemenceau, culminating with the Prime Minister bidding Brandes *"adieu"* in his journal *L'Homme enchaîné*, was especially painful. So too was the pressure to take sides from friends such as August Rodin, the hateful letters that piled up in his apartment, and the accusations that his refusal to blame Germany for the war amounted to treason, given Prussia's defeat of Denmark in 1864. "It is terrible how my contempt for humanity has intensified," he wrote to a friend. "I almost can't stand the sight of other people. When I go out, I walk along those streets where I am least likely to run into anyone."

The two major biographies that he wrote during the war, *Wolfgang Goethe* in 1916 and *François de Voltaire* in 1917, bear the imprint of his retreat from the theater of humanity. He described Goethe's Olympian "contempt for the ignorance and loquaciousness of the masses," his "painful familiarity with the ignorance, the envy, the prejudice of the human horde." Voltaire, meanwhile, was to be admired for vanquishing the piety and superstition of the masses, for serving as a beacon of enlightened hope. "Throughout his long life he awakened generation after generation to the might and power of reason," Brandes wrote, a little defensively.

Setting aside his misguided retreat into the intellectual dead-end of genius worship, Brandes' suspicion and even contempt for the masses was not without justification. (You might even say that, for a Jew in interwar Europe, suspicion of the masses was a condition of survival.) After all, he had been a victim of chauvinistic smear campaigns, reported on the Dreyfus affair, defended vulnerable minorities against their powerful neighbors, and witnessed an entire continent engulfed by a murderous war in which even the press, the politicians, and the intellectuals were complicit. He felt he was living through an era of unprecedented collective madness.

"What is Europe?" he asked. "Transformed into hundreds of battlefields, thousands of cemeteries and hospitals, one enormous bankrupt estate, and one immense insane asylum."

A year before his death, he was described in *The New York Times* as "a European who has outlived Europe." Brandes was inclined to agree. When he suffered a fall just a month before his death, he committed the following to his diary: "It's over. Everything is deserting me. Sight, hearing, smell, mobility. I've outlived myself and my generation. The new one is ten times worse." He knew that the liberal cosmopolitanism he had, in his myriad ways, spent his life espousing now belonged to what Zweig called "the world of yesterday." And yet he had no illusions about the future, either. The First World War's "destroying hatred," he had written in 1916, "will live long after the war, and will inevitably give birth to new wars. The longer the war lasts, the shorter the coming peace will be." The poignancy is enormous. Brandes' faith in reason had left him poorly prepared for reason's eclipse. He regarded the war as a regression, a betrayal of civilization, rather than as its unavoidable shadow: "I am convinced that future generations will look upon the great days we are living in as we look upon the days of witchcraft and the Inquisition." We would do well to remember Brandes: his grand agon with liberal universalism and the politics of unreason is one that continues to bedevil us today.

CHAIM NACHMAN BIALIK

God Has Not Shown Me

God has not shown me in nightdreams
and no sorcerer has divined
where my last day will overtake me
and how my end will look, that I may know.

Whether in my tent, on my couch, I will die
with all my cherished close to me,
every one of them camped mutely around me,
sentries of love and sanctity at my bed,
who will count my last breaths in the bosom of my God
as one would count coveted attainments.

Or, scorned and despised, in the ire of God and man,
hated by my fellows and a fugitive from my family,
on a pile of straw in a forsaken cell
I will emit my vacant and impure soul.
Nobody will attend my spirit's release
and no hand will shudder over my snuffed-out eyes.

Or perhaps, in my hunger and my thirst
for life and its delicacies,
with loathing in my soul,
in spite of the Creator and his wrath,
I will kick away His gift
and like hurling a soiled shoe from my foot
hurl my soul at His feet.

Or maybe my soul will wait long and longer until it rots,
from too much expectation and too much silence,
and spill upon the earth in my bitterness
as I vomit it like blood from my heart.

Or it might drop like a pearl with my last teardrop,
the light of the world within it, trembling,
and shine many generations later
for eyes that never beheld me.

Or perhaps like a butterfly, dancing and leaping
around the flame, my soul will depart.
Or like the flame itself, before it consumes the wax,
in the throes of its death my soul will flutter
and flicker and smoke for many days, an optical illusion,
until suddenly it plummets into a dark abyss
and is extinguished forever.

Or perhaps like the sun before it sets —
abruptly all its beams ignite
and it disperses its flaming torches across the clouds
and its pyres among the mountaintops,
and thousands of eyes open wide and gape
at the approach of its final radiance.

Who knows, my God may be cruel to me
and I will die while still I live,
and they will bundle my soul in shrouds of paper
and bury me in a bookcase,
the mold in the house will grate my bones
and a rat in a hole will gnaw at me,
and I will stand with my own feet in my own grave
and recite the kaddish with my own mouth for myself.

Or perhaps my death will arrive small and without sense,
and not as I had hoped:
on a furious winter night,
like a starving dog behind one of the fences,
I will freeze.
The gentle snow will cover the black stain
and erase the shame of a man and his life,
and the last rattle of my teeth as I curse my death
will be scattered by the raging wind.

*Translated by Leon Wieseltier,
in loving memory of A.B. Yehoshua and Meir Shalev*

WILLIAM DERESIEWICZ

The Quality To Be Tragic

Elizabeth Hardwick is having a moment — and why not? The last two years have brought *The Uncollected Essays*, an addendum to *The Collected Essays* of 2017; Cathy Curtis' biography, *A Splendid Intelligence*; and *Come Back in September*, Darryl Pinckney's memoir of his writerly apprenticeship at Hardwick's feet. Like Joan Didion, a very different sort of talent and sensibility, Elizabeth Hardwick was a lion of the 1960s and 1970s (and 1980s and 1990s). Lavishly frank, instinctively original, elegant, intimate, and when she wanted, very, very funny, Hardwick was one of the great critics and great prose writers of the second half of the twentieth century. It is fit and fine that her work and example be forwarded to a new generation of readers.

My own interest in Hardwick is tangled up in a larger obsession with the New York intellectuals, that storied gaggle of talkers and writers — cultural critics, political philosophers, editors, polemicists, controversialists — who bestrode American thought in the decades after World War II. Readers conversant with the group may be surprised to hear this, for of the figures typically enumerated among its members — Lionel Trilling, Alfred Kazin, Dwight Macdonald, Irving Kristol, Irving Howe, Sidney Hook, and a dozen or two others — Hardwick has never been one. It is not because she was a woman: Hannah Arendt was a key presence; Susan Sontag, the youngest of them all, is regarded as a kind of last hurrah. It is not because she wasn't Jewish, though Macdonald and Mary McCarthy, Hardwick's best friend, were the only gentiles. It is not because she didn't share the same milieu. Hardwick lived in New York throughout the 1940s, left for ten years, then returned for good. She went to the parties, holding her liquor and holding her own. She was a mainstay of the journals: *Partisan Review*, and then, for more than forty years, the *New York Review of Books*, of which she was among the founders. She was universally esteemed, and not infrequently feared.

It is because she wasn't, strictly speaking, an intellectual. I don't mean this as a deprecation; quite the opposite, in fact. Like Henry James, she had a mind so fine that no idea could violate it. More than any other critic I'm aware of, Hardwick possessed the ability to speak with great incisiveness about a work, an author, without recourse to general conceptions: no theses, no theories, no larger arguments, oftentimes no arguments at all. "She stayed away from academic criticism, theory, analytic philosophy," Pinckney tells us, while

"Marxism made her distrust ideologies of criticism." Though her reading was vast, she eschewed comparison, allusion, discussion of genres, movements, genealogies. Instead, she focused like a lover on the writer before her, bringing her entire self to the encounter, which she enacted in prose of incomparable suppleness and energy. She didn't "review"; she metabolized.

What she shared with the other New Yorkers, though, was larger than her differences. Like them, she came of age at a time when the life of the mind was lived without reference to the university — when the models were Paris and Vienna, not Harvard and Yale. Critics now are academics first: if not professors or disappointed PhDs, then former literature or "studies" majors trained in the accepted points of view. Among the New Yorkers, even those who taught steered free of academic sensibilities, manners, jargon, frames of reference. They eschewed professionalization; they stood on the authority of their own aesthetic. Hardwick enrolled in a doctoral program (at twenty-three, in English), but she found her professors uninspiring, and scholarship unappealing, and she soon dropped out to write — to be a writer, to have a different kind of mind and life. "They are critics and have good taste," wrote Kazin of a pair of academic acquaintances. "I am a writer and interested in everything I can see and read and feel and touch." Like others among the New Yorkers, Hardwick saw herself, and was, a bohemian — unsalaried and uncredentialed, living hand to mouth on freelance checks and books. Like them, she self-educated, stubbornly and idiosyncratically. With them, she gathered to debate, to individuate, not to align and conform. Like theirs, her style of thought and writing was unique.

Nothing in her background prophesied her destiny. The modal New York writer was a Jew from the outer boroughs, maybe the Lower East Side. The city was their native ground, texts and arguments their birthright. Hardwick was from Lexington, Kentucky, and despite her later reputation for gentility, she grew up working-class, at the wrong end of town. Her father, who didn't make it past the seventh grade, was a sometime plumber and full-time wastrel. Her siblings, ten in all, would come to include a beautician, a steamfitter, a postal clerk, and a couple of teachers — this last the highest she was meant to reach for. There is simply no accounting for her gifts. She was a unicorn, born among horses.

The only thing that Hardwick ever wanted in Kentucky was to leave. Lexington had scarcely forty thousand people in her youth. Small towns, she would later write, were scenes of a "galling, busy puritanism...moving on the wheels of disgrace and scandal, drunkenness and deceit." Her ticket out was books. As an adolescent, Curtis writes in her biography, she "read her way through the classics" at the local public library. College, at the state university downtown, introduced her to communism, "European émigré professors," contemporary literary currents, and "a group of clever young Jewish men from New York." These last determined her direction. She was, she later said, like a provincial out of Balzac "yearning for Paris." A year out of college, she turned down a fellowship at LSU in favor of Columbia, boarded a Greyhound, and headed for the Emerald City.

That was in 1939. In 1943, after sojourns in a women's dormitory, then some nearby rooming houses (the latter an experience she'd call upon in fiction), Hardwick shifted to the Hotel Schuyler, a grotty den of transients and failures —

Liberties

"spotted rugs and walls," "greasy, smoking ovens," "people who slept all day in their graying underwear" — a short stumble from Times Square. She stayed for years, sharing an apartment with a gay young man she knew from home, then a call girl and her pimp. Other neighbors included a middle-aged woman, barroom pianist by trade, who borrowed fifty 1940s dollars (more than eight hundred in today's money), then, by way of repayment, called Hardwick a "dirty cunt." When the pimp cornered her in the hallway and rubbed himself off on her coat, she decided it was time to leave.

Meanwhile, she wrote: fiction first, then criticism also. Her maiden novel failed to find a publisher. A second manuscript, *The Ghostly Lover*, appeared in 1945. It was not well received — reviewers called it "removed from reality," its characters "strangely suspended in air" — but it won the attention of Philip Rahv, the editor of *Partisan Review*. In general, Hardwick's fiction of the 1940s and 1950s — some fourteen stories plus a second novel, *The Simple Truth*, about a murder trial in Iowa City, which she seems to have started as a way of dealing with living, for a semester, in Iowa City — is well-constructed but excessively controlled: stylistically cautious, self-consciously premised and plotted, lacking a genuine pulse.

It was in the essay, starting at *Partisan Review* in 1945, that Hardwick found her voice, her freedom. She took chances; she had fun; she let it fly. An early piece, on Simone de Beauvoir's *The Second Sex*, begins: "Vassal, slave, inferior, other, thing, victim, dependent, parasite, prisoner — oh, bitter, raped, child-swollen flesh doomed to immanence! Sisyphean goddess of the dust pile!" Her style took shape. There were her famous adjectives. That paragraph on de Beauvoir goes on to offer "madly sensible" and "brilliantly obscure" as descriptions of that landmark tome. Later she will give us "the clamorous serenity of [Frost's] old age" and "the mournful, expensive defeat of Fitzgerald's last years," Plath's "ambitious rage" and "the sumptuous, taciturn resonance" of Bartleby's "I prefer not to," the "aggressive simplicity and shy opulence" of the old New York aristocracy and the "intimidating revelation" of contemporary girls in string bikinis. Hardwick's adjectives aren't decorative; they are load-bearing. They create volume. They tell a story in a phrase, and it is always one of life's impossible conjunctions, its vitalizing oxymorons.

Then there are her similes. Some are marvelously simple, homespun. A character is "as dry as an old lemon rind." An account of Dylan Thomas' disastrous, drunken visits to America is "as flat and true as a calendar." The names of old Boston worthies such as William Ellery Channing "remain in one's mind, without producing an image or a fact, as the marks are left on the wall after the picture has been removed." Others draw upon her eye for social types. Boswell hung about Johnson's coattails "like an insurance salesman after a policy." The owners of jazz clubs, always changing, quickly failing, "started out with the embezzler's hope and moved swiftly to the bankrupt's torpor." The most brilliant of Hardwick's similes crystallize a situation in a single image. Delmore Schwartz, in his last, mad years, was "given by paranoia to the shedding of friends and wives, angrily plucking them off like flies on the worn threads of his jacket." A pair of poor, aging women who roam the streets of her neighborhood "wander about in their dreadful freedom like old oxen left behind." The naïve and friendless heiress Catherine Sloper, in Hardwick's dazzling account of *Washington Square*, "is as alone as an animal in a field." Morris Townsend, the adventurer who seeks her fortune, "goes for Catherine's attention with the watchful concentration of the sportsman waiting for the game to fly in the range of the gun."

Liberties

Her wit — dry, sly, sticking in the shiv before you even see the flash. Ted Kennedy was "no guardian of his reputation." Rabbit's wife in *Rabbit, Run* "is confused, sore, exhausted, and not sober." Apropos the O.J. Simpson trial, "It is not easy to imagine Lawyer Dershowitz in discomfort about his life decisions." Epigrammatic: "the example of the great is seldom a deterrent to the mediocre." Deflating: "swapping" was for "wives and husbands who had read sex manuals and radically wanted more of life even if it had to be, like pizza, brought in from around the corner." Just plain wicked: for Truman Capote, the South was "there to be called upon...as a sort of *spécialité*, like Key lime pie and conch fritters" — this from an essay-length draught of vivid vinegar ("crocodilian celebrity," "ruins and works of art he declined to get off the yacht to see") composed at eighty-one, an age at which writers are usually napping or dead.

Above all, her sentences: their moves, their turns, their variety and unpredictability, their sinuosity and steel, the way they gather and release their force.

On *Jude the Obscure*:

"Every single character fails and falls, in great pain, each one." The sympathy is in the syntax.

On the subjects of Frans Hals' *The Regents of the Old Men's Almshouse*:

"The laughing cavaliers perhaps had eaten too many oysters, drunk too much beer and died a replete, unwilling death, leaving the poor, freed by a bitter life from killing pleasures, to shrivel on charity, live on with their strong, blackening faces." Nearly every phrase, sometimes every word, turns us in a new direction.

On Capote's Black and White Ball to celebrate the publication of *In Cold Blood*: "The party at the Plaza acquired the fame of a coronation for the very successful book, still a work of riveting interest for its portrait of the misshapen bodies, language, highway felonies and idiotic plans and dreams of two savage, talkative, rawhide murderers, Perry Smith and Dick Hickock." A syntactic cascade, phrase falling into phrase; a thread that ties the happy famous to the heartland refuse on whose wretchedness the book was built.

And this:

> Updike went on to Harvard and, as a young writer, came under the benevolent paternalism of *The New Yorker*, married early, had children, moved to Massachusetts, and with an uncommon creative energy wrote stories, novels, poems, essays, and still writes on and on with great success about suburban landscapes or small-town ones efflorescent in observed detail, prodigal in image, and brashly knowing and accomplished in the rhythms of current dialogue and steaming with the orifices and bodily fluids of many fluent copulations.

Form follows function, a prodigal sentence for a prodigal talent, remaining aloft, with its unexpected "ands" ("and still writes on," "and steaming with"), like a basketballer torquing toward the hoop, and finishing, like a spent adulterer, in a superfluity of fluids.

There are no flat patches in Hardwick's prose. Every inch is as detailed and colored as a Renaissance landscape. All is taut, condensed; there is pressure on every word. "She writes like a poet," said Robert Silvers, eternal editor of the *New York Review of Books*. "The leaps are so precise and dramatic that they open up the mind." Yet Hardwick had it tougher than the poets, for as a critic she was more constrained by sense, by the demands of clarity and fact, by the expectations of the form. She had to look before she leapt. Still, it's no surprise to discover, from Pinckney, that she believed in reading poetry before one sat down to write prose, because it "opened up the possibilities of language in your head." Nor that she composed like a poet — "line by line," he says. "She couldn't go on to the next sentence if the one before it wasn't right." Curtis reports that it could take her six months to write a fifteen-page essay. Her dedication to criticism as a high literary calling, an art form of its own, is virtually without parallel.

Was there something too precious about all this, as some have said — a cult of the sentence, of style for style's sake, for which Hardwick, along with some of her contemporaries, was responsible? I don't think so. Style, for Hardwick, was an instrument of exploration, a way of pushing language to the point of discovery. Writing, she once said, is "the only time in your life when you have to think." As both a reader and writer, she possessed an absolute belief in the value of art as a way of knowing: independent of politics, superior to journalism and the social sciences, indispensable for understanding. That conviction, so essential to the New York writers as to not require naming, has over the ensuing decades gradually been submerged — under scientism, under the frivolity of garbage entertainment, under, lately, ideology — and is one of the cultural resources that Hardwick can help us recover.

Hardwick did not enter the New York literary world at a good time. She entered at the best. She raised herself above provinciality at exactly the moment America did. The great nineteenth-century American writers were isolatoes, one-offs:

Poe, Melville, Whitman, Dickinson. Then came the expatriates: James, Stein, Eliot, Pound; Hemingway and Fitzgerald. Now, after the war, New York was the center, a city of refugee geniuses and incandescent offspring of working-class immigrants. In the Greenwich Village circle, at cocktail parties at the Rahvs, one can only picture the commotion that Hardwick and McCarthy caused, two brilliant, sexy gentile women from the exotic heartland. "The dull Communist wives," Pinckney reports, "didn't like...their double act. They said challenging things, wore bright red lipstick, and were pretty."

It was at one of those parties, in 1947, that Hardwick met Robert Lowell, a year younger and well on his way to establishing himself as the leading American poet of their generation. The marriage lasted more than twenty years and knew as much drama as all of Aeschylus. Lowell's endless infidelities were frequently the prodrome to a re-eruption of his mania. Again the mental ward, the verbal abuse, the brave face to family and friends, the false, returning hope — a Sisyphean repetition. "All night I've held your hand," he wrote in "Man and Wife," "as if you had / a fourth time faced the kingdom of the mad /.../ and dragged me home alive." And that was only 1959. Hardwick's was a deep and wounded love. "I would kill myself if it would cure you," she wrote in 1965. The good times were extraordinary; his intellect opened up worlds. Five years later he abandoned her for good, taking up with Caroline Blackwood, an aristocratic Englishwoman who'd already burned through Silvers, Lucien Freud, and others.

It was devastating. It was also liberating. Artist couples, Hardwick later wrote, "share in perceptions, temperament, in the struggle for creation, for the powers descending downward from art, for reputation, achievement, stability, for their own uniqueness — that especially." That especially.

She had changed her name when she married, but she hadn't changed her byline. "Elizabeth Lowell never wrote anything," she said. But the relationship, particularly as it staggered through the 1960s, cost her as an artist. "I love Lizzie," Lowell once told Sontag, "but she's such a good writer. One can't have one's wife writing *Madame Bovary* in the kitchen." He needn't have worried: the tumult of their home life made the necessary concentration unobtainable. By the time they split, she hadn't attempted a novel since *The Simple Truth* in 1955, hadn't published a story since 1959. But soon, with Lowell gone, she set out upon the work that would develop into *Sleepless Nights*, her great accomplishment in fiction. First, however, she produced a volume of essays that represented both "an act of self-rescue," as Pinckney puts it, and the height of her achievement as a critic.

Seduction and Betrayal, from 1974, is anomalous among her books. Her other collections — *A View of My Own* (1962), *Bartleby in Manhattan* (1983), *Sight-Readings* (1998) — represent the harvest of many years of freelance work, and each covers a wide range of subjects, including, in the first two cases, politics, theater, and travel. The essays that make up *Seduction and Betrayal* were written in a concentrated burst, during the three years immediately following Lowell's departure, and on a single theme: women and literature — the Brontës, Ibsen's heroines, Plath, Woolf, Zelda, Dorothy Wordsworth, Jane Carlyle, and, in the title essay, Tess, Clarissa Harlowe, Hester Prynne, and others.

The list is telling in its heterogeneity. Hardwick's approach as a critic was to place the characters of fiction on the same plane as real people. She treated them alike, because she was interested in the same questions with regard to both. Questions, precisely, of character, in its twin senses: one's moral composition, as shaped, in part, by place and family and history ("deforming conditions," she calls them), and one's way of facing those conditions. That is, the why and how of action and its consequences. You can call this gossip, as Hardwick sometimes playfully did. It is also an exalted version of the kind of thing that every reader — every "common reader" — does. This is the point of Hardwick's refusal to read like a specialist. She read for the reasons that everyone reads, or everyone who hasn't been debauched by learning: aesthetic bliss, and knowledge of our fellow human creatures, who were for her an endless fascination.

In *Seduction and Betrayal*, those questions of character largely revolve around what might be called the drama of the gifted woman. Charlotte Brontë and her heroines, Nora in *A Doll's House* and Rebecca West in *Rosmersholm*, Thomas Carlyle's wife and William Wordsworth's sister: intelligent, spirited figures constrained by the condition of being a woman, by their limited options in life. How did they respond, and at what cost? The autobiographical dimension here is not hard to spot. Hardwick sees Zelda Fitzgerald as someone whose creative potential was sacrificed to her husband's convenience and ego, and Jane Carlyle as a brilliant intellect and wit who spent her energy, as Hardwick did a lot of hers, on housework. Yet we shouldn't overstate the parallels. For one thing, Hardwick was looking back, mostly to the nineteenth century. Her own life straddled old and new: born to traditional expectations, she had had the chance to overleap them as Sue Bridehead or Jane Eyre had not. These essays were themselves the proof of that.

For another, she did not believe that conditions, however deforming, were determining. We all face them in one form or another. The question, given that, was what was inside you and what you did with it. Dorothy Wordsworth, Hardwick judged, had the gift of minute observation (as demonstrated in her celebrated journals) but "did not understand meter" and "lacked generalizing power." Her own poems were "not good," and her existence as her brother's sidekick ("she lived his life to the full") was in fact a blessing. Jane Carlyle, who wrote wonderful letters but never became the novelist we imagine she might have been, "lack[ed] ambition and need — the psychic need for a creation to stand outside herself."

"Ambition": a sacred word for Hardwick — it repeats in her essay on Plath — as was "discipline." She understood the gulf between potential and achievement and what it took to cross it. She also understood the difference between writing — real writing, finished work — and domestic substitutes. She admired Jane Carlyle and she respected housework, but the "truly staggering Victorian energy" that poured four years into *Oliver Cromwell*, and thirteen into *Frederick the Great*, belonged to her husband. "This is altogether different from nailing carpets and shaking out curtains." Dorothy's contribution to her brother's poetry — the shared walks and feelings — was an "illusion of collaboration." "This is the way for gifted, energetic wives of writers to a sort of composition of their own." Hardwick was, or had been, married to a writer, but she was not a writer's wife. She was a writer. Ambition, discipline, achievement.

And, in Hardwick's case, as these examples demonstrate, brutal frankness, a quality for which she was famous and feared — in the parlor, the classroom, the pages of an essay — and that is nowhere more in evidence than in the volume's title piece. The seduced, she loudly implies, want to be: "guile and insistence are clever at uncovering pockets of complicity." As for the betrayed, they shouldn't be surprised. That is love:

it goes wrong. For those who merely suffer under their betrayal — Hetty Sorrel in *Adam Bede*, Arthur Dimmesdale in *The Scarlet Letter* — Hardwick feels pity but no respect. Dimmesdale "cannot ask fundamental questions about life." Hetty "hasn't the quality to be tragic. Instead she is something smaller and lesser — she is miserable." The tragic qualities are courage, dignity, fortitude, endurance, and these depend on an acceptance of "the griefs of experience," "the command of necessity" — the reality of "life." They mark the difference between the victim and the heroine. Tess is the latter: "She is not surprised by loss and rejection and therefore never degraded by it." In light of the circumstances under which they were written, those words were an act of self-rescue indeed. "The betrayed heroine," Hardwick goes on, "unlike the merely betrayed woman, is never under the illusion that love or sex confers rights upon human beings."

The composition of the essays in *Seduction and Betrayal* coincided not only with Lowell's fresh abandonment but also with the heyday of second-wave feminism. *Ms.* was founded in 1971; the ERA passed Congress in 1972; *Roe* was decided in 1973. The volume went against the movement's grain and was received within it less than gladly. Assertions like the notion that Clarissa's rape "may be a crime, but it is not exactly a betrayal of her expectations" — from the title essay, which was first delivered as a lecture at Vassar, no less — were not designed to flatter the party line. Hardwick's own view of the movement was dim, seeing it as mostly "bad writing, bald simplicity, and simple-mindedness."

In retrospect, the limitation was partly hers. Having lived from old to new, or relatively new, she couldn't imagine the next step, a world of full equality in which Elizabeth Lowell split the household duties with their husbands fifty-fifty (in which Elizabeth Hardwick didn't have to be Elizabeth Lowell at all). But she also knew things that she saw the movement — and the era's social utopianism more broadly — as having failed to learn. She knew that human beings, women no less than men, tend to disappoint the roles that ideologies script for them. Women have an erotic relationship to caregiving, she sometimes implies, for example, as men do to power. She also knew that while the tragic qualities may be in short supply, tragedy itself is not a choice. "Flirtation, surrender, pregnancy, misery. This is the plot of existence." Sex, she told the age of Kinsey and the pill, is not the solution — "the body is a poor vessel for transcendence" — nor even is love, "love with its ancient distresses." What she mourned was not this, but the loss of a sense of the tragic in fiction and life — the era's slick mobility, its desperate insouciance. She turned and returned to an earlier age, the great age of the English novel, to find the depth she felt so lacking in the present.

Hardwick realized her own great novel not by emulating traditional forms, as she had in her earlier fiction, but by inventing her own. The true American artist, Harold Rosenberg had written, surveys their situation and "searches for the principle that applies, even if it applies only once." In *Sleepless Nights*, it applied only once. The work appeared in 1979, and, in its associative movement, owes something to Renata Adler's *Speedboat* (1976) and to Didion's fictions of the 1970s, *Play It As It Lays* and *A Book of Common Prayer*, but it is unique, in Hardwick's corpus and the world. She never wrote another novel; one feels she didn't need to. It is one of those books in which a writer states their entire being. It is a novel with no plot, no character development, no resolution. It is a memoir, fictionalized, that avoids discussion of the self. It is largely a series of sketches of people she has known, from Billie Holiday to the woman who does her laundry, interleaved with invisible art. It has no apparent structure, yet its structure feels unshakable, recalling Lily Briscoe's thought in *To the Lighthouse*: "on the surface, feathery and evanescent, one colour melting into another like the colours on a butterfly's wing; but beneath the fabric [is] clamped together with bolts of iron." It is all voice, mood, sensibility, address.

She is lying awake — the title's premise, not explained until the final line but everywhere implied. She is writing "Dearest M" (Mary McCarthy), calling out in thought, composing letters in her head. She is reassembling her life, her self, from fragments of memory glued together by imagination, yet finding that the self does not cohere so much as flow: "On the battered calendar of the past...I had imagined there would be felicitous notations...And myself there, marking the day with an *I*...And yet the old pages of the days and weeks are splattered with the dark-brown rings of coffee cups and I find myself gratefully dissolved in the grounds as the water drips downward." She is thinking of others, mostly women, mostly distressed, downhearted, downtrodden. Hardwick's sympathy for ordinary people was the treasure that she carried with her from Kentucky. That laundress, Ida; bag ladies; a "failed mezzo," Miss Cramer; a local girl who turned to prostitution out of willfulness or nameless need; her mother — refracted selves, paths she might have taken or could still. It is a book about time, what it does to us.

Much of the novel happens elsewhere — in Kentucky; in Maine, where she summered; in Boston, where she and Lowell lived for much of the 1950s; in Amsterdam, where they spent a year — but it is thoroughly a New York book. Its movement is the movement of memory, of gossip, one story calling forth another, but it is also the movement of a walker in the city, of serial encounters on the sidewalk, figures looming up, fates etched on faces, then dropping back, receding. Hardwick lived on West 67th Street, a few doors down from Central Park, for nearly fifty years. "I never heard Elizabeth Hardwick say, 'I took a walk in the park,'" Pinckney writes. "What she wanted when she went out were shops, sidewalks, traffic, to be among strangers on Main Street, the small-town girl's dream." In fact, the whole book happens in New York, in her bedroom, in the mind of a New Yorker, consciousness sending out feelers, reaching around corners, peering in windows. In the background is "the birdsong of rough, grinding trucks in the street."

Manhattan, she would later write, "is not a city of memory, not a family city." People come and go; the city is always destroying itself, "overthrow[ing] the future before it arrives." She makes a memory for it, gathering an ad hoc family of New York strangers. The final chapter centers on the rooming houses where she passed her early years. Working women, talkative and secretive, some young and transient, some older, defiant, "as if to say: You cannot destroy a ruin." Solitary New York women, together in "the strange apartment with its peculiar cells for the protection of a vast, overwhelming privacy." Lives lived apart in close proximity. "Someone is running a bath, someone is listening to the late-night preacher on the radio." Now, forty years later, the narrator is old herself, is solitary once again, is back to listening to noises from the nearby rooms, the sounds of other lives, which keep her company across the sleepless nights.

The novel changed the way that Hardwick wrote. It was followed by a set of stories that were even more associative in form. "Cross-town," "The Bookseller," "Back Issues," "On the Eve": set in New York, they read like outtakes from the book, or further thoughts, more New York lives recorded in her loose and brisk notation, colored by her sympathetic irony. But her criticism grew associative as well. She taught herself to make an essay travel like a conversation. This was her late style, which she practiced through her middle eighties. Instead of laying out an argument in sequence, she would hover over points, digress, move on, circle back. Transitions became abrupt, or absent, or occurred within a paragraph. Sometimes paragraphs themselves were mini-essays, related to each other only by accumulation. And yet because she somehow seemed to be able to talk about several things at once — the work, the life, the biography under review — she could always recover from the digression, pick up a dropped thread, move on in whatever direction she chose. She would end with an aside, an evocation rather than conclusion, or with an unexpected point that she had, as it were, just thought of. She had more to say but her time was up, so she was going to say goodbye now, the end.

ADRIAN NATHAN WEST

The World as an Institute

In August 1990, the recently retired Dutch ethnologist Johannes Jacobus Voskuil had a dream: he lay in his coffin and was carried to his grave while a song he had heard hundreds of times — Sidney Bechet's rendition of "Nobody Knows When You're Down and Out" — played in the background. He heard the crunch of gravel under the pallbearers' feet. After a while, the soft swaying over others' shoulders stopped, and he felt himself being lowered to the ground. As faint murmurs arose, and the footfalls died away, he lifted the lid of his coffin and sat up to watch the attendees depart. Those at the tail of the funeral train he didn't know; those at the head were now too far away to recognize. Lying back, letting the lid settle over him again, he remained awake, "overwhelmed by a feeling of limitless sorrow."

A month later, Voskuil began work on *Meneer Beerta* (*Mister Beerta*) an autobiographical novel chronicling eight years in the life of his alter ego, Maarten Koning, at the Bureau for Dialectology, Folklore, and Onomastics in Amsterdam. By July 1991 he had moved onto a sequel, *Vuile Handen* (*Dirty Hands*). He would continue writing at an average pace of around four pages a day, until by 1995 he had finished the longest novel written in Dutch, and one of the longest novels ever written, entitled *Het Bureau* (*The Office* or *The Institute*) which appeared in seven volumes from 1996 to 2000.

On its surface, the premise is anything but promising: a not-quite-young man in need of work looks up a former professor, who offers him a job as a researcher for an Atlas for Folk Culture, investigating such topics as beliefs about the *kabouter*, a sort of leprechaun or gnome. Maarten accepts the post against the spirited protests of his wife Nicolien, because he must have a job, and because he feels that, of the two of them, he will better tolerate steady employment. For five thousand pages, he goes to work every day, produces an exhaustive record of petty squabbles, malingerings, and the vicissitudes of his field of *volkskunde* — commonly translated as folkloristics or ethnology, though neither term fully encompasses the breadth of the Dutch, especially given the transformations *volkskunde* underwent in Voskuil's time. Well over half of the novel consists of dialogue: transcriptions of committee meetings, domestic arguments, conversations with barbers or shopkeepers, and a decades-long exchange with a psychologically disturbed friend named Frans Veen. As transformations overwhelm his workplace, the former

Bureau for Dialect, Folklore, and Onomastics, known from 1979 onward as the A.P. Beerta Institute, Maarten chooses to take early retirement, only to find that the backdrop of his life has disappeared, and he is "adrift like a balloon in the sky."

He returns to the office periodically, to finish a few lectures and essays; his colleagues greet him first with tolerance, then indifference, then hostility; finally, his desk is taken away and his papers piled up in the corner. He never believed in his work, and had described himself and his coworkers as "belonging to a reservoir of superfluous intellects society no longer needs, who must be given some pointless task to keep them off the street." What had kept him going for thirty years, he believed, was solidarity, but he now realizes that it was a mirage. "Despite his skepticism, and against his better judgment, he had wanted to believe, deep in his heart, in his people, as like Gideon's band of three hundred. Only now, with the slow passage of time, did he realize he had knowingly deceived himself."

There is no sex and no romance, there is scant adventure only apathetically described, there are no noble heroes, no dastardly villains, no deathbed penitence or hidden treasure. Yet *Het Bureau* has gained a hold on the Dutch imagination comparable to the fever caused elsewhere by *Harry Potter* or Stieg Larsson's *Millennium* trilogy. It has sold hundreds of thousands of copies, is perpetually out at the libraries, has inspired a radio play and a graphic novel adaptation; for a time the Meertens Instituut, the real-life counterpart of Maarten Koning's office in the novel, offered guided tours, and there was even an exhibition at which institute employees mentioned in the book stood at their desks, ready to converse with fans. There have been reports of Dutch office workers nicknaming their colleagues after those they most resemble in the novel. More than one person, chronically ill, sought special permission from Voskuil's publisher to see proofs of the novels later volumes before release, in order to die in peace, knowing how Maarten's story ended.

In my own experience, mention of the book among the Dutch gives rise to an almost conspiratorial sort of amity like that which once brought together fans of *The Wire* in the United States, but with an added note of gratitude, because the Netherlands is a country that outsiders rarely bother to learn much about. The untraveled and uncultured can trot out stereotypes about snooty Frenchmen, lusty Latins, stolid Russians, and orderly Germans, but how many under fifty have any sense of the proverbial frankness and frugality that inspired the terms "Dutch uncle" and "going Dutch"? Neither in Europe nor in the United States have I had the sense that Dutch culture matters much to anyone: Rembrandt, sure, or the diary of Anne Frank, or Cees Nooteboom or Gerald Reve for the really well-read, but these references run out soon, and pale in comparison to the significance of Amsterdam as a budget airline destination for the cannabis-and-sex-tourists who have made much of its historic center almost uninhabitable. For these reasons, and perhaps because of the relatively scant attention received by Gerd Busse's heroic translation of the entirety of *Het Bureau* into German, critics have debated whether there is something specifically and irreducibly Dutch about Voskuil that would impede his success in other languages.

This is nonsense. *Het Bureau* is a masterpiece almost unique in its accessibility, dense with humor and sorrow, and ecumenical in its concerns. It is the sort of book you live with, feeling sorrow as the pages turn, and in the weeks since I finished it I have more than once felt maudlin, wondering when my copies of Voskuil's diaries would arrive so that I can get another fix. Even now, reopening the first volume to check something, I was consoled by the recollection that it was still there, and I could start over whenever I wished.

Frequently remarked upon is Voskuil's capacity to show the interest in boring things, the interest even in boredom itself. In volume four of *Het Bureau*, his protagonist, Maarten, tells one of his closest colleagues, Ad Muller, about his research into threshing techniques. Ad replies he could get excited over a simple farming implement, and Maarten counters, "When you immerse yourself in something, it becomes interesting as a matter of course." *Het Bureau* depends on this principle of immersion, and its form is intended to frustrate readers who imagine they can skim and still get the point. On this, Voskuil was categorical:

> A book should be thick, a book should be detailed, a book should be "tedious" for those who are not my true readers. If you are able, you should scare readers away. Then, you'll be left with those you can trust.

[All translations are mine throughout.]

This principle is nicely illustrated by Maarten's minute observations of his *bête noire*, Bart Asjes, a fellow researcher whose variations on the phrase "I have serious objections" have a rhythmic Bartlebyesque insistence. At first one forgives his peculiarities, before growing frustrated with his finickiness and finally beginning to sense something sinister in his supposed probity, the lone effect of which is to stall or derail every possible initiative, while offering no constructive alternatives because, as he never wearies of reminding Maarten, that is *his* responsibility. Their relationship at times takes on a morbid quality, with Maarten's attention to him a form of tormented distress, as Bart's every movement is subjected to surveillance in anticipation of discord in the wings:

> Bart returned from the card catalogue room. He greeted Ad, sat at his desk, and began to type with short, hard strokes. "Hey!" he said every time he made an error. He then erased the incorrect letter and typed the right one in its place.

The moment is mundane, the prose is lacking in ornament; what gives it its bizarre power (and this is true of *Het Bureau* as a whole) is the patient reprisal of related incidents, like the inexorable lapping of waves, that gives shape to a character not as a pendant to the protagonist's story but as a quantum of his life.

Voskuil shows, like Natalia Ginzburg or Chekhov, that syntactic virtuosity is often a matter more of self-regard than art, and may introduce an air of contrivance that is detrimental to real pathos. At some point in the discussion of any long novel, you have to get it over with and talk about Proust, so I may as well say it here: weepy as I get when Bergotte dies on a settee at an exhibition of Dutch paintings after admiring the "patch of yellow wall" in a Vermeer, the scene strikes me, if I'm honest, as flowery babble, and almost dishonorable in its sponging of religious principles in pursuit of aesthetic rapture. There is no "world based on kindness, scrupulousness, self-sacrifice… which we leave in order to be born on this earth," and

Liberties

since it does not exist, we will not return there, and Bergotte inhabits no ether where the precepts of his heart reign, he is just dead and rotting in a coffin.

Contrast with this the death of Maarten Koning's father, a disillusioned old socialist and newspaper man, who in retirement continues to write editorials every morning that he then tears into tiny pieces and throws away. He grows grumpier, his gait slows, his mind wanders; one day he is taken to the hospital; he despises the doctors' cluelessness, and the nurses telling him when to drink, when to eat, when to piss, asking him patronizingly whether the flowers his son brought him aren't nice. When Maarten wishes to know whether he is afraid of dying, he responds, with unsettling honesty, "I'm not... But of course I don't know whether I will be afraid when the moment comes." "God, what an end," he says elsewhere amid interminable bedside conversations crowded with bromides, insipid gossip, medical trivia, words uttered to pass the time. One day Maarten's wife tells him that she thinks his father wants to hold his hand. Maarten does so gingerly, but realizes that the old man is asleep, and the couple goes home. An hour later, Maarten's brother calls him to tell him their father is gone.

A similar tenderness is evident in Voskuil's portrayal of Nicolien's mother's dementia, which begins with an untoward crying fit when Maarten and his wife change residence and ends with her in a nursing home, unsure where she is and who is who, constantly repeating "Oh, yes," as though understanding were still possible, as though she could yet hold onto all the facts needed to retain a clear picture of the world. It is there, too, in rare moments of joy, as when Maarten recovers his pipe the day after the bowl detached from it and rolled into the waters of the bay as he was knocking it against a stone bollard. The pipe has no history; it is not a prized inheritance from a favorite uncle, a keepsake from a long-lost friend, a costly indulgence or a reminder of happier days. It is just something Maarten likes, a piece of his world, and when he lies in bed holding back tears because he thinks it gone, Voskuil doesn't coddle the reader with explanations why.

I might remark here on the contrast with another, more famous, comparably massive fictional project: the six volumes of Karl Ove Knausgaard's *My Struggle*. At the peak of Knausgaard fever in America, one had the sense that this was something unprecedented, but even within European literature *My Struggle* already formed part of a tradition of long novels that struggle between the competing tendencies of radical intimacy and radical objectivity in the search for autobiographical truth. Exemplary in this regard are Gerhard Roth's *Archive des Schweigens* (*Archives of Silence*), Peter Kurzeck's *Das alte Jahrhundert* (*The Old Century*), and *De harde Kern* (*The Hard Core*) by Voskuil's friend Frida Vogels, who appears in *Het Bureau* under the name Henriette Fagel. Knausgaard shares with some of these older writers, and certainly with Voskuil, what Frederic Jameson has called the "itemized" approach to description. Knausgaard distinguishes himself from them through the consciously metafictional nature of his endeavor: *My Struggle* cannot be separated from the public and private scandals around it, which form much of the material of the later volumes. It also evinces a confidence in the author's analytical powers, with regard to autobiographical memories and even with the thoughts of others, that has more in common with the omniscient first-person of the eighteenth- and nineteenth-century novel than with the hesitancy to explain that characterizes both *Het Bureau* and the projects mentioned above.

This hesitancy is essential to *Het Bureau*'s effect, which

combines a feeling of profound familiarity with bafflement, even despair at why things happen as they do. Voskuil shuns the mantle of creator: he is instead a chronicler (he repeatedly insists that nothing in the book is invented and that conversations are recorded verbatim) whose concern is to intrude as little as possible on the transcript of events. Though in all aspects Maarten Koning's life resembles his own, the third person that Voskuil employs is unusually opaque: even his most private thoughts, in the form of diary excerpts, are artifact rather than proof. Voskuil strives for a representation of a single subjectivity in the most objective possible terms — a subjectivity that is also subjection to the myriad realities, some material, others impalpable, that define an individual self, but of which that self is never master.

Het Bureau is a self-contained story, but Maarten Koning exists elsewhere — in the novel *Bij nader inzien* (*Upon Closer Inspection*), written in 1963, and in *Binnen de huid* (*Within the Skin*), written between 1964 and 1968 but published a year after Voskuil's death. Both books show a protagonist at odds with the world: in the first, he is a radical university student taken with the illusion that he and his friends might live together, true to their values, forever, and who stands by in disappointment as they marry, get jobs, and adapt to the demands of convention. (Not immune to the allurements of revenge offered by the *roman-à-clef*, Voskuil used *Bij nader inzien* to send a message to his comrades: "This is what you said, and this is what you did.") *Binnen de huid* is an account of Voskuil's own capitulation in turn. In it, Maarten is married to Nicolien, and his friend Paul is married to Rosalie. Maarten and Nicolien disdain her

— she is the one, they think, who turned Paul from a Francophile would-be poet to a teacher and paragon of bourgeois conformism. Yet Maarten falls crazily in love with Rosalie, and Nicolien begins a relationship with Paul. Neither affair leads anywhere, and Maarten learns that he, too, lacks the courage of his convictions: "I began to suspect that betrayal was the only way of staying alive, and that all I'd done thus far was postpone the execution."

Ironically, Maarten becomes a teacher himself — briefly — in Groningen, in the north; he quits this job just before *Het Bureau* begins. I hasten to add that there is no need for pious distinctions between biography and fiction, or boring reflections on auto-fiction, in the case of Voskuil. He is quite straightforward: in interviews, he refers to himself and his protagonist interchangeably; in histories of the Meertens Institut, more than one writer has mistakenly referred to real people by the names Voskuil assigns them in his novel; and in *Binnen de huid,* when Paul comments on the mistake of confusing an author with his main character, Maarten chides him, "That is the only way you should read."

Those acquainted with the earlier novels will recall Voskuil's contempt for science — *wetenschap* in Dutch, which, like *Wissenschaft* in German, describes not just the hard sciences but the systematic pursuit of scholarly knowledge in general. Maarten's willingness to make an exception for *volkskunde* is partly a result of his indolence — he needs to do something, daydreams of being a farmer, or a baker like his grandfather, but seems to sense that fate has marked him to be an urban intellectual — and partly of his impression of the disreputable nature of the field. Dominated, since the mid-nineteenth century, by a search for what used to be called "the genius of the people," Dutch folkloristics had long placed special emphasis on supposed continuities among Germanic peoples in a way that dovetailed with the Nazis' racial thinking. Several significant figures in Dutch folklore studies and ethnology were prominent supporters of the Nazi occupiers, and the broad rebuke to the discipline after the end of the Second World War led to a more discreet approach, with a focus on documentation to the detriment of grand theories. For Maarten, this means the opportunity to labor in the dark: to send out questionnaires, conduct field research, clip newspaper articles, and fill out file cards free from the obligations entailed by institutional prestige.

Maarten pursues his work under the auspices of Anton Beerta, a fussy and aloof gay man who drops frequent, tacit hints about his sexuality while at the same time scorning what he calls "homos." The Atlas for Popular Culture, which he hires Maarten to work on, is "a Dutch-Flemish initiative that dated from the time before the war, when Beerta, like so many of his persuasion, was an ardent believer in the idea of the Greater Netherlands," that is, the unification of Dutch-speaking territories severed during the Eighty Years' War into the Dutch Republic and the Catholic Netherlands — precursors to the modern Netherlands and Belgium, respectively. Beerta's enthusiasm has vanished by the time of Maarten's arrival, and his chief passion has become the joining of as many committees as possible. Maarten looks to Beerta as a paragon, "the living proof that it was possible to shield oneself from the world so much that one became untouchable." To his friend Klaas and to his wife, who would have preferred that he become a postman, Maarten explains:

> If Beerta hadn't offered me the job, I wouldn't have sought it out. I accepted it because we were out of money

and I think Berta believes in nothing, just as I do. He has built the perfect alibi for himself, and in its shadow he can live a life of his own. At present, I feel that's the only solution. At least if you don't want to hold your hand out and beg.

Nicolien suspects from the first that Maarten's employment in the office is a mistake. Her interminable, hysterical grousing is one of *Het Bureau*'s high points; it is impossible not to laugh at her limitless indignation as Maarten cowers, and is scolded for cowering; clams up, and is scolded for his silence; protests, and is exposed to infernal fury. That so little resentment ensues from their fights is due to Nicolien's role as Maarten's conscience: she knows that he won't stop at being a researcher, that papers and lectures will follow, that a late evening at the office or a Saturday spent polishing an essay are not fleeting obligations, but harbingers of a future in which he will commit himself rigorously to a respectable role in a society he has always claimed to despise.

Some of the novel's greatest moments of humor are owed to the tension between Beerta's outsized pretensions and Maarten's indurate skepticism. After Beerta promises the Commission — Voskuil favors such vague designations as the Office, the Main Office, the Commission — that the Atlas of Folk Culture will be completed by his retirement, he asks Maarten how long it will actually take. Reminding Beerta that he has worked for twenty-five years on the yet-to-be-published first volume, or better twenty, subtracting five years for the war, and that the Atlas is projected to run to twenty volumes, he arrives at the figure of four hundred years. "But I was the only one here," Beerta tells him. "And now I have you." "Fine, two hundred years," Maarten replies.

In fact, the *Volkskunde-Atlas voor Nederland en Vlaams België*, edited by P.J. Meertens and Maurits de Meyer (Anton Beerta and Jan Vanhamme in the novel), which began to appear in 1959, met a somewhat ignoble end, ceasing publication after four volumes. It was criticized for the superficial nature of its analysis, its haphazard selection of themes, and a lack of rigor in its approach to the diffusion of folk customs. Volume IV, *Het ophangen van de nageboorte van het paard* (*The Hanging of the Afterbirth of the Horse*), written entirely by Voskuil, consists of a hundred-page commentary on a single map showing where, in Belgium and the Netherlands, the afterbirth of horses is traditionally burned, buried, thrown on a dung heap, or hung from a tree. In *Het Bureau,* Maarten is proud enough of his work on the subject, which represents the first time the Bureau has managed to locate one of the cultural boundaries that are in principle essential to its labor, that he scolds Beerta's failure to recognize its "historical significance." But Maarten himself cannot well say why this difference exists, and eventually, he will forsake the geographical method, abandoning the idea of fixed cultural tendencies in favor of a study of processes whose relationship to tradition is rarely reducible to practices persisting across time.

Were the years not marked — these are the only chapter divisions in the book — readers of *Het Bureau* might struggle to situate it in time. History intrudes overtly only when it affects Maarten Koning's life: the Vietnam War appears twice, once as Maarten's justification for voting for the Pacifist Socialist Party, and once when he and his wife attend an antiwar demonstration. The most significant mention of apartheid occurs when Maarten turns down an offer of collaboration from a professor at the University of Stellenbosch and must defend himself to the Bureau and the

Commission. Yet there are aspects of history that ought not be ignored. The fate of the Bureau, for example, is dependent on economic developments in the Netherlands: political shifts and GDP growth as high as eight percent per annum from the early 1960s to the late 1970s encouraged massive social spending in a climate in which, as one historian put it, "a successful minister was defined as one who could get a larger share of the pie."

In this context, the bureaucracy expands vertiginously, leaving Maarten to fight for resources with his colleagues in Dialectology and the Music Archive. (Onomastics, the preserve of Beerta's successor Jaap Balk, seems barely to exist for him.) A symbol for this expansion is the card catalogue that Maarten maintains, which by 1976 has reached one million cards and continues to grow at around fifty thousand entries per year, recording the sleeping attire of informants in the countryside, details about threshing practices, the text of press clippings, the titles of books, and cross-references to superstitions involving the severed fingers and hands of thieves. So long as things are flush, no one bothers asking whether this endless notation has a point, and when Maarten's staff asks he gleefully tells them there isn't one; but with economic stagnation, austerity measures make their appearance in 1980, along with the new managerial language of productivity measures, self-evaluations, efficiency, and output.

Before this happens, however, Maarten has a revelation about his work. It comes in volume five, *En ook weemoedigheid* (*And Melancholy, Too*), which takes its title from the penultimate stanza of the modern Flemish writer Willem Elsschot's haunting poem, "Marriage," in which a husband dreams of beating his wife to death, setting fire to his home, and running away:

> But bludgeon her he didn't, for between dream and deed
> Stand laws and practical objections,
> And melancholy, too, which no one can explain,
> But comes in evening when we go to sleep.

At conferences for the European Atlas of Folk Culture, one of the many obligations that he has piled on himself in the course of his career, Maarten comes to condemn the geographical method favored by Beerta and, previously, himself, and casts doubt on the very idea of culture and tradition. Already in volume four, he tells his staff that *volkskunde* stands at a crisis point: the idea that the distribution of customs contains clues to a distant past has been disproven, and a new basis must be found if the science is to move forward. This new basis he finds in a psychological approach to ethnology. Traditions, he believes, respond to psychological needs; he will later describe them as remission points in historical processes that address anxieties about changing identities.

Illustrative of Voskuil's thinking here is his essay "*De weg naar luilekkerland*" ("The Road to the Land of Milk and Honey"), described in *Het Bureau* with characteristic dismissiveness as his "bread research." Voskuil begins by noting the longstanding stereotype of a north-south divide between rye and wheat bread consumption that was dispelled when he mapped informants' responses about bread consumption for the Meertens Instituut in 1974. He did find a clear geographical divide, but it was between east and west, which was logical given the appropriateness of the two grains to the clay soils of the southwest and the sandy soils to the east. He explains anomalies in this general pattern with reference to rinderpest, which forced a transition from cattle breeding to grain cultivation; the importation of wheat from the Baltics; and eventual improvements of infrastructure, which flooded the Netherlands with cheap American wheat and eliminated availability as a factor in dietary preferences. He attributes the persistence of a partiality to rye bread to "a rapid expansion of the intellectual elite."

> The new intellectuals are a product of the provinces and the lower middle classes, and much later of the working class. They enter a milieu where they find it difficult to adjust and have problems with their identity. To compensate, they may attempt to adapt fully to their new environment; on the other hand, they may adopt a defiant posture based on the ideal image they hold of the class they proceed from. This representation will be ideal because they are psychologically cut off from the values of their elders. This may manifest itself in coarse manners, coarse clothing, coarse food, coarse language, and (if their numbers are large enough) in a change in prevailing norms.

Reading this, I couldn't help but think of the paradoxes that produce, say, the mixologist who keeps his ice saw in a leather tool belt while making high-priced tiki drinks for hedge funders, or tech millionaires in hoodies and jeans, or the class ambivalences that inspired Nordstrom's Barracuda Jeans with their artificial mud coating and Balenciaga's eighteen-hundred-dollar "super-destroyed" sneakers.

Het Bureau presents few indications of Voskuil's theoretical forebears, and given the contrast between his narrow research interests and his fundamentally literary inclination, it is hard to say which of his ideas are borrowed and which he hit upon independently. He mentions *Tristes Tropiques*. He must have been aware of Georg Simmel. The most prominent thinker he cites is Norbert Elias, who resided in Amsterdam for the last decade of his life and whose book *The Civilizing Process* provoked heated debates among Dutch sociologists beginning in the late 1960s, when the revised German edition appeared. Maarten's first mention of him is contemptuous, but increasingly his own research will similarly renounce broad-brush conceptual explanations (the German sociologist Peter Gleichmann referred to Elias's approach as "concept avoidance") in favor of a model of social change rooted in alterations in the self-interpretation of individuals when their *habitus*, that is, the practices that define them as members of a given social group, must react to novel circumstances.

Strange here is the total absence of Voskuil's near-contemporary Paul Feyerabend, the philosopher of science who was a convinced positivist in his early years but became one of the most trenchant critics of established science. In his paper "The Problem of the Existence of Theoretical Entities," Feyerabend controversially subverted the distinction between objects observable to the senses and those present only to the mind. With the phrase "all empirically observable entities are theoretical entities," he both furnished a sensory basis for theoretical constructs and introduced radical uncertainty as to the possibility of any one perspective establishing priority in its understanding of the world.

To the extent that *Het Bureau* embodies a kind of ethnology of the office, its observational rigor is aligned to an almost solipsistic adherence to a single perspective. This gave rise to objections among those portrayed in it, not only privately but in the press and on television. Ton Dekker, the model for Ad Muller, has mounted a particularly vigorous rebuttal of Voskuil's portrayal of him. Responding to his critics, Voskuil was at once blithe and peremptory: the novel was not about other people, it was about his experience of other people. Moreover, "they should be happy to finally hear how I experienced them in all these years. After all, you never really hear what someone thinks of you."

Pournelle's Iron Law of Bureaucracy states that with time, the control of bureaucracies inevitably passes from the hands of those devoted to the ends for which the bureaucracy was conceived into the hands of those devoted to the perpetuation of the bureaucracy itself. Maarten sees this in action as the long arc of *Het Bureau* draws to a close. Anyone who has worked in Europe and seen the absurd psychology of institutional-legitimation-through-English will roll their eyes when a new director comes on board with the ambition of transforming the Bureau into a "Center of Excellence," while higher-ups at the Ministry float the proposal that the Bureau's yearbook, concerned exclusively with Dutch dialectology, onomastics, and folkloristics, be published in English to give their research an international reach.

These institutional changes, which only accelerate as Maarten announces his imminent retirement in 1987, accompany more profound changes in Maarten's frame of mind. He is getting old. He is scared of foreigners and young people; the constant din of automobiles maddens him; new policies giving women priority at university strike him as absurd. There is a sort of contemporary reader, nourished on writers who use fiction to promote an ideal version of themselves so that their admirers can in turn fabricate ideal versions of themselves, who will find this degree of sincerity distasteful; but I would defer here to Lousje Voskuil, who stresses the central role of accountability in her late husband's writings. Gerard Rooijakkers writes that for Voskuil "the one freedom a person has is the freedom of (self) reflection: to find out how and why things happened, how people (willingly) misunderstood each other, and, of course, the overpowering inevitability of it all." And Voskuil was not one to deny himself this freedom simply to look good before others.

Maarten's aging has much in common with Jean Améry's notion of the elderly person as "outmoded in an incurable way," watching a new era come into being before his eyes at the same time as it recedes from his grasp. He rails against the incursion of the computer into the Bureau, is dismayed when his colleague Ad Muller puts in an order to replace his old, sturdy wooden chair for a "bigshot chair... a jerkoff chair," a padded office chair. Maarten's disappointment doesn't grow with the passing of years, because he has never had the illusion that his life at the office had meaning. In *Meneer Beerta*, he tells a friend, "With every step I take, I have the feeling I am moving further away from myself." Five thousand pages later, in *Afgang*, which I will translate for convenience's sake as Debacle, he confirms the truth of this intuition, adding that even the pretense that he would know himself better when he was old has failed to hold up. Het Bureau is a novel not of revelation, but of dogged persistence in error and of the refusal to mitigate the gravity of this error by indictments of the malfeasance of others or the cop-out that everyone does the best they can.

A commonplace among reviewers of *Het Bureau*, put forward to buttress critics' perplexity that a novel so superficially banal should prove so deeply engaging, is that nothing happens in it. But this is not true in the least. What disarms readers, I think, is the lack of hierarchy among its events. In most fiction, there is little doubt about what you must attend to and what you can ignore. In Voskuil, either everything counts or nothing does. There is a sense in which things speed up in the later volumes, but this is a question less of fictional constraints than of time: in *Afgang*, Anton Beerta, Frans Veen, and Nicolien's mother all die, because Maarten has reached the age when people start dying. These figures are portrayed movingly, and their end has a clear import, but the undeviating rigor of Maarten's introspection, and the discontinuity of any given episode in the novel, biases readers in favor of whatever instant is before them, whether it be one of Maarten's strikingly rendered dreams, the pettiness of a colleague trying to appropriate more room for his department, or the contemplation of a coffee bean on the floor:

> While sweeping the kitchen floor, he found a coffee bean. He went to throw it in the trash with the dust, but changed his mind. A bean like that had been grown in South America, had been plucked, shipped, roasted, and packaged. This is nonsense, he thought, but he couldn't bring himself to throw it out, and he dropped it into the coffee grinder. When, after grinding, he spilled some coffee on the counter, he hesitated before wiping up, but this time, only as a matter of consistency. Because a ground bean meant nothing to him, no more than a piece of meat in which he no longer recognized an animal.

Liberties

At the end of his retirement dinner, preceded by a ceremony at the Bureau with gifts, honors, and speeches, Maarten, walking home with unsure steps, turns to his wife, full of feeling, and tells her, "Anyway, I think they liked me." When she keeps silent, he continues, "Don't you think?" Nicolien responds, "I don't know." The final volume of *Het Bureau*, *De dood van Maarten Koning* (*The Death of Maarten Koning*), will show how little his life has meant. If earlier he described himself as an ape in a cage, he now struggles with the unmitigated open. He starts repairing things around the home, to Nicolien's consternation, takes long walks around Amsterdam, rides his bicycle, gives direction to strangers, more an observer than a participant in the world. He has a dream one night that he is back at the office, and Karel Ravelli, Beerta's longtime companion, calls him. "I thought you were retired," he says. Maarten tells him he still has a few matters to take care of. "Yeah, that's what everyone says," Karel responds. Maarten's work at the Bureau, which consisted of combing through endless primary sources in order to extract data on abstruse topics for the buttressing of dubious hypotheses, was by its very nature an endeavor not subject to conclusion, but his guiding delusion has always been that its incompleteness demanded redress; and even when he is not compelled to go there, the feeling of things unfinished at the office continues to exert its pull.

But there is something more here, something difficult to grasp, related to the perception of time in Voskuil's writings, which he hinted at in a radio interview in 1996. "The curious thing about working at such an office is that as soon as you turn your back on it, melancholy ensues." Voskuil then describes the experience of attending conferences, which are an unqualified torment for Maarten and inevitably occasion migraines and fits of vomiting: you are brought together in a small space with people you don't like, but "you turn your back on them, you go home, and it seems you have left behind an oasis of peace." This is a small example of the way Voskuil disentangles the perception of the objects of thought in past, present, and future. His great virtue lies in the renunciation of any attempt at reconciling these modes of time, the admission that there is no true and final account of experience. In his arguments with Nicolien, or his attempts to grasp what his life at the office has meant, he concedes that even the act of recollection exerts a distorting effect on the thing being recollected. In sum: his work has been meaningless, and it has also been his primary source of meaning; the office was once purgatory, and now it feels as if it had been a haven.

Complicating this is an unstated vision of personality as a tension between elemental feelings, which prey upon Maarten independent of his environment. Vulnerability is perhaps the most basic of these: "Maarten felt threatened" is the most frequently repeated sentence in the novel. For nearly thirty years, the threats come from colleagues and rivals in the profession. But when he retires, instead of vanishing, the peril merely migrates: now he worries about nuclear war, surly young people on the train, death, the decline of culture. His essential posture is fearful and defensive, longing for a safe harbor that is always somewhere else.

Maarten's initial excuse for returning to the Bureau is to hand in a set of page proofs. By this point, even the colossally irascible Nicolien has thrown in the towel. She asks if he couldn't just send them; he responds that doing so is a nuisance; she tells him, "You know best." When he rings the doorbell at the Bureau, an unfamiliar doorman lets him in. Maarten tells him he used to work there, adding pathetically, "Look, there's my name." Initially he is received warmly, but there are nefarious doings afoot. Maarten's replacement is a careerist, "a Catholic tyrant, a brute," and still worse, "the author of fifty-two articles." (Maarten has previously declared that if less was published, "it would be an act of charity toward humanity.") The new head of the Institute, Dick van de Marel, a theoretical linguist who, Maarten suggests, applied for the job only to escape falling victim to budget cuts at the university, pushes out staff and institutes publication quotas, ignoring Maarten's warning that the quality of research will suffer in consequence. Worst of all, Ad Muller readily connives with both men to destroy Maarten's legacy.

The climax of *De dood van Maarten Koning* comes at the farewell gathering for Eef Batteljee, an employee in the Music Archive whom Maarten hired a decade before. None of the higher-ups at the office invite Maarten; Eef himself informs him privately that he is emigrating to work in his family's business in South Africa. When Maarten brings him a gift, Eef reveals the depths of Ad's betrayal: "Everything changed the very day you left... Everything you stood for has been dismantled and desecrated, and all in the name of a higher production." On his way out, Maarten sees his former colleagues in the stairwell, taking their cups of coffee to the celebration: one turns up her nose at him, one looks away, one stares at him with a triumphant smile. Later, two remorseful employees visit him at home (a third sends his greetings but stays away, afraid it will be bad for his career). From them, he learns how much he was hated by the people he supported and looked after.

The Swiss writer Hermann Burger uses the word *Grus* (in English, offal), a term of art from the tobacco trade for useless leavings that have fallen to the ground, to examine the problem of the superfluous in literature. Ilyusha's mother's fascination with the toy cannon in *The Brothers Karamazov*, the small string of tobacco that lies "coiled like a brown maggot" in *The Green Hat* — these are a kind of *Grus*: they have no obvious connection to the plot of the books they feature in, and yet they are things without which fiction has no point. *Het Bureau* abounds in these sorts of anecdotes, cameos, and finely observed details, and together they make the novel far more poignant and beautiful than anything I can convey here. I am thinking of when Maarten, in Hungary for a conference, asks a peasant woman whether her life has improved under communism, and an interpreter translates her response: "No, because she was young before, and back then her husband was still alive." Or of the fate of poor Slofstra, an eccentric older man sent to the Bureau by the employment office, whose favorite joke is to walk around repeating the phrase, *"Je parle toutes les langues, exceptée la langue française, parce-que c'est une langue très difficile."* Beerta compares him to a robot, but for Maarten he is "authentic," someone who has arrived at the Bureau because society has nowhere else for him. One day Slofstra brings Maarten a drawing of a farmhouse as a gift, because his wife, whom he met through a marriage agency, has told him that she can't stand looking at it anymore. When she decides to stick him in a nursing home, not because he is ill but because she is tired of having him around, she calls the Bureau to make sure his internment will not disrupt her collection of his retirement payments.

No less touching are the moments of vulnerability, such as the late nights in bed when Nicolien confesses her fears of old age and death. Hers is precisely the "special way of being afraid" that Philip Larkin described in "Aubade," made doubly bitter by the knowledge that she has gotten so little of the man she loves because he has given his life to an institution. And I have barely mentioned Voskuil's gift for comedy, which is in evidence on nearly every page: when Nicolien berates him for his audacity at moving a shelf, and his every attempt at fixing the error drives her to further degrees of outrage, I had to wipe tears of laughter from my eyes.

If we accept the idea that greatness in art partakes of the universal, then here I must come back to Proust and his points of comparison with Voskuil. Most of us never see the drawing rooms of the aristocracy or have an epiphany over a cup of tea, and few of us will glimpse in their involuntary memories a cathedral-like structure whose grandeur justifies our days of pampered idleness; but all of us, rich or poor, at some point in our lives, and many for the better part of our lives, will be made to sit in a chair and do something pointless which we will be told is the height of urgency. None is spared the sense that life, which could be the vessel of so much kindness and beauty, is stolen, frittered away in the need to fill out forms and surveys, make phone calls and xeroxes, attend to correspondence, all in an effort to justify one's existence on the basis of a job that one would rather have not had in the first place. This exasperation in the service of futility is a defining experience of the modern age, and *Het Bureau* is its epic.

ANNA BALLAN

Forever Taking Leave

Roland Barthes asked if we are "condemned to the adjective" when speaking of music, when attempting to put into words music's special way of pulling heartstrings and twisting guts; and in the case of Gustav Mahler one feels especially so condemned. It is difficult not to rhapsodize about Mahler. The descriptors accumulate on the tip of the tongue; a deluge of feeling engulfs us, and we can only in turn unleash our own deluge — of words. But words are pallid and limp before such beauty. Mahler induced even Arnold Schoenberg to rhapsody, a bit of purple prose to which I will return, while Daniel Barenboim lamented Mahler's status as "the only composer who is discussed mostly in non-musical terms" (the "only" here is arguable). One associates Mahler with the discourse of sheer feeling, not with "musical terms," for which we may have Visconti's *Death in Venice* happily to blame. And there is worse. Namedropped in Woody Allen films, indexed in Sondheim's "Ladies Who Lunch," framed as the preoccupying obsession of a certain Lydia Tár — one further associates Mahler with the glib stuff of urbane conversation, his rough edges sandpapered off in the smoother interests of sophistication and "culture." One can wearily sympathize perhaps with the anti-Wagnerian critic Eduard Hanslick:

> An intelligent musician will, therefore, get a much clearer notion of the character of a composition which he has not heard himself by being told that it contains, for instance, too many diminished sevenths, or too many tremolos, than by the most poetic description of the emotional crises through which the listener passed.

And yet one doesn't wish to dissect music like a cadaver. Bruno Walter, for his part, instructed that "no evaluation in strictly musical terms can be just" when approaching Mahler's corpus, for "his work was the outcome of his entire inner life... human as well as aesthetic values must enter in." Mahler himself seemed to invite such grandiose and holistic readings: in an exchange with Sibelius in 1907, he made his immortal remark that "the symphony must be like the world, it must embrace everything" (countering the austerity of the Finnish composer, who had declared that "I admire the symphony's style and severity of form"). It is a high-wire act, writing about music: to call up the aesthetic experience in all its aliveness, to analyze while avoiding death by analysis, one must tread carefully, barely grazing the edges of the thing to leave its integrity, its wholeness, and its separateness from ourselves intact. One must recognize it as an autonomous aesthetic reality even while attending to the overflowing subjectivity from which it sprung.

I want here to tread carefully over *Das Lied von der Erde*, "The Song of the Earth," the penultimate symphony that Mahler composed. I aim to give a brief chronicle of it, to ask what it means, and to begin to traverse its aesthetic, conceptual, and historical significations. It is a symphony that bids farewell to existence, looks death in the eye, radiates outward in a thousand shades of feeling: therefore I wish also to ask after its correspondence with life. "Nothing beautiful is separable from life," said Valéry, "and life is that which dies."

Das Lied von der Erde is popularly associated with the sources of acute grief that occasioned it. There was the death of Mahler's beloved daughter Maria; the revelation of his own congenital heart condition; the kindling of antisemitism in Vienna and the political maneuverings of his colleagues, culminating in his resignation from the Vienna Court Opera in 1907. Death in assorted guises had come knocking at the door. Completed in 1909, the orchestral song-cycle — whose full title reads *Eine Symphonie für eine Tenor und eine Alt (oder Bariton) Stimme und Orchester (nach Hans Bethges Die chinesische Flöte*, or "a symphony for tenor and alto (or baritone) voice and orchestra (after Hans Bethge's *The Chinese Flute*)" — was conceived as a setting of Bethge's collection of loosely translated and paraphrased Chinese poems, published in 1907, the beauty and clarity of which had cut through Mahler's thick fog of grief at just the right moment.

Harmonically, *Das Lied's* East Asian influence is clear,

particularly in its frequent use of the pentatonic scale. But the piece absorbs disparate influences, opening for instance with a *Trinklied* or drinking song, in A minor, its repeated refrain more melancholy than raucous: *Dunkel ist das Leben, ist der Tod*, "dark is life, is death." The gloomy phrase is pitched, as in the *"mein Vater"* of Schubert's *Erlkönig*, slightly higher in each iteration — steadily raising the stakes of its misery, like a beer-clutching drunkard growing more wretched and hollow-eyed as the party wears on. Yet with its horn fanfares and energetic cross-rhythms, establishing a jaunty mood of festivity, this opening movement is not as passive or bleak as its lyrics suggest. It is also richly chromatic, anchoring *Das Lied* in the sonic ambiguity for which Mahler's late style would become renowned.

The piece's middle ranges from the slow second movement to a spirited three-part scherzo, all occupying that same continuum between pleasure and despair, between celebration of life and grief at its evanescence. "The sweet fragrance of the flowers has fled; / A cold wind bends down their stems... My heart is weary" — with its suggestion that fading and fatigue are cruelly inevitable, as harsh winds lay waste to spring's flowers — is redolent of Keats at his most doleful. We are located in a natural landscape both lovely and indifferent, both alive and withering into decay; we imbibe the sap of life and are face to face with death.

These movements alternate between the respective songs of the alto and tenor — the song-cycle form here is fully assimilated into that of the symphony — and coalesce into an orchestral song-cycle or "song-symphony," as some call it (a form that Mahler did not invent but made his own, as in his *Kindertotenlieder* of 1904). A song-symphony is a flexible hybrid organism. It coheres into a large-scale whole as a symphony does, but its songs can nonetheless feel self-contained, like set-pieces or vignettes loosely strung together. As legend has it, this was Mahler's attempt at transcending the fabled "Curse of the Ninth," a late Romantic superstition owed to the fact that Schubert, Beethoven, and Bruckner all died with their tenth symphonies unfinished. Mahler's genre-bending *Das Lied von der Erde* ventured to dodge this fate, the fear of which had apparently preyed on him continually.

His widow Alma Mahler, who survived him by fifty years, recalled his musing that "no great symphonic writer was to live beyond his Ninth," though she is something of a bête noire among Mahlerians for her unreliable and often seemingly self-serving narratives — the "Alma Problem." It was a fate to which Mahler would eventually succumb: following his Ninth Symphony of 1909, also the music of farewell, Mahler died with his tenth symphony incomplete. Schoenberg reflected rather mystically on the phenomenon in an essay on Mahler. "He who wants to go beyond [the Ninth] must pass away," he intoned. "It seems as if something might be imparted to us in the Tenth which we ought not yet to know, for which we are not ready. Those who have written a Ninth stood too close to the hereafter."

Das Lied's expansive, slow-burning final movement, called "*Der Abschied*" or "The Farewell," proceeds lightly, mostly lacking in the Wagnerian thunder of the cycle's opening. Its orchestration is a feat of naturalism, featuring the gong, the celesta, simulated birdsong, and the tam-tam — the instrument of death par excellence, often brought to bear in funeral marches. Only select groups of instruments are wielded at a given time; no individual instrument's color is effaced or sacrificed to a wall of sound. Many have observed that this delicate touch lends the movement the feel of chamber music. The piece climaxes with lines altered considerably by Mahler himself and, unlike the often tightly compressed verses of prior movements, his rhetoric is overwhelmingly lyrical. Here we witness the protagonist wandering the mountains alone, seeking an elusive peace.

> A cool breeze blows in the shadow of my fir trees.
> I stand here and wait for my friend.
> I wait for him to take a last farewell.
> I long, O my friend, to enjoy the beauty
> Of this evening by your side.
> Where are you? You leave me long alone!
> I wander to and fro with my lute
> On pathways which billow with soft grass.
> O beauty! O eternal love-and-life-intoxicated world!

A purely orchestral interlude intercedes — a funeral march of sorts — and at length *Das Lied von der Erde* concludes with lines written by Mahler alone:

> The dear earth everywhere
> Blossoms in spring and grows green again!
> Everywhere and forever a blueness lights the distance
> Forever...forever...

"Ewig...*ewig*...": it would be the last word that Mahler set to music. Voiced as a falling second, its melody descends two whole steps downward, from E to D and from D to C. Though on one level simply a routine cadence, the interval of the falling second had been associated, ever since Beethoven's Piano Sonata No. 26 in Eb major ("Les Adieux"), with the theme of parting and farewell; hummed aloud, it has the innocent ring of goodbye. *Ewig* also hints at self-quotation, recalling the monumental finale of Mahler's Eighth Symphony, with its repeated horn-and-strings-backed cries of *"ewig, ewig."* Where the Eighth's *ewig* had proclaimed the eternal triumph of love and human creativity, in the final words of Goethe's *Faust, Part Two* — *das Ewig-Weibliche zieht uns hinan*, "the Eternal Feminine draws us onward" — the *ewig* in *Das Lied* is cast in a decidedly muted palette. The "forever" is repeated, over and over, unfurling like a chant, growing gradually quieter, finally dissolving into an icy, deafening silence.

With its irregular cadences and incorporation of silence, *Der Abschied* has thus far moved centripetally toward this end. But when does the silence really reign? I have seen audiences momentarily freeze, unsure whether the sound waves have merely stopped reaching their own strained eardrums or whether the piece is indeed over. Or the opposite phenomenon: following a performance of the piece recorded for Leonard Bernstein's Young People's Concerts, the audience erupts in applause preemptively, before the final bars of music have passed away. When is the alto's soft intonation swallowed up by quiet, the "forever" engulfed by nothingness? It is haunting to think that the earth and this very song of the earth will one day cease to be. But is the suggested impression that it is not the song that ends, but we who stop hearing it? Heard melodies are sweet, but those unheard are sweeter, and so on. "Therefore, ye soft pipes, play on…"

It was one of the last concerts I attended in-person, in January 2020, before the pandemic overturned and pulverized life as we knew it. The faint whiff of death was already in the air; the threat was still immaterial and our fears still insubstantial. The New

York Philharmonic had paired *Das Lied* with Schubert's Fourth, or "Tragic," Symphony. Could there be anything more quintessentially Romantic, I thought, than the impulse to immortalize a communion you fear to be already lost — a "forever" you suspect to be slipping through your fingers like sand, or one whose other name is nothingness? The declaration of "forever" seemed always to contain the recognition of its opposite, of finitude and the pit of non-being. *Das Lied*'s misty escape-into-landscape finale, like that of Wordsworth's "Tintern Abbey," features a speaker anxiously awaiting the arrival of a friend — one whose face and voice and fervor would affirm for the speaker the truths that he so ardently desires to believe, the truths he feels receding from him even as he insists on their self-evidence.

I do not mean through overwrought association to imply that Mahler read Wordsworth or was otherwise influenced by him. I am simply stitching together my own influences and long-accrued associations. Simply to identify Mahler with a Romantic ethos requires elaboration: he is properly regarded as both a paragon of late-Romantic style and a precursor of modern music, a kind of bridge between the two — expanding tonality to its outer limits without collapsing it entirely, only taking up Schoenberg's injunction to "emancipate the dissonance" so far. And this is not even to acknowledge the distinct meanings of "Romantic" in music and literature. Mahler, at any rate, had his suspicions about the term. In a letter to a friend, discussing Goethe, he had this to say:

> What Goethe says on the meaning of the terms Classical and Romantic is this: 'What is Classical I call healthy, what is Romantic sick... Most modern work is Romantic not because it is modern but because it is weak, sickly and ill, and old work is not Classical because it is old but

because it is strong, fresh, joyful and healthy. If we distinguish Classical and Romantic by these criteria, the situation is soon clarified.' The inner connection between my argument and Goethe's should be obvious.

Mahler leaves ambiguous what "my argument" is. We can only wonder if and how he applied these criteria to his own compositions. Is *Das Lied* hale and hearty or dour and morbid? Brimming over with hope for renewal or baldly nihilistic? Does it engender in its listener the proverbial desire to take to the sickbed? These oppositions aren't necessarily useful ones; plainly, music need not *do* anything, and in the best of cases may do the wholly mysterious. Even Nietzsche, in his polemic against what he came to perceive as Wagnerian sickliness, recognized in it the essence of modernity — "a diagnosis of the modern soul" — and that "there is no way out: one must first become a Wagnerian." The Nietzschean mandate may be one of health-through-sickness, or, put in modern terms, spiritual inoculation ("sickness itself can be a stimulant to life: only one has to be healthy enough for this stimulant"). It was he who remarked that whatever did not kill him made him stronger.

It is notable that Mahler should have thought along these lines at all, toward the physiological sphere of sickliness and heath, though I suppose one could chalk it up to his reading of Nietzsche or the larger concern of his culture with degeneration and vitality. (Mahler moved in intellectual circles saturated by Nietzsche and Schopenhauer; he nearly called his Third Symphony "The Gay Science" and, in its fourth movement, set *Zarathustra*'s Roundelay to music.) Privately Mahler mused about a potentially despondent audience response to *Das Lied*, allegedly grilling Walter: "What do you think? Is it at all bearable? Will it drive people to make an end of themselves?" Caustic or impish as the question may have been, Mahler evidently held on some level that his music did do something to its listener, that it bred and reared something considerable in her breast. What is it *Das Lied von der Erde* effectuates or demands — and if we privately experience it as some sort of call, toward what duty or vision are we being summoned?

The attentive reader will have noted my relative lack of attention to the symphony's conclusion, without which such questions are dead on arrival. *"Ewig"* on its face may bring comfort, and the broader musical structure of *Der Abschied*, with its progressive tonality, would seem to express uplift; it possesses an affecting, consolatory C minor to C major tonic scheme. Musically we experience a sublime feeling of breakthrough and transformation — a renewal of spring, if you will. But the hard-won release does not feel like a triumph, exactly, nor like what we may call joy. Like the low murmurous adagio of Mahler's Ninth, this finale breathes a great sigh of resignation, its peace achieved at the threshold of extreme suffering. If this is bliss, it is the bliss of anguish borne and surpassed. It is also perhaps a self-negation in the face of what Buddhist and Hindu texts term *upādāna*, attachment, a kind of death to the flux of this world. To be sure, *Das Lied* closes out with a protracted, non-metrical decrescendo that some compare to a slow dying-away of breath, a deadening pulse. *Der Abschied* begins *"schwer,"* or "heavily," and ends *"gänzlich ersterbend,"* or "completely dying away": life's weight has been lifted, the lightness of non-being attained. Yet even this interpretation, with its Schopenhauerian thread, feels only skin-deep.

Benjamin Britten would say of the piece's final chord, "I cannot understand it," marveling in a letter to Henry Boys that "it passes over me like a tidal wave — and that matters not a jot either, because it goes on forever, even if it is never performed again... that final chord is printed on the atmosphere." What is this apotheosis "printed on the atmosphere"? The music radiates a mood of gentleness, of pain melting into joy and vice versa: the effect is achieved in part by a final series of arpeggiations, so that the music unwinds itself in horizontal concatenation before gathering itself up into vertical concord. The notes form a blended whole only to unfasten themselves, floating dreamily back into arpeggiated sequence, the cycle beginning once more.

And what are those notes? Above the final chord drifts the vocalist's melody on the E—D—C motive. The melody does not, at long last, resolve to its tonic, C: the final note of the final *"ewig"* is in fact C's supertonic, D. It's as if we have taken a step, expecting once more to feel solid ground beneath our feet, but instead we find ourselves still suspended in mid-air. This may be a farewell, but closure eludes us. And the musical climax here is doubly unresolved. The terminal chord of *Das Lied von der Erde* is C major (made up of the notes C, E, and G) with an added A, the sixth scale degree of C major; this results in what is known today as a C major sixth chord. The major sixth, in traditional tonal harmony, is a consonant interval, but here the added A forms an extreme dissonance with another chord tone of C major (a second with G). For the interval of the major second, picture two white keys lying side by side, struck in unison; they clash, too close for comfort. Mahler leaves the dissonance unresolved. This was quite a choice: before the twentieth century, before its assimilation by jazz, an unresolved major-sixth chord existed as an acceptable tonic primarily in ragtime and cakewalks. This A sits above middle C, voiced too low in the chord to sound like it'll slide easily downward to G — a customary resolution — and yet not low enough in the bass to alter the chord's sonority from C major to A minor.

Yes, C major is bound intimately to A minor, the key with which *Das Lied* begins. A minor is the relative minor of C major, meaning they share the same notes, but differ on their tonics or resolution tones. The faint evocation of A minor through a resounding C major, dissonant though it may be, is an all too effective case of sublation: the opening movement's essence is at once preserved, nullified, and transcended. This whisper of the original tonic refreshes our memory, reminding us that — on top of the C minor to C major of *Der Abschied* — the work as a whole possesses a broad-scale progressive tonal architecture, wending its way from A minor to C major and toward its own transformation.

The effect of an unresolved dissonance is typically one of infinite ache, and this is no exception. But what is unresolved can by definition seem to be without end. The essential, protean simplicity of C major encircles us, and the dissonant A lingers on indefinitely as a color, an atmosphere, a promise of endlessness.

This farewell, this leave-taking — what is it? For Leonard Bernstein, *Der Abschied* is a farewell to tonality: the high water mark of tonal expansion before dissonance would flood it completely, and Mahler's intensely pained farewell to German Romanticism. "It was Mahler's destiny to sum up the whole story of Austro-Germanic music and tie it up," he proclaimed of the end of *Das Lied*. "And not in a pretty bow, but in a fearful knot made out of his own nerves and sinews." To be a Romantic in an increasingly post-Romantic age requires negotiation with the death of aesthetic culture as you know it. This is, for Bernstein, what Mahler attempts over and over, unable to loosen his grip without anguish; part of him would cling to a tonal temperament "forever." Like Hans Castorp humming Schubert's "Der Lindenbaum" in the corpse-ridden landscape of the Great War, headed toward his own extermination, this is an elegy for Romanticism as an era, a mood, a climate of feeling, and for the music that had once expressed its spirit. That spirit, felt to be ebbing in an increasingly mechanized age of world war and mass culture, had to be mourned. Yet, in what I will call the Bernstein reading, there is a Romanticism that steadily and remorselessly blooms in the soul of twentieth-century man — even as it outwardly might be elegized.

The Mahler we have today is in a certain sense Leonard Bernstein's Mahler. He could still remark, in 1960, that "Mahler isn't one of those big popular names like Beethoven," and while today we would disagree, it is in large part owing to his influence. Bernstein hardly plucked Mahler from oblivion — Bruno Walter, Otto Klemperer, and Jascha Horenstein, among others, had already put him on the map, and Aaron Copland had been a longtime advocate — but Bernstein almost single-handedly mainstreamed the composer in the United States, inaugurating a major revival of interest in his work. His conducting of the New York Philharmonic in the 1960s made Mahler a classic in repertories thereafter; he featured Mahler in his popular televised lectures; and he pulled off the first complete recorded cycle of Mahler's symphonies. In the United States, certainly, the ubiquity of Mahler — as opposed to, say, Strauss or Bruckner — is partly a function of Bernstein's gigantic celebrity.

Bernstein's cheerleading made for a tangled legacy. One senses in his televised programming a determined overidentification with Mahler: they were both Jewish-born conductors of the New York Philharmonic, though it didn't bear that name in Mahler's day; both conductors *and* composers; both thereby afflicted by what Bernstein called a "double nature." There was a funny effect whereby the two figures were forever linked in the public mind. Yet Bernstein was not without his critics. He was occasionally accused of conducting at a slower tempo than was typical for Mahler, and for taking infelicitous liberties with his rubato. Pierre Boulez, a great Mahlerian in the concert hall and in recordings, noted in a late interview how frequently Mahler's tempo markings implore their conductor not to drag. Mahler, he felt, was afraid that his music might sink under the load of excessive emotion.

Bernstein was on that basis charged with sentimentalism. Some found his melodramatic public persona in poor taste. He swayed on the podium, eyes closed intermittently, registering an extremity of emotion that looked a lot like ecstasy. The man was possessed: dripping with sweat, almost giddy, his physical charisma tremendous. One wants to watch Bernstein as much as one wants to listen to the music he is conducting. Through him, Mahler became all but synonymous with ostentatious, even histrionic, emotionalism. Bernstein was himself a spectacle, but his innate musicianship, his profound understanding of Mahler in particular, was undeniable — and he had the platform and the desire to propound his grandiloquent thesis. Ever the Romantic interpreter, it was often a Keatsian mood with him: in his personal introduction to *Das Lied*, recorded during rehearsal breaks with the Israel Philharmonic in 1972, he recites from a touchstone of English Romanticism, Keats's "Ode to a Nightingale":

> Darkling I listen; and, for many a time
> I have been half in love with easeful Death…

[Bernstein murmuring, "that is almost exactly the quality of the end of this piece."]

Was it a vision, or a waking dream?
Fled is that music: — Do I wake or sleep?

[Bernstein, pausing: "That is the essence, that is all, of *Das Lied von der Erde*."]

Yet what might it mean for a composer to part with Romanticism? It will help to first sketch a faint picture of Romanticism in music, concentrating for the most part not on theory but on what all of this sounded like. An admission first: there was perhaps for some a whiff of derision to the term "Romantic" — a sense that it meant surrendering form to feeling, wallowing in emotion, and not living up to the "strong, fresh, joyful and healthy" standards of classicism. Less polemically, one can regard Romanticism as a temporal designation, referring loosely to a kind of long nineteenth century in music. Some variation on the Beethoven-to-Mahler genealogy would suffice.

The term was first applied to music by E.T.A Hoffman in 1810, in his review of Beethoven's Fifth Symphony, where he alleged that music was in fact the only truly Romantic art. For Hoffman, the term implied expressive triumph. Romantic music was the music of the artist qua artist, responsive to the throbbing dictates of his own soul — overfull, unchained from reason, prevailing over the banal and the finite to bear witness only to the fiercely real. "Beethoven's music stirs the mists of fear, of horror, of terror, of grief, and awakens that endless longing which is the very essence of romanticism," Hoffman wrote breathlessly. Hold on to that notion of "endless longing," which would later become a standard cliche of Wagnerism. Other attributes of the Romantic temperament would be a delight in the natural world, a taste for folklore and the Gothic, and an incorporation of extra-musical material: songs, tone poems, program music generally. But lofty passions and stormy sensations — emotional extremes — remain the calling card of musical Romanticism.

Formal compositional revolutions whirled alongside the thematic ones. Abetted by the public concert hall and the rise of the domestic salon, the period saw musical works expanding and contracting in scale, tempo, and dynamics, the better to pour out every species of feeling. Romantic music remained perceptibly tonal but moved just as perceptibly toward harmonic ambiguity. The graceful harmonic sequences and well-proportioned melodies of Haydn and Mozart yielded in Schubert, Chopin, and Liszt to a new and mottled sonic universe: chromatic saturations, dissonant intervals, mysterious harmonies, modulatory surprises.

One cannot breathe a word about Romantic music, of course, without addressing Wagner, though some would position him later in the story, as a late-nineteenth-century neo-Romantic. Wagner's monumental music dramas appeared at first blush to erode fixed keys, or at least to resolve themselves into unexpected keys, breaking down large-scale durational unity into "brief tonal particles which follow each other in line, connected like links in a chain rather than assembled round a common center," as Carl Dahlhaus elegantly put it. And beyond Wagner's generally soupy tonality was his famed Tristan chord, debuted in 1865. The chord — made up of the notes F, B, D♯, and G♯ — was inscrutable, harshly dissonant, and strangely beautiful, impossible to predict in its path toward resolution. Wagner seemingly was not the first to use the chord, but the first to use it as the structural principle of a work: listeners of *Tristan und Isolde* were made to molder in its ambiguity, seemingly interminably. Wagner eventually rounds off the repeated cadence into ecstatic consonance, but not until the last thirty seconds of an opera whose running time is approximately four hours. The delectable tension is released — so belatedly that release becomes almost an afterthought. There lurks in this dynamic an element of masochism perhaps ever-present in Romanticism's longing for longing: Schiller, following Kant, had identified the experience of the sublime as at once "a joyous state, that may rise to rapture" and "a painful state, which in its paroxysm is manifested by a kind of shudder."

Wagner's innovation will be better understood against the backdrop of common-practice tonality, developed in the Baroque period through the nineteenth-century. It was poised on the axis of the musical key: in the key of C, C is the tonic or pitch of central interest; the tonic and its chain of corresponding relations form the basic syntax of tonal music. Tonal compositions often depend upon dynamics of tension and resolution: on straying potentially far from one's tonic chord only to return home faithfully in due course. In such a scheme, dissonance — however seductive — must ideally be annulled or transcended, and can be only a temporary excitement, a roadblock on the path to eventual consonance: an exotic spice sprinkled to enliven but never to overwhelm.

Dissonance is a nebulous concept whose meaning has evolved over time. Select intervals have been hotly contested, such as the fourth: it was for some an open-and-shut dissonance and for others a quite perfect consonance. ("It is not, therefore, the human ear or nervous system that decides what is a dissonance, unless we are to assume a physiological change between the thirteenth and fifteenth century," Charles Rosen admonished.) The introduction of the keyboard as we know it had divided the octave into twelve equally spaced pitches, approximations of intervallic frequencies existing in nature; of the intervals on a keyboard, only what we call the octave and the fifth exist as "consonances" scientifically (if you strike a string and hear its reverberations, the ensuing series of overtones naturally includes these intervals). If the understanding of what counted as dissonance was mostly historically contingent, so too was that idea of dissonance itself — but the rigors of tonal scaffolding came to behave like a set of natural laws in the classical period. A momentary dissonance, a chromatically altered C major, at the start of Mozart's nineteenth string quartet got it branded "The Dissonance Quartet" for the next couple of hundred years. It was such a scandal to its nineteenth-century interpreters that they insisted on doctoring it, overwriting its dissonant early bars at public performances. I have heard it drolly claimed that the "emancipation of the dissonance" dates back to this.

Broadly speaking, Wagner and his contemporaries undertook to throw a wrench in tonic-oriented musical organization. Wagner disdained what he called "quadratic compositional construction," the tightly symmetrical and balanced compositions of his predecessors. Whether composers such as Wagner (or Chopin or Liszt) were flouting arbitrary aesthetic calcifications or the very laws of nature — no matter. This was inexorably where music was headed: harmonic ambiguity became its own destination, and desire more desirable than consummation. Well before "modern" music, then, and well before the twentieth century, there occurred a gradual unfocusing of tonal music's accepted contours — and Mahler had one foot in both camps.

The boundaries of modern music are porous. To speak of separate camps is not quite misleading but not quite useful. If modern composers and their tonal murk did not arise *ex nihilo* in the twentieth century, and were nourishing growths whose roots lay as deep in the soil as Mozart, what accounts for that special modern sound? You know it when you hear it: it concentrates itself around the year 1900 and gains momentum around 1914, spurred to maturity in the crucible of the Great War. One can think as far back as 1889, to Strauss' *Don Juan*; to the dissonant, nearly atonal shrieks of his one-act opera *Salome* in 1905; to the riotous premiere in 1913 of Stravinsky's *Rite of Spring*, with its mammoth polychords and barbed rhythms; to the impressionism, so-called, of Debussy and Ravel. Adorno meanwhile would call Mahler's Ninth Symphony "the first work of the new music."

In this regard, one man outpaces the others in the minds of many to this day. Arnold Schoenberg was the most controversial composer of his age, striking ire into the hearts of audiences and bewildering those who found his style self-indulgently cacophonous. It is claimed that he secured a definitive break with tonality. Or was he merely playing out the consequences of the Wagnerian upheaval? Schoenberg, to be sure, invented a newfangled system to replace functional harmony. But even his twelve-tone technique can be treated as a late flowering of the process of harmonic expansion already underway. Thomas Mann had called Wagner a "cultural Bolshevik" already "on atonal terrain"; he may have been better describing the father of the Second Viennese School.

Schoenberg had been cautiously testing the limits of tonal music as early as 1899. In that year's masterpiece of a string sextet, *Verklärte Nacht*, in the ravishing *Gurre-Lieder* of 1900, and in the chromatically saturated *Pelleas und Melisande* of

1903, he still moved discernibly in the ambit of Beethoven and Wagner. In 1909, the year Mahler completed *Das Lied*, Schoenberg was already dabbling in free atonality (or pantonality, a term he seems to have preferred). In his fully formed twelve-tone technique, completed by the early 1920s, no single pitch or key center was to take precedence over another: the twelve pitches of the chromatic scale were to be used equally, without repetition, abrogating the hierarchy of tones necessary to establishing a tonic. The epiphenomena of functional harmony — major chords, minor chords, diminished and augmented chords — were to be left in the dust.

If you deploy twelve pitches equally and without repetition, treating consonance and dissonance as kindred substances, your music will give the impression of jumping around, of rising and falling too swiftly to sort itself out into a key or assume definite shape. What sounded to some like unfocused, scattershot noise — pitches flitting through the air like so many nameless particles of sound — was in fact a highly structured and purposefully engineered musical ambiguity. "Tonality is no natural law of music, eternally valid": these were Schoenberg's fighting words.

> The appeal to tonality's origin in nature can be refuted if one recalls that just as tones pull toward triads, and triads toward tonality, gravity pulls us down toward the earth; yet an airplane carries us up away from it. A product can be apparently artificial without being unnatural, for it is based on the laws of nature to just the same degree as those that seem primary.

Taken side-by-side with another statement of Schoenberg's — "I have made a discovery that will ensure the supremacy of German music for the next hundred years" — one glimpses a curious thought process irreducible to contemporary intellectual frameworks. Schoenberg was perhaps a revolutionary conservative, revolutionary in the service of preserving an unbroken line of "German music": a chain of aesthetic inheritance in which he placed himself without hesitation and in whose supremacy he believed. One feels as if his twelve-tone technique and the ambiguity it systematized was, at bottom, an attempt to replicate the soul-rattling power of the composers who had enthralled him — a way of realizing their staggering, discomposing beauty for a new age.

Schoenberg worshipped Mahler. He arranged *Das Lied* for chamber orchestra, to be performed in his exclusive Society for Private Musical Performances in Vienna. The admiration ran so deep that the first edition of his *Theory of Harmony*, published shortly after Mahler's death, bears the following dedication:

> This book is dedicated to the memory of GUSTAV MAHLER. The dedication was intended to give him some small pleasure while he still lived. It was also meant to express reverence for his immortal compositions, and to show that these works, which academic musicians pass by with a shrug of the shoulders, indeed with contempt, are worshiped by someone who is perhaps not entirely ignorant either. Gustav Mahler was denied greater joys than my dedication was meant to provide. This martyr, this saint, had to pass on... now he is dead, I want my book to win me respect, so that nobody can pass by when I say, 'That was one of the truly great men!'

What would Mahler have made of the panegyric — and of Schoenberg's musical novelties, for that matter? To study the convergence of these figures is another way of straining to situate Mahler in the shifting sands of late Romanticism and early modernism, to stamp Mahler and his legacy for good. Music composed in the middle and later nineteenth-century, up until right about 1910, is a no man's land, up for grabs by those inclined to throw labels around. We would do well to recall Rosen's advice in *The Classical Style*: "Every period of time is traversed by forces both reactionary and progressive. Beethoven's music is filled with memories and predictions... Instead of affixing a label, it would be better to consider in what context and against what background Beethoven may be most richly understood."

Against what backdrop, then, is Mahler most richly understood? To suggest that he must be grasped in relation to Schoenberg and the serialists as much as in relation to his Romantic forebears — though on one level patently obvious, and elucidated by many scholars and critics — may grind the gears of some. Labels and camps may be limiting or arbitrary, but the partisan hothouse of twentieth-century musical culture, a culture we fall heir to today, would make their effects actual.

Mahler certainly hewed closely to Beethoven, Schubert, and Wagner, the Romantic luminaries in whose shadow he and his contemporaries composed — and more specifically to the motif of farewell. For Mahler's *Das Lied* does more than distill a century's worth of tonal expansion; as a song-cycle it forms a late entry in the genre of the German *Lied*. The *Lied* or art song tradition was where the poetry and the music of German Romanticism merged. The enormous output of Schubert, especially his *Winterreise*, typifies the genre and looms over Mahler's body of work. Mahler's *Abschied* was not the first of its kind; Schubert had composed scores of *Lieder* in the leave-taking mode, many with that very title. What is the farewell lyric all about, if we can get a fix on such a thing? If it is true that the human being is chronically contorted in such a pose, so that by our nature and despite our very best efforts we are habitually poised on the axis of farewell — turning, lingering, suspended on one threshold or another — what is the content of this existential orientation? In his Eighth Elegy, Rilke asks a plaintive question — "Who has us twisted around like this, so that/ no matter what we do, we are in the posture/ of someone going away?" — and goes on:

> Just as, upon
> the farthest hill, which shows him his whole valley
> one last time, he turns, stops, lingers —
> so we live here, forever taking leave.

How does the composer render this essence musically? Is this essence uniquely Romantic, and how does Mahler's farewell fit in?

Let us begin with Schubert's litany of farewells. They include "Abschied" (D. 578), a farewell to a friend; "Abschied von der Harfe" (D. 406), a kind of farewell to music; "Willkommen und Abschied" (D. 767) and "Auf dem Strom" (D. 943), farewells, in their own ways, to beloveds; and a bleaker consideration of love, "Abschied" (D. 475), among others. It is hardly surprising that most farewell songs concern romantic parting and abound with the tears and sentimentalism of doomed lovers. But there are musical partings with a more contemplative cast, with the end-of-life awareness exhibited by Mahler. There is, for instance, Schubert's "Abschied von der Erde" (D. 829), with text by Adolf von Pratobevera, composed in 1826, in which we move from a slate of particularized farewells to a sweeping farewell to life.

> Farewell, beautiful earth!
> I can understand you only now,
> when joy and sorrow
> pass away from us.
> Farewell, Master Sorrow!
> I thank you with moist eyes!
> Joy I take with me,
> you I leave behind.
> Be only a gentle teacher
> and lead all men to God;
> in the darkest nights
> reveal a little red streak of dawn!

Schubert's song is scored for spoken voice and piano, meaning it has no vocal melody and is instead performed like a dramatic recitation. Its score is marked *langsam*, or slow, but it provides no further rhythmic direction for its vocalist: much is left to the discretion of the reciter in electing where to place dramatic emphasis, if any. It is fascinating that Schubert felt that these words did not cry out for melody or firm pacing — that he wished to impart to them a kind of conversational fluidity, as if the vision of life and death they gave voice to were being worked out in the very act of speaking. The lyric positions its listener in neither supreme ecstasy nor supreme doom: at the moment of farewell, all emotional excess has been drained away, and only a delicate mode of "understanding" remains. The soft red glow of dawn streaks across the sky. Friedrich Hölderlin's poem "Abschied" partakes of a similar emotional extinguishment. "I may drink with you, all things/ Hate and love be forgotten then," he advises his beloved. The poet shows his hand, admitting that "to be gone is my wish," but he equivocates: "Later perhaps one day,/ Diotima, we'll meet — here, but desire by then/ Will have bled away." With its soft watercolor palette, its suggestion that parting and death are inducements to ultimate repose — states of nonbeing where extremes, including the exigencies of desire, are nullified and melt away — Hölderlin's poem feels like the melancholy lover's mirror image of Schubert. The perfume of renunciation lingers about them both.

From Haydn to Beethoven to Liszt, there were musical farewells, but it was the Schumanns who most visibly took up the mantle. Here renunciation is not quite the point. Robert Schumann's *Waldszenen* ("Forest Scenes"), a set of solo piano pieces composed in the late 1840s, cycles through a dizzying array of emotional states to examine the ambivalence of man in nature. Its final movement, "Abschied," is sweetly beautiful, pulsating softly and gesturing toward a realization of peace and uplift in nature. He would take up the *Abschied* theme again on several occasions, including in his final song-cycle *Gedichte der Königin Maria Stuart* (1852). Its fourth song, "Abschied von der Welt," features the soon-to-be-beheaded queen embracing death with open arms. She cries out for the cessation of her earthly torments; the joy of death is all that remains.

Crudely speaking, the respective farewells of *Waldszenen* and *Gedichte* reflect perhaps two sides of Schumann's bifurcated persona in the public mind, as well as the innate doubleness of the *Abschied* form, brought into bittersweet unity by other song composers. They notably included his extraordinary wife Clara: her song *"Beim Abschied,"* with a text by Friederike Serre, is a farewell dripping with ambivalence (and one that gently refuses to regard itself as one, even as it bears the traces of the farewell lyric). It opens:

> A purple glow shines from afar,
> Golden now the bright day sinks...
> One more greeting, now goodbye,
> No farewell, no departure...

Notice, as in Mahler, how frequently a soft glow glints in the distance (here it is purple; in *Das Lied* it is blue). Farewells are linked with archetypical consistency to shifting light: in them light waxes, wanes, dissolves, flickers, tinges, envelops. Morning-glow and evening-glow, standard settings of transition, are images befitting the literal contingencies of parting, but they also suggest the merging of one's undulating ambivalences with the earth's eternal cycles. The dim light that the scenes impart also matches their mood of existential pause — their aura of quiet stillness and shadowedness. I like to think of this clustering of images, associations, and resonances as part of the lyrical-musical atmosphere that Mahler absorbed, knowingly or not, almost in the manner of a cultural unconscious.

Mahler's farewell temperament is echoed in a song such as Richard Strauss's exquisite "Morgen!" (op. 27, no. 4) in 1894: it is not quite a farewell, and not quite about death, but it bears traces of the tradition under consideration. As its title — Morning! — suggests, the song looks toward the morrow. It sets forth an image system by now familiar — "this same sun-breathing earth," a landscape of "blue-waved bliss," and so on — and it joins together the sense of an ending with a perception of the eternal:

> And tomorrow the sun will shine again
> And on the path that I shall take,
> It will unite us, happy ones, again,
> Amid this same sun-breathing earth...
> And to the shore, broad, blue-waved,

Forever Taking Leave

> We shall quietly and slowly descend,
> Speechless we shall gaze into each other's eyes,
> And the speechless silence of bliss shall fall on us...

After completing two identical harmonic progressions in G major, the piece concedes its vocal melody ("and the speechless silence of bliss shall fall upon us...") over an unresolved dominant chord. After a dramatic pause, the piano picks up where the vocalist leaves off, and music supersedes language: in the ensuing purely instrumental realization of the G major cycle, we can feel the sun breaking through, shining again once more, even as all human presence has left the frame. (I am perhaps alone in preferring the bare piano and voice version to the fully orchestrated one.) This is a restatement of musical material made magical and salutary through simple repetition — and, if you will, a belated resolution to the tonic. It is an evocation of nature resuming its course, operating independently of human will and expression: the subject of Strauss's song is the aftermath of human departure. He returned to this spiritual terrain many decades later, in the fourth of his *Vier letzte Lieder,* or *Four Last Songs*. In these songs I recognize the lineaments of a Mahlerian ethos, clear as day.

Thresholds and suspensions are Romantic in nature, are they not? Schlegel, for instance, declared that "the poetry of the ancients is the poetry of possession, while ours is the poetry of longing... the former is rooted in the present, while the latter hovers between remembrance and anticipation." Recall that *Das Lied*'s "hovering," its suspension, is harmonic and literal. Indeed, I know of no better harmonic language to match these lyric modes than Mahler's C major sixth. In its resounding C major-ness and intervallic sixthness — the piercing ray of incongruous light imparted by its A — *Das*

Lied's musical climax feels both shut and open, both inevitable and impossible, the sort of farewell that cuts you to the core.

In Mahler's leave-taking mood, we find an affirmation of death as life's precondition and vice versa — but not the Romantic-Wagnerian longing for death as completion, consummation, or redemption. *Der Abschied* bleeds out anticlimactically, while Schubert's "*Abschied von der Erde*," one of its closer analogues, lacks vocal dynamism. The Strauss pieces simmer but never boil over; they are slow, steady, wistful, reconciled. Contrast these subdued forms of yearning and fulfillment with the soaring raised stakes of the *Tannhäuser* and *Lohengrin* preludes, or the achingly sweet and long-awaited consonance of Isolde's *Liebestod* — a harmonic release both sacred and sexual, one that coincides with the expiration of the human body onstage and of the music itself. Baudelaire's famous account of being ravished by Wagner's music is barely distinguishable from the logic of orgasm. Orgasm is, of course, perennially coupled with self-extinction, as Elizabethan puns on the word "die" and the French "*la petite mort*" suggest. But death is not orgasmic or glorious in Mahler, nor is extinction construed necessarily as a deliverance or refuge into "holy night" (as in *Tristan*). From such nocturnal fantasies, from such voluptuous death-addled aestheticism, *Der Abschied*'s lyrical voice departs decisively. It decouples death from the claustrophobia of eros and opens up onto a plane of fresh mountain air, infinite space, and brightening horizons. To grasp death unblinkingly in the bright light of day is quite a different matter than to lust after it in the dark.

I have situated Mahler amid eclectic and freely overlapping traditions, against a broader backdrop of Romantic forms — staging a musical and lyrical scene and populating it with definite, though gauzy, shapes and figures. This context brings Mahler's aesthetic-cultural source material into sharper focus. But it should be noted with equal emphasis that Mahler's posture was not strictly a backward-looking one. Mahler was also a curious and cautious enthusiast of the "new music." He welcomed the young Schoenberg as a disciple of sorts, keeping up the correspondence even after the latter's style had begun to perplex him. Though sometimes irritated by Schoenberg's arrogance, he stood resolutely by the younger composer, and apparently had to be restrained from attacking hecklers at the premiere of Schoenberg's First String Quartet. Legend has it that when Mahler told the audience they had no reason to protest, someone replied: "I hiss at your symphonies too!" The exchange hints at the continuity and the likeness that the composers possessed in the minds of many of their contemporaries, for whom they signified all that was modern. (Mahler's modernized re-orchestration of Beethoven's Ninth provoked a backlash in Vienna as early as 1900. One critic called it "barbarism.")

Schoenberg's full embrace of serialism may have baffled him, but Mahler was himself headed in an expressionist direction late in life, flirting with atonality in his final symphonies. There is a point at which late Mahler's and the early Schoenberg's styles seem close to converging, though Mahler died before the dynamic could play itself out. In 1909 he wrote to Schoenberg: "I have your quartet with me and study it from time to time... But it is difficult for me." The letter concludes movingly, if cryptically: "I'm so terribly sorry that I cannot follow you better; I look forward to the day when I shall find myself again (and thus find you)."

Mahler completed his Ninth Symphony that same year — his final symphony, composed shortly after *Das Lied*, and a critical document of his "late" style. Its first movement is a little ghastly, touched by bitterness. Though it opens in D major, this D major is in troubled waters, wrestling with D minor for dominance throughout and easily swamped by dissonant explosions. These clashes are eerie, even nightmarish, and stray far from the relatively smoother surfaces of Mahler's earlier works. The work's final movement, like *Das Lied*'s, has been interpreted as expressing a kind of death drive: in its final bars a high A♭ voiced whisperingly by the first violins, trickles away until it is swallowed up by a closing D♭ major triad, and with an icy silence. Both *Das Lied* and the Ninth are farewells, but the Ninth terrifies in its utter opacity. Explicit hope of renewal, of an abiding "*ewig,*" seems less of a sure thing. I hasten to add that not everyone would agree with such a reading: Bruno Walter, who conducted the piece's premiere in 1912, described its final movement as a "peaceful farewell; with the conclusion, the clouds dissolve in the blue of heaven." I think Schoenberg gets a little closer to capturing its fearsome power: "[Mahler's] Ninth is most strange," he writes. "In it, the author hardly speaks as an individual any longer. It almost seems as though this work must have a concealed author who used Mahler merely as his spokesman, as his mouthpiece."

This eclipsing or emptying out of the self, this surpassing of merely personal expression, could help to explain the tendency among some Mahler enthusiasts — I share it — to explain away his late drive toward maximal dissonance and disintegration. Such sonic violence must be Mahler's intimation of a future to be mourned: political catastrophe, civilizational decline, aesthetic decay. As if someone had forced Mahler's hand, as if he had looked straight into the maw of fascism and were crying out in prophetic sorrow. Bernstein claimed that Mahler's symphonies "foretold all," referring to the horrors of the twentieth century. Is this really so? Is all bleakness in early twentieth-century art a prophecy of historical catastrophe to come? There can be a curious mental block in considering that what sounds demonic in Mahler is being expressed not as commentary but for its own sake, or for a sake otherwise unknown to us.

And there is his unfinished, often atonal-sounding Tenth Symphony to consider, beside which the tempests of the Ninth may appear quite consonant, though the cobbled together version we possess bears an uncertain relationship to Mahler's original intentions. When one contemplates the arc of his late output, one wonders where Mahler would have gone musically had he lived past fifty — had he lived even a few more years. In its form and tonal contours Mahler's Ninth, especially its first movement, has always seemed to me to be blood brothers with Schoenberg's *Pelleas und Melisande*, composed within the same decade, and with Anton Webern's *Passacaglia* in D Minor, Op. 1, composed one year earlier. To pigeonhole Mahler as a mournful bookend to the Romantic age, as a late Romantic grieving a vanishing world and clinging to the last scraps of tonality available to him, would be to paper over his compositional range and evolution — and to neglect his flesh-and-blood immersion in his space and time. Tonal dissolution gripped Mahler, mystified him, and unnerved him; he gestured toward it increasingly. One wonders, in other words, what terrible storms Mahler could still have called forth.

After the Second World War, tonalists and serialists waged their own battle. "The compositional currents of an age shed light on the way it interprets past music, and vice versa," Dahlhaus remarked. "It would distort their place in music history if we neglected to analyze the overlap between post-serial music and the Mahler renaissance." Dahlhaus is in turn somewhat scathing on the term "late Romanticism," seeing in it a blinkered "failure to take seriously enough the age's sense of its own identity" — and worse:

> "Late romanticism" is a pejorative and polemically loaded term used in the 1920s by adherents of neo-classicism and the Neue Sachlichkeit [the New Objectivity] to separate themselves from the immediate past... [Turn-of-the-century modernism] saw itself as a fresh start in a new direction. It was the next generation that turned it into a historical denouement, a dead legacy, using terminology as a means to commit, as it were, historiological patricide.

It is doubtless difficult to picture a composer sitting down to write "late Romantic music" or regarding himself with this vocabulary of overripeness; it smacks too much of historical hindsight. We do not like to think of ourselves as latecomers, artists least of all. It seems plausible rather that a composer would identify with what is newly brewing within and around him. But Dahlhaus touches on what makes the question a difficult one, namely its "pejorative and polemically loaded" dimension — its considerable political proportions. The mood of the twentieth-century musical scene was indeed feverishly political.

Composers such as Schoenberg, Webern, and Berg held that functional harmony had atrophied: it was no longer enough to seize on dissonant chords and intervals, scramble tonal boundaries, or modulate into tonal nether regions as Wagner had done. An attack at the root was in order. Serialist theories, or variations on them, would become dogma thanks to some of Schoenberg's more rabid students, to the René Leibowitz-descended school from which Boulez emerged, as well as to the serialist catechisms of Adorno. Popular audiences never quite caught up with the modern sound, finding it less than beautiful; it was incomprehensible noise to many of them, and they thirsted for music they could understand and adore. Later composers such as Milton Babbitt did not conceal their utter contempt for audience tastes. A chasm was widening between aesthetic factions who regarded each other with near-venomous enmity. The Mahler Renaissance bloomed in this era of ideological ferment.

And then there was the matter of Mahler's Jewishness. The Third Reich had famously embarked on a scorched-earth campaign against modern art and modern music, inveighing against the jazz influences coursing through Weimar culture and nearly banning atonal music altogether (it was felt to possess a distinctly Jewish effluvium). The art historian Henry Grosshans writes that for Hitler "modern art was [seen as] an act of aesthetic violence by the Jews against the German spirit." While it embraced and exalted the machinery of modern warfare, Nazism was on some level a neo-Romantic movement. It expounded and exploited the eminently Romantic longing for a pre-alienated past — a past that is always hypothetical and out of reach, but that one senses deep in one's gut, buried but perhaps recoverable. This is the private imaginative soil upon which fascism preys.

A particularly potent strain of antisemitism identified Jews with all that was discomfiting about modernity, including its critical spirit: modern art was too brainy for those Germans "who thought with their blood," as Peter Gay put it. Jews were Oswald Spengler's "decomposing element" in culture, and more broadly, a perfect stand-in for the early twentieth-century sense that art and life had grown disenchanted, fragmented, and drained of innocence. The twisted Otto Weininger, himself a Jew, had argued as much in his explosive tract *Sex and Character* ("inner ambiguity, I repeat, is absolutely Jewish," he wrote, and "simplicity is absolutely un-Jewish"). This was a people fated to wander, foreigners in every land and yet mysteriously intellectually dominant therein. Jews were the ur-types of existential alienation, "rootless cosmopolitans" detached from the *Volkskörper* upon which they could only be parasites. The sickness of modernity was in essence a Jewish sickness and it could be fumigated with poison gas. That such an animus would abet the hypermodern death machine of the Third Reich is one of history's most pitiless ironies.

Mahler, of course, was Jewish, born in 1860 to a petite bourgeois family in Kaliště and raised in Iglau, a small village on the Bohemian border. His family were German-speaking Jews in a sea of mostly Czech-speakers. After a stint of conservatory training and a slew of conducting appointments throughout Central Europe, Mahler arrived at the Vienna Court Opera in 1897, the same Vienna in which the famed antisemite Karl Lueger had recently been elected mayor. Mahler would convert to Catholicism in the year he took up the post, a conversion of the sort that Heine famously described as the "ticket of admission to European culture." Lingering antisemitic feeling among his colleagues and resistance to the maestro's severity would cause him to be driven out in 1907, and he accepted an appointment at the Metropolitan Opera in New York.

It was a tenuously assimilated Viennese milieu in which Mahler moved. It was also, as is well known, a climate of Jewish intellectual preeminence; the man who towered over it all was that skeptical and ambivalent and idiosyncratically proud Jew, Sigmund Freud. Hitler reported in *Mein Kampf* that his teenage immersion in Vienna cured him of his formerly Jew-friendly politics. The enlightened secularism of turn-of-the-century Jews was less than irrelevant to the Third Reich: conversion was an empty facade to those for whom Judaism was a race, and for whom race was deeply metaphysical. Despite Mahler's conversion and thoroughgoing secular assimilation, and despite a substantially tonal body of work, his music would be effectively outlawed in Germany following Hitler's rise to power in 1933 (though Richard Strauss, as onetime president of the Reich Music Chamber, had advocated for the continued performance of his symphonies). A bronze bust of Mahler's intensely expressive face, sculpted by Rodin in Mahler's final years — and Alma's gift to the Vienna State Opera in 1931 — would be destroyed by Nazis. Mahler's niece, a virtuosic violinist and a baptized Protestant, would be deported in a cattle car to Auschwitz in 1943. The concepts and the vocabularies of the political sphere may leave art itself, not to mention the very notion of aesthetic quality, untouched — but the same is not true of artists, who may be silenced, crushed, and destroyed.

In the ashes of the postwar age there sprang up among some a desire to recover, and to honor, the "degenerate art" that the Nazis had loathed. The Third Reich had, to put it mildly, politicized music: who could blame those who politicized it in return? Ernst Krenek, who fled to the United States in 1938 and was himself briefly married to Mahler's daughter, once explicitly claimed to write twelve-tone music to steer clear of fascist tastes: "My adoption of the musical technique that the tyrants hated most of all may be interpreted as an expression of protest."(His jazz-opera *Jonny spielt auf*, which became a European sensation when it premiered in 1927, would be banned by the Nazis and in caricatured form became the poster image of the "Degenerate Music" exhibit in Düsseldorf in 1938.) After the Nazi conflation of Jews, modernism, and degeneracy — and their heralding of Beethoven and Wagner at official state events — it was difficult to simply get on with the usual programming. That unbroken chain of inheritances, Schoenberg's "supremacy of German music," was felt to be rotting from within. Some seemed to flinch from the beauty that once delighted them. Perhaps there was even a suspicion of the sweeping quality of Romantic music, its appeal to unreason, its sonic pull away from all limits and toward the infinite. Atonal music, by contrast, may preclude instinctual submersion, the annihilation of the self. It is a series of interruptions and roadblocks, defamiliarizing itself at every turn, forcing its listener moment by moment to begin again. Every successive sound punctures and slices up the silence anew.

The Mahler revival flowered in this charged historical moment. Serialists and tonalists warred. Accusations of wrongthink abounded. Popular taste and conservative opinion shrunk from modern music, while universities and composition departments by and large embraced it. (It was difficult in some cases to get a faculty position as a tonalist in the later twentieth century, which yielded perhaps its own aesthetic sclerosis). Bernstein, a hero of this story, admirably tried to split the difference. He posited in his Norton lectures that two trends would define music in the coming century: the Schoenbergian break and the Stravinskian expansion, with Stravinsky personifying the maximization of harmonic ambiguity within tonal bounds. Mahler was a paragon of tonal expansion, in Bernstein's eyes; on this he and Boulez agreed. Bernstein, though himself a tonalist inclined toward the Romantic, and though a bearer of incomplete theses, ultimately eschewed the dogma that insisted he take a side. He was comfortable declaring Mahler to be the very peak of German Romanticism *and* happy to acknowledge Mahler's link to the modern school, in his embrace of tonal puzzles. Bernstein apprehended Mahler's wistful backward glances but never denied his unflinching forward ones. Mahler was lucky to have had such a level-headed champion.

Alma Mahler left a recollection of her husband's final moments, and though it may be a little too good to be true, it is worth reproducing.

> During his last days, while his mind was still unclouded, his thoughts often went anxiously to Schoenberg. "If I die, he will have nobody left. Who will protect him from the mob?" Then the end. Mahler lay with dazed eyes; one finger was conducting on the quilt. There was a smile on his lips and twice he said: "Mozart!"

There it is, in all its poetic symmetry.

Upon completing *Das Lied,* Mahler had only four years to live; he was never to hear his work performed, and Walter would conduct its premiere in the wake of its creator's untimely death. Death marked the work's gestation and it would mark the work's reception. This seems altogether fitting: the song of the earth is after all a song of death, and life and death, death and re-birth, constitute our notion of what a cycle is. Mahler's song-cycle dies with "*ewig*" on its lips and leaves us rattled with paradoxical emotion. We hunger for resolution but it is denied us; we strain against the necessity of the end, but the end comes. To pinpoint the decisive moment would be impossible: we are not up for the task, and we imagine its arrival either too late or too soon. It is mysterious, the moment this beautiful dissonance slips into silence, like the moment the sun recedes from view — leaving the world strangely bright for a while, until suddenly it goes dark.

MIRON BIAŁOSZEWSKI
Gray Eminences of Rapture

Oh how I rejoice
    that you are sky and kaleidoscope
    that you have so many artificial stars
    that you glow in a monstrance of brightness,
        when I place your perforated
        half-globe
        over my eyes
        under the air.
    How unstrained in abundance,
    oh colander spoon!

The stove too is beautiful:
it has tiles and chinks,
it may be grizzled,
    silver,
        gray—even drowsy...
but especially when
it shuffles its glints
or as it sets
and through the whole rhythm of its imperfections
whitely poured
        in charred bells
it flows into elements
of monumental bedding.

This apartment can be inspired

the window's wing
I'm in my nook
my ears hum
weeds carried on Noah's line
in the painting, it's incomplete,
old brown greens fluttering
for three hundred years
and an angel's bent elbow

———————

what is this art
when centuries fly
interplanetarily
us knocking at our own doors
all will dissolve
still something calls for
a gesture
seeking
an angel's elbow

My Jacobs of Weariness

To Artur Sandauer

Higher
    reveilles of shape
        habitations of touch
    all weathers of the senses...

Lowest — I
    the staircase of reality
    rises from my breasts.

And I feel nothing.
Nothing succulent.
Nothing colorful.
    I'm not only not
    a testament hero
I'm worse than a flounder
    glued to the river's deathbed
    with bunched balloons of breath
    fleeing upwards
worse than a potato mother
    who sprouted vast antlers of roots
    herself wizened
    almost gone

Smite me
oh construction of my world!!

Self-Verified

    A chair stands:
    article of truth
    sculpture of itself
    tied into one knot
        reality's abstraction

    It broke.
    That's a form too
        yes — candelabra
        yes — bull's face.

    A chair's abstract calling
    now summons
    whole crowds of reality
    ties them in one knot
    inside the stockroom of truth
        reality's abstraction.

Nights of Inseparation

1. Night.
    The bridge's scent.
    The fence lets in roots.
    Water shines for the earth.
    A listening stone.
    A hair sings.

2. Night.
    Road.
    Your own knees lost in suppositions.
    There is no separate green.

    A different epoch of the hand,
    a different time of swaying.

    Moths and stars
    watch each other;
    they point crosswise
    to night's rims of horizons
    a glass jar.

3. Night.
    Now we all grow together, we rotate,
    potatoes people dogs roofs...
    Who's going? Who's breathing?
    You above me and farther up—

a branch, let's shake on it,
we won't tread on one another,
    oh my stony leg,
oh bark oh fish
speak say whatever...

you feel how our heart beats
    under scales under shells
oh, that anxiety
    let's get rid of it—
    we die together

Testimony of Sleep

Past the fences of beds
we are movie sheds
of sleep.

We can't stamp
or clap.

At best
we shriek in monkey speech,
our old dialect,
about the latest things.

And then we
truly live through
our own civilization.

Translated by Clare Cavanagh and Michał Rusinek

HELEN VENDLER

The Artless Art

The Lamb

      Little Lamb, who made thee?
       Dost thou know who made thee?
Gave thee life, and bid thee feed
By the stream & o'er the mead,
Gave thee clothing of delight,
Softest clothing, wooly, bright,
Gave thee such a tender voice,
Making all the vales rejoice?
      Little Lamb, who made thee?
      Dost thou know who made thee?

>   Little Lamb, I'll tell thee,
>   Little Lamb, I'll tell thee;
>   He is callèd by thy name,
>   For he calls himself a Lamb.
>   He is meek, & he is mild,
>   He became a little child.
>   I a child, & thou a lamb,
>   We are callèd by his name.
>   Little Lamb, God bless thee!
>   Little Lamb, God bless thee!
>
>   WILLIAM BLAKE

Nothing is harder to comment on than a piece of art which successfully pretends to artlessness, to be "merely" transcribing what a voice utters — or seems to utter: in real life nobody actually converses in rhyme, but readers of rhymed or rhythmic poetry accept the pentameters of "To be or not to be" as Hamlet's "natural" way of speaking, just as audiences of opera accept the convention that whatever Rodolfo is "saying" to Mimi will be conveyed in song. In the rhyming lines of William Blake's "The Lamb," we hear a single voice speaking, in rhyme; there is no narrator, no editorial comment, no concluding summary. And no self-revelation by the artist-author.

Although Blake was fiercely concerned with politics, and within a few years was to write long poems called *The French Revolution* and *America,* his little illustrated booklet called (and I imitate the original typeface) SONGS *of Innocence,* which appeared in 1789, offered poems of a simplicity that was hailed then (and sometimes even now) as "pure," "childlike," "transparent," "sweet," and of course "innocent." The *Songs* utterly baffled me — as the productions of a grown man —

The Artless Art

when I first encountered them in high school, and I set them aside in favor of any poem (from Milton's "Nativity Ode" to Keats's "Ode on a Grecian Urn") which seemed properly and deeply reflective in thought and language. (Poems are meant, said Stevens, "to help us live our lives," and in high school that was what I wanted from them.)

Later I decided, before even entering a doctoral program, that I wanted to write a dissertation on W. B. Yeats, but I knew that I had first to understand Blake. Yeats, in his twenties, had co-edited Blake's works, and derived from them aspects of his own theory of poetry. When I entered Harvard's graduate program, seeing that no course was addressing Blake in detail, I asked one of my professors to direct a semester-long "reading course" on Blake for me. Since he generously agreed, we met every week and read all of Blake's poetry. My teacher tolerated our initial pursuit, but when my later papers began to concern Blake's long "prophetic books" — mythological, obscure, and stormy fantasies about weirdly named people ("Oothoon") living in weirdly named places ("Golgonooza") — he groaned and said, "Helen, the *awful* things you are having me read!" But Yeats, following Blake's declaration that "I must Create a System or be enslav'd by another Man's," indeed developed his own erratic mythological system, called *A Vision,* and my (imperfect) absorption of Blake gave me an entrance to writing on it. (My dissertation on Yeats became my first book, and I am still grateful to that reluctant teacher.)

Blake's long poems, composed, like oratorios, of arias and choruses, are accompanied by his stunning but mysterious illustrations. (They may be found online in *The Blake Archive*.) They puzzled me, but I was still more puzzled by the ostentatious simplicity of "The Lamb" and other poems in his *Songs of*

Innocence. Was there more to this artless art than I could see? I had faith in the sincerity of Blake's promise to his readers in *Jerusalem*, composed between 1804 and 1820:

> I give you the end of a golden string,
> Only wind it into a ball,
> It will lead you in at Heaven's gate
> Built in Jerusalem's wall.

But how to find the golden string? An unforgettable lyric usually startles by some original feature, some conceptual or linguistic thread calling attention to itself. With intuition and investigation, the clue glows, the golden ball is wound up, and the poem assembles itself into an intelligible structure. But I could not find, for many years, any such golden string of entrance into "The Lamb."

Before introducing "The Lamb," and explaining my dissent from the usual readings, I must add something about the origin and form of Blake's two lyric sequences, *Songs of Innocence* and *Songs of Experience.* Even before he issued his engraved *Songs of Innocence* — with its appealing title page, elaborately designed, minutely populated, and beautifully colored — Blake had composed, as we know from his notebooks, dark poems, shocked and shocking, centered on female betrayal and male jealousy. In 1793, with *Songs of Innocence* completed, Blake published some of those despairing notebook poems with other lyrics in a collection called (I reproduce the text-format) SONGS *of* EXPERIENCE, emphasizing the difference from the earlier sequence by repudiating the italic font of *Innocence* in favor of roman for EXPERIENCE. He released only four copies of this booklet because he had changed his mind about the actual relation of the two sequences to each other. They should not, he realized, be presented as opposites but as complements. The following year — and ever after — he published the two sequences together, inextricably twinned in a single volume which bore an expansive and informative title page, cunningly expressive via the fonts ROMAN and *italic,* changing even the small introductory word "of" in its first two appearances to expose the contrast in the sequences: SONGS of *Innocence and Of Experience, Shewing the Two Contrary States of the Human Soul.* At the foot of the title page lie the prostrate figures of Adam and Eve wearing fig-leaves after their expulsion from Eden.

In spite of Blake's blunt assertion that his poems convey "the two contrary states of the human soul," readers persisted in identifying Innocence with Childhood and Experience with Adulthood, identifying the two "Contrary States" as successive life-periods rather than as fluctuating emotional and intellectual moods. If the two states of the human soul ("the" restricts them to only two) are recurrent from infancy to death, they might more accurately be designated Naïveté and Knowledge. They can in fact be two equally true renditions that allegorize a single event, as in, for example, the paired poems about the birth of a child, "Infant Joy" and "Infant Sorrow." In *Innocence,* under the title "Infant Joy," a young mother imagines a virtual dialogue with her newborn but as yet unbaptized child. "Infant Joy" could more properly be called "A Mother's Joy," since it describes her state of mind. The speechless infant (Latin *infans,* "unable to speak") seems to be requesting that the mother confer on it a pre-baptismal "human" name in lieu of the ecclesiastically required saint's name:

"I have no name:
I am but two days old."

The mother immediately responds, deferring to the baby's implied wish,

"What shall I call thee?"

The infant names itself (or, rather, the mother, once again, imagines what she would like to have the baby say):

"I happy am,
Joy is my name."

And the mother offers a hopeful prayer for her child:

"Sweet joy befall thee!"

The baby's "self-chosen" name, perhaps imagined by the mother (as Leo Damrosch suggests), as the capitalized female name "Joy," is thus made identical with its hoped-for fate (a lower-case "joy") and the elation of reciprocal exchange ("Joy" from the infant, "joy" from the mother) in the (imagined) dialogue begins to be felt.

The baby's original "self-chosen" adjective was "happy," and the mother in the second stanza, where dialogue ceases, provides the second of her own two adjectives (she has already uttered "sweet," necessarily true of the abstraction "Joy"). Now, gazing at the bodily form of her infant, she chooses "pretty," an aesthetic characterization, suitably small:

> "Pretty joy!
> Sweet joy but two days old,
> Sweet joy I call thee:
> Thou dost smile,
> I sing the while,
> Sweet joy befall thee!"

The young mother addresses her silent baby in Blakean baby-talk, cooing in repetition her "pretty" and "sweet," while recording the mutual and simultaneous happiness of mother and child. "I call thee sweet joy," says the mother, caroling a series of praises in her delusion that she understands what her baby is "saying" and that it understands what she is "saying back." It is actually her own upbrimming joy that the singing mother projects into the "smile" of her infant in this "innocent" ventriloquial, alliterating, and rhyming companionship: "Thou dost smile, / I sing the while."

By his conclusive title-page-twinning of *Innocence* and *Experience* in 1794, and by characterizing the two nouns as "Contrary States," Blake is embodying the law he had announced a year earlier in *The Marriage of Heaven and Hell*: "Without Contraries is no progression." He now asks himself to enlarge his perception by imagining a Contrary to maternal joy, expanding from Joy to Sorrow as he holds contrary moods in his mind at the same moment. While the fond mother is preparing her soul to dote on her child, what must be the state of soul of the actual newborn infant?

"Infant Sorrow," the baleful song of *Experience* corresponding to "Infant Joy," is an enraged monologue from the infant as he (who is ungendered in the poem; I use "he" for convenience) recapitulates the ignominy of his birth. With three paralleled verbs ("groan," "weep" and "leap") he fuses his tortured and unarmed birth-leap into dangerous Infant-Experience with the simultaneous dismal fall into Parent-Experience of his appalled mother and father. He pipes his birth-cry as his mother groans in agony and his father bursts into tears:

> My mother groan'd! my father wept,
> Into the dangerous world I leapt:
> Helpless, naked, piping loud,
> Like a fiend hid in a cloud.

Who is thinking that the baby, with its unintelligible scream, is arriving like a monstrous "fiend hid in a cloud?" Its mother, of course, as we know from Blake's draft of a different poem, "A Little Boy Lost," in which a child — a truthteller like Lear's Cordelia — says that it cannot love its parents more than itself. Hearing that reasonable assertion, the mother cries out in revulsion, "O that I such a fiend should bear!" (That Blake ultimately transfers the word "fiend" to a sadistic priest who burns the baby alive in "a holy place" does not erase, from the mind of the modern reader who knows the draft, Blake's initial impulse to let the demonic epithet emerge from the mother.)

Just as he had "channeled" in "Infant Joy" the young mother's delusion that she and the baby are in dialogue, so, as he continues "Infant Sorrow," Blake "channels" the resentful baby's angry thoughts as he announces the elements of his state, binding them by alliteration — he struggles, strives, and sulks:

> Struggling in my father's hands,
> Striving against my swaddling bands,
> Bound and weary I thought best
> To sulk upon my mother's breast.

The Artless Art

Although the infant writhes to escape the constraints of both nature (his father's grip) and culture (the binding swaddling bands), he finds himself helpless, and sinks back, with no "Infant Joy" at all, to sulk upon his mother's breast. And since Joy and Sorrow are two contrary states of the human soul, the allegorized Joy (in a mother) and Sorrow (in an infant) can arrive simultaneously on the poet's page. The mother's idea of the joyous internal state of her baby is pathetically naïve, while the baby's infernal idea of itself — from its first horrible Experience — is entirely credible.

It must not be forgotten, in reading such songs as "Infant Joy" and "The Lamb," that every single poem in *Songs of Innocence* has been written by an adult being who knows exactly what Experience always brings. The reader's consciousness of the concealed adult author of *Innocence* must figure in any account of Blake's art in the artlessness of "The Lamb." I differ from earlier readers in believing that the poem "The Lamb" is — when we look at its companion poem in *Experience,* "The Tyger" — composed by the author-as-Tyger looking back with pity, on its deluded childhood state. The Tyger, accustomed in his early life to being a docile Lamb, has suddenly awakened in a wholly unfamiliar body, burning with the inner flame of appetite and armed with teeth and claws. We must see the nature of the child-speaker through the Tyger's lens, because we too are Experienced (as well as perpetually Innocent), passing constantly, in each episode of life, from Ignorance to Knowledge, from naïveté to awareness. Throughout our life, if we do not refuse perception of our soul-states, we continue to undergo successive falls into Experience. In Blake's long poem *Vala,* one character (speaking, we understand, for Blake himself) sums up the price of the soul's repeated passage from ignorance to awareness, from error to wisdom, from hope to desolation:

> What is the price of experience? do men buy it for
>   a song?
> Or wisdom for a dance in the street? No, it is
>   bought with the price
> Of all that a man hath, his wife, his children.
> Wisdom is sold in the desolate market where none
>   come to buy,
> And in the wither'd field where the farmer plows
>   for bread in vain.

What, then, are we to make of "The Lamb?" It was sometimes carelessly thought that Blake was speaking in his own voice to the Lamb, but the single line, "I a child, and thou a Lamb," establishes that Blake has created a fictional child, who speaks to an equally fictional Lamb. The two initial questions put to the Lamb by the child seem innocent enough, since they reproduce the first question in the Christian catechism as adapted for children: "Who made you?" (This calls up its answer, "God made me.") Any churchgoing Christian of Blake's day would recognize the child's Biblical allusions: from Psalm 23, "He maketh me to lie down in green pastures; he leadeth me beside the still waters"; and from Psalm 114, a metaphor of nature expressing lamb-like joy: "The mountains skipped like rams, and the little hills like lambs." There seems nothing here to "interpret," once one recognizes the Christian references echoed by the churchgoing child-speaker: he knows that God made the Lamb; that

John the Baptist called Jesus "the Lamb of God" and that Jesus applied the epithet to himself; that God (as Jesus) became a "little child"; and that Jesus said "Learn of me, because I am meek and lowly of heart." The Christian reader would also know that the child has sung Charles Wesley's two hymns for children (published in 1742): "Gentle Jesus, meek and mild, / Look on me, a little child," and "Lamb of God, I look to thee; / Thou shalt my example be; / Thou art gentle, meek and mild, / Thou wast once a little child." It seems that the child is now charmingly conveying his religious knowledge to a "little lamb," met in the meadow. The invisible author of the poem is presumably delighting in his vignette of a young child as innocent "teacher."

The child makes his first departure from religious echo-paraphrase into unconscious originality as his attention turns — with no feeling of impropriety — from received doctrine to his bodily senses of touch and vision. Lambs in the meadow are to him huggable pets, and as he recalls embracing them, he imagines a God who has bestowed on the Lamb his unBiblical "softest clothing, wooly, bright." In fact, Blake reproduces the "hug" in *Innocence* via the poem called "Spring," in which the child-speaker converses (in wholly sensuous terms) with a Lamb: the child has not yet been brought under the Vicar's indoctrination.

> Little Lamb
> Here I am,
> Come and lick
> My white neck.
> Let me pull
> Your soft Wool.
> Let me kiss
> Your soft face.

I propose that Blake knowingly composed "The Lamb" as an ironic text. Because the poem has a child-speaker, Blake has decided on stylistic simplicity in its stanza form, rhyming, rhythm, vocabulary, grammar, syntax, and two-stanza structure. Critics have had very little to say, therefore, about "The Lamb," preferring by far to expatiate upon its paired *Experience* poem, "The Tyger."

> Tyger! Tyger! burning bright
> In the forests of the night,
> What immortal hand or eye
> Could frame thy fearful symmetry?

The speakers of the two poems seem like wholly different personages, and the animals they address could hardly be less alike: the child-speaker of "The Lamb" seems to have fellow-feeling for the Lamb, while the speaker of "The Tyger" is terrified by the predator that has appeared before him. The Creator of the beast is imagined as an immortal and inscrutable artist, using both physical force ("hand") and conceptual design ("eye") to inaugurate an unprecedented visual symmetry, not the familiar symmetry of beauty but one of fright and fear. Since selections in anthologies have reinforced the notion that Blake composed *Innocence* about childhood and *Experience* about adulthood, the "paired poems" of the two sequences are examined for difference rather than for resemblance. Yet one must arrive at some view considering the Lamb and the Tyger as Contrary States rather than Opposite Animals.

An ironic reading of "The Lamb" arises from our scrutinizing the little drama between child and lamb. Under what circumstances did the child learn the truths that he is teaching the lamb? We deduce that the child has just begun attending the lessons in Christian belief offered to the youngest children of the Infant Class at Sunday School. On the child's first day, the Vicar has humiliated the newcomer by omitting any kind of welcome such as "Little Child, I greet thee, / Little Child, I greet thee", which would match his closing "professional" dismissal: "Little Lamb, God bless thee! / Little Lamb, God bless thee!" Instead the Vicar situates his little student at a disadvantage by putting to him the first question in the catechism — "Who made thee?" — to which the child, not knowing the answer and feeling ignorant, remains dumb. Refusing to reveal the correct answer, the Vicar once again exhibits the child's vacancy of mind, insisting a second time on the question, this time revealing the child's lack of knowledge: "Dost thou know who made thee?" The child hangs his head in embarrassment. Having established the child's inferiority, the Vicar finally, in the second stanza, offers the missing answer. "Little child, I'll tell thee," he says, then grandly repeats his intention with "Little child, I'll tell thee," implicitly boasting of his own superior knowledge and demonstrating the child's earlier inadequacy of response.

We find ourselves asking, as we think about the poem, why the child has chosen to address a lamb, but as soon as we raise the question, we realize that every local child who has preceded Blake's child in the Infant Class surely knows the answer to the opening question, so that for the child the only available creature younger and more ignorant than himself is the Lamb. The whole drama now presents itself to us as a role-playing drama arranged by the child, in which he is playing the Vicar and the Lamb is cast as his own first-day self. When he, imitating the Vicar, poses the question in its variant form as a determiner of the child's cognitive capacity — "Dost thou know who made thee?" — the Lamb is helplessly silent (as the child himself had been). The Lamb, questioned, is satisfactorily speechless, and now the child, addressing the "ignorant" Lamb, can take on, in the second stanza, the satisfactory (if evil) role of the twice triumphant Vicar: "Little Lamb, I'll tell thee, / Little Lamb, I'll tell thee."

The Vicar, as we deduce from the poem's reflection of his Infant-Class teaching, has been carefully selecting and sanitizing the portions of Christian belief purveyed to the child. The Vicar's lessons never mention the vengeful God of Isaiah and the Psalms, nor the violent Jesus who drives the moneychangers from the temple, nor why Jesus calls himself a Lamb (metaphorically anticipating the Passover when he will be slaughtered). In fact, although the child has been told the Christmas story ("He became a little child"), the tragic story of the Passion and Crucifixion remains concealed from him, as does the divine virtue of violence in moral condemnation, defamation, or exclusion.

When a child hurting from a visit to the dentist replays the visit with a younger child, the former victim must become of course the pain-inflicting dentist: the whole point of the role-playing is for the child to reverse the roles, to take on the triumph of the victor and thereby triumph over his past passivity. We become spectators of the child's "innocent" sadism as he humiliates the Lamb (thereby revealing the way in which he was himself humiliated by the Vicar). And our heart sinks at how much the child will ultimately have to learn about the life of Jesus—above all, the harsh tragedy of the Crucifixion. The implicit cruelty of the child, as, unaware of his own ignorance, he complacently and proudly dominates the Lamb, represents his first step into Experience as he (by design) defeats the hapless Lamb, his ideal (because language-less) victim.

Even before composing "The Lamb," Blake understood

that there never has been, nor could there ever be, a time of entire and sinless Innocence. In a marginal inscription in the manuscript of *The Four Zoas* (never illustrated, never published) he writes:

> Unorganized Innocence, An Impossibility.
> Innocence dwells with Wisdom but never with Ignorance.

The animal Blake chose as the contrary to the "innocent" Lamb is the Tyger. And the poem, in its short-form lyric drama, recounts, in my view of it, the frightening passage into Experience as the (male) adolescent undergoes it. The little child, formerly clothed in the soft white garment of the docile Lamb, wakes up overnight to sexual power and aggressive physicality as he discovers himself metamorphosed, with no warning, into a Tyger. He has become a predator whose substance is flame and whose habitation is darkness. Apprehensive questions, as rhythmic as the anvil-strokes of the Maker at the forge, burst out of the adolescent as he becomes the protesting witness of his own overnight transformation — by some unseen and apparently malevolent agent — into an unrecognizable and "evil" creature.

This Beast is the result of a Blakean seventh day of Creation. God has already said, "Let us make man in our image, after our likeness." And since a man was indeed created in the image and likeness of God, according to Genesis, can it be that the Tyger is another image and likeness of the divine? And since God has pronounced his creations good, did he smile in approbation as he contemplated his creature of savage strength, the Tyger? The angelic Stars, seeing the Tyger, regard its creation as a catastrophe, because it reveals that human erotic desire and human lust for aggression must be understood as aspects of God: "Did he smile his work to see? / Did he who made the Lamb make thee?" Later, in his illustrations to the book of Job, Blake gives his definitive answer to the adolescent's frightened speculation. The divine "voice out of the whirlwind" represents himself to Job as the creator of two monsters, Behemoth and Leviathan, praising their nature and their powers. In Blake's engraving, the Behemoth of land and the Leviathan of sea, both magnificently hideous, share a single design: inside a circle, Behemoth stands above on land and Leviathan twists below in the sea. The design bears as its subscribed title God's own words to Job: "Behold now Behemoth, which I made with thee." "Did he who made the Lamb make thee?" Yes, the voice has implied, and he made you, Job, and with you Behemoth and Leviathan, the sacred monsters who are as holy as any other creature. "For everything that lives is holy, life delights in life, /Because the soul of sweet delight can never be defiled." With those two lines in his *America*, Blake entered his fundamental creed in 1783, even before he twinned *Innocence* with *Experience*.

The adolescent investigating the burning state of his soul knows, as he frames his questions to the Tyger, that there are two fires in nature: the celestial fire of the sun and the volcanic fire underground. Where did the maker find the molten raw material for the Tyger? "In what distant deeps" (of Hell) — and then he must extend the boundaries of the question to the alternative — "or [celestial] skies" — "burned the fire of thine eyes?" He answers his own question by admitting the need to search out the fire by ascent into the air: "On what wings dare he aspire?" The fire lives with God: the human soul would be incomplete without sexuality and aggression, lust and war;

otherwise the soul would find itself permanently arrested in the Contrary state, the naïveté of *Innocence*.

The mild appearance of the Tyger in Blake's engraving accompanying the poem has often been criticized, even mocked. But because this Tyger is an image and likeness of God, we must see him as one of the transfigured predators in "the Peaceable Kingdom" prophesied in Isaiah 11: 6-7, in which not only does the Wolf dwell with the Lamb, but the carnivores are transformed into herbivores:

> The wolf also shall dwell with the lamb, and the leopard shall lie down with the kid; and the calf and the young lion and the fatling together; and a little child shall lead them.... And the lion shall eat straw like the ox.

Blake had once thought (in "Night" in *Innocence*) that this transformation could take place seamlessly, in a final heavenly phase of the predators' existence: after the predators have massacred the herbivores, the "mild spirits" of the sheep inherit celestial new worlds. The celestial lion, weeping tears of gold, joins them there as the guardian of the sheepfold, who tells the lamb, that he, the lion, newly herbivorous, can follow him in grazing:

> "And now beside thee, bleating lamb,
> I can lie down and sleep;
> Or think on him who bore thy name,
> Graze after thee and weep.
> For, wash'd in life's river,
> My bright mane for ever
> Shall shine like the gold
> As I guard o'er the fold."

In this transcendent state of "Organized Innocence," Innocence is no longer ignorant and Experience is no longer destructive.

But Blake found no relief in castrating the Tyger (or the Lion) into a herbivore cohabiting with the Lamb. Instead, in the apocalyptic *Four Zoas*, he constructed a Last Judgment in which the roaring Lions regain all their strength. The ninth night has come, the grapes of wrath are being trampled, and the harvest grape-wagons are brought to the winepress by "ramping tygers" and "furious lions":

> Then Luvah stood before the Wine press; all his
> > fiery sons
> Brought up the loaded Waggons with shoutings;
> > ramping tygers play
> In the jingling traces; furious lions sound the song of joy
> To the golden wheels circling upon the pavement
> > of heaven, & all
> The Villages of Luvah ring.

Blake, without dismissing individual sexual emotions, aged into despair over collective evils. He declared Love to be the true religion of Jesus, and preached peace by the forgiveness of sins and the eternal brotherhood of man. He ended his last and longest "prophetic book," the *Jerusalem* of ninety-eight illuminated engravings, in visionary prophecy of a redeemed time. In its grand rhetoric, he has come farthest from the concise art and artlessness of *Innocence* and *Experience*.

Does it make any difference to represent "The Lamb" as a poem constituted by irony instead of by innocence? Yes, if it renders a truer account of Blake's representation of Innocence. If the art concealed by its artlessness enlarges our view of Blake's capacity for moral subtlety, then we may see, among his thousands of vigorous lines, more such subtleties. It is not until we have the two poems before us that we perceive the Lamb's four-beat verse-speech to be technically identical (as trochaic tetrameter rhyming couplets) to that of the Tyger, establishing their indivisible continuity of being. Only in the Vicar's word-for-word repeated formal "staging," opening and closing each stanza of "The Lamb" does the child imitate the Vicar's original words: "Little Child, who made thee?... Little Child, God bless thee!" (The child merely substitutes "Lamb" for the Vicar's "Child.") Only the lines reproducing the Vicar's "professional" speech are written in three-beat form: this is the Vicar's ungenerous rhetoric. But as soon as we move into the Lamb's hazy recollections of church-instruction, we see that he, by contrast, speaks in four-beat lines, ampler than those of the Vicar. The Lamb's utterances are "smooth," with "sweet" rhythms, even though their metrical signature of successive downbeats is not usually a mild music. The four-beat equally trochaic lines of "The Tyger," with their truculent "anvil-beats," reproduce the "grownup" form of the Lamb's four-beat mildness. We take no particular notice of the meter as we read, "Gave thee life, and bid thee feed / By the stream & o'er the mead"—but who could fail to notice the distortion of sentence-form and the hammering percussive questions in the heated, equally trochaic, downbeats of "The Tyger?

> What the hammer? What the chain,
> In what furnace was thy brain?
> What the anvil? What dread grasp
> Dare its deadly terrors clasp?

Keeping the same meter, Blake "acts out" for us the metamorphosis from placidity to terror as Innocence discovers itself mutating from ignorance into Experience.

The art of the artless tempts every artist: its "vitreous finish" (Heaney on Yeats) repels explanation of its effect. It can be childish (as in "The Lamb") or unbearable ("Those are pearls that were his eyes"). In music it is idyllic (the shepherd's pipe), in art confounding ("This is not a pipe" accompanying a pipe). It grounds theology ("I am that I am") and establishes morality ("Thou shalt not kill"). It can be the quintessence of sublimity: at the heavenly banquet Herbert's final words are "So I did sit and eat." It can have a deadpan humor: "What do you read, my lord?" "Words, words, words." But it is in tragedy that the art of artlessness reaches its greatest eloquence: Desdemona, dying, when asked "O, who hath done this deed?" replies, "Nobody — I myself." And the broken Lear, bending over the dead Cordelia, comes to the end of language:

> Thou'lt come no more.
> Never, never, never, never, never.

After an unbearable death, nothing comes to mind but Lear's five-word line.

CELESTE MARCUS

The Shape of a Question

A fragile creature that cannot be broken is confounding, and this juxtaposition of delicacy and strength renders it freakishly powerful. Isabelle Huppert is so constituted. This is evident from almost every one of the dizzying number of films in which she has appeared. Her aura is incongruously encased in an exceedingly slim frame. Animated by the whirling of an inhuman engine, she provokes awe, disgust, lust, and adoration. She has said that the art of acting requires a peculiar combination of passivity and power, and passive power is precisely what she exudes. It emanates from her with unmistakable and inexplicable force. Huppert is just over five feet tall, and thin in a way that would be grotesque if she were slightly taller. If you held her with your hands on each of her hips, pressing your thumbs down along the slope of her hip bones, you would feel as if you could break her in half. She would look you dead in the eyes and invite your violence.

It is impossible to identify which combination of her physical characteristics confers beauty — she is slightly too pretty to be plain and not by any conventional standard sexy enough to justify her undeniable physical magnetism. Huppert burns even when she is icy. She always does — every variation of her, in all of the hundreds of films and plays in which she has been serially reincarnated. Some believe that it is an actor's job to camouflage herself so that the person playing the part seeps entirely into the character and disappears. For some, that is what is meant by "acting." Huppert thinks otherwise. In all of her roles she is always also herself. This is especially remarkable because of her subtlety, her utter lack of interest in "pulling focus"; she is not always Isabelle Huppert in the way that Al Pacino is always Al Pacino and Vanessa Redgrave is always Vanessa Redgrave. She says that her filmography is a kind of autobiography, which is to say that she has been hundreds of women, and all of them are charged with her electricity, her passive power, her sex and heat and frigidity.

Annick Huppert, née Beau, gave birth to her fifth child on March 16, 1953 in Paris' sixteenth *arrondissement*. She and her husband, Raymond, named their baby Isabelle and raised her in Ville d'Avray, a suburb seven and a half miles from the center of Paris. (It is the setting of the movie *Les dimanches de Ville d'Avray,* which won the Oscar for best foreign film in 1963, as

Huppert proudly repeats.) Raymond was a Russian Jew who married a Catholic, and the Hupperts sent all their children to the St. Cloud Gymnasium, a Catholic school which Isabelle attended until she was sixteen years old. (Her parents married directly after the war. She has never spoken publicly about how her father made it through that catastrophe, or how being the daughter of a Jew who survived the Nazi occupation hardened, softened, or in any other way altered her.)

Encouraged by her mother to pursue a career in the arts, she enrolled at the Conservatory of Versailles, and then earned a BA in Russian Literature from the *Institut National des Langues et Civilisations Orientales* before studying at the *Conservatoire National Supérieur d'Art Dramatique* in Paris. Her teachers were Jean-Laurent Cochet and Antoine Vitez, who furnished French cinema with the next generation's Milky Way, producing stars such as Gérard Depardieu, Daniel Auteuil, Emmanuelle Béart, Fabrice Luchini, and of course Huppert. When asked what she learned at the conservatory, Huppert insists she learned nothing at all. She either never absorbed or willfully purged its teachings. She attended the school because it was where young people who wanted a career in theater and film taxied before takeoff. She and her peers took part in the ritual of knocking on the doors of directors they admired looking for work, a rite of passage among young theater students.

In this way she won her first film role in 1972. She achieved national recognition five years later as Pomme in *The Lacemaker*, a tragedy about a shy girl driven insane by her own timidity. For this part she won the BAFTA award for Most Promising Newcomer. Claude Chabrol, a director whose temperament and philosophy of cinema were preternaturally compatible with hers, cast her as his lead in *Violette Nozière* in

1978. If a director agrees to work with Huppert, he must be prepared to cede significant freedoms, since her film style is unique and immovable. She changes the ether of the movie. Chabrol didn't mind: her ether enriched his. The two would go on to make seven movies together. (He died in 2010 while their eighth collaboration was incubating.)

Violette Nozière recounts the true, gory tale of a Parisian murderess who, in 1933, poisoned both her parents and incensed all of France. She was the Lizzie Borden of the French *petit-bourgeois*, only without the acquittal. The film earned Huppert the first of her two best actress awards at Cannes, and is the earliest instance of a stereotypical Huppert part: severe, disturbing, mysterious, riveting, somewhat opaque, and deepened by a feral intelligence. Throughout the 1980s she worked with some of the greatest directors in the world, including Jean-Luc Godard (*Every Man for Himself,* 1980, and *Passion,* 1982), Joseph Losey (*La Truite,* 1982), Diane Kurys (*Entre Nous* 1983), Andrzej Wajda (*The Possessed,* 1988), and of course Claude Chabrol (*Une Affaire de femmes,* 1988).

Today Huppert is considered one of the greatest actresses alive, in both theater and film. A.O. Scott has called her the world's greatest actress, and in *The New York Times* list of "The 25 Greatest Actors of the 21st Century," published in 2020, Huppert came in second behind Denzel Washington. This status was secured over a long and frenetically busy career, but it was cemented most powerfully in 2001 by her unforgettable performance as Erika Kohut in Michael Haneke's *The Piano Teacher*. She played an emotionally stunted, self-mutilating pianist who lives in a small apartment with her monstrous mother. Erika, who has been capable of experiencing passion only through music, suddenly discovers to her horror that she has fallen in love with one of her students.

Driven by a ferocious appetite that she cannot constrain, she begs him to engage in sadomasochistic sex. His compliance and subsequent disgust are equally devastating to her. Early in the film she slices inside her own vagina with a razor blade; in the final scene, she plunges a kitchen knife into her shoulder while walking out of a performance hall. Her self-contempt is excruciating to witness.

2016 was the most impressive year of her film career to date. She received her first Oscar nomination for *Elle*, a movie about a rape victim who seeks out and seduces her rapist, and *L'Avenir*, a film about a middle-aged professor, was heralded as one of the best movies of the new century. The similarities between her characters in the two films have been noted, but the differences between them are profound and significant. In the public imagination Huppert is caricatured as a perverse exhibitionist. Michèle, the protagonist of *Elle*, is the kind of role that viewers assume she would choose to play because it is known that her characters are often weirdly sexed. But that is hardly what is most interesting about Huppert's character in *Elle*. Michèle is hypnotically complicated. We witness her struggle in every realm of life: as a mother, a daughter, a businesswoman, an erotic being, and a victim. That complexity is what drew Huppert to the role. But the role of Nathalie in *L'Avenir*, a professor attempting to make sense of her life after a series of personal and professional catastrophes, is equally Huppertian. She doesn't choose roles because they are edgy. Edginess is just another familiar category, but Huppert is not governed by familiar considerations. For her even the edge is too close to the center. Her art takes place on another plane.

Huppert's relationship to her medium is strange, and not only for the obvious reason that she often plays similarly discomfiting, unpleasant, and unusual people. She is doing something uncommon through acting, and whatever this strange project is it defies articulation. Huppert's belief in the limitations of language is mystical. It is symptomatic of a sophisticated lack of faith in human reason. She is impatient with ordinary human trust in language's communicative capabilities, and with the common intolerance for mystery that language is often enlisted to dispel. She thinks that human behavior is chronically incomprehensible, and she makes films which reflect such a conception. Her films do not tell their viewers how to interpret them. As she puts it, she makes movies "in the shape of a question, not in the shape of an answer." She vivifies characters without fully understanding them, and she chooses characters who thwart transparency and defy explanation. She is certainly uninterested in cultivating the kind of intelligibility that viewers crave in movies and people crave in life. Huppert does not harbor those cravings. She has remarked that "we always feel slightly misunderstood and misjudged in life. We should gain strength rather than weakness from it. I always feel misunderstood, and yet that is what I seek." She does not analyze her roles, she feeds herself into them, syncopating herself to their rhythms or mixing their rhythm with hers.

There are actors and directors and viewers for whom cinema offers the opportunity to present coherent narratives made up of legible characters who do the things they do for discernible reasons. Sometimes these reasons and the actions that they precipitate are morally reprehensible and sometimes they are morally sound. Sometimes they are both these things. Rarely are they wholly bewildering. For the kinds of actors and directors who make films which broadcast who is good and who is bad — and they are the sort whose products sell at the box office — the characters in their movies respond to stimuli the way people have been taught to think they ought to respond. "Cinematic" here means, among other things, comprehensible, transparent, even obvious. When horrible things happen to them, the characters get upset. When a character commits horrific crimes, the viewer knows why she does it and so does the character herself. Villains are unattractive unless it is made clear to the audience that they are somehow contrite, or at least victims themselves. A great actress is expected to know precisely why the character she plays so much as cocks an eyebrow, and to communicate this understanding to the audience so that the audience acquires the same knowledge, and learns, if not to like the character, then at least to understand her. Understanding is paramount. Bafflement, mystery, irrationality — all endemic to the human experience — are not seriously treated. One of the illusions upon which we have come to depend in film is that, as Jean Renoir imperishably instructed, everyone has his reasons.

But in life, far more often, no one does. That is Huppert's creed.

Consider the following vignettes from three of Huppert's most representative works.

From *Violette Nozière* (directed by Claude Chabrol, 1978):
Violette Nozière sits quietly at the kitchen table beside her balding father and watches him with thickly lined, unblinking eyes. He swallows all of the water mixed with his allotment of white powder, which she has told him and her mother the doctor prescribed for all three of them. She had brought the powder home in her purse, carefully encased in three paper

packages with one of their names on each. When his glass is empty she raises her own, which she has filled with milk to disguise the fact that it contains no powder, and downs its contents in one gulp. A trickle of white glimmers at the corner of her lip which she curls slightly while looking into her father's eyes. The red nail polish on the hand grasping the glass complements her deep lipstick and the auburn hair elegantly curled close to her head. She is out of place in the drab, cramped apartment with her dowdy father and mother. Violette replaces the glass on the table and, still unblinking, says that "It tastes better that way." He turns to his wife and instructs her to add milk to her concoction. "I don't like milk," she grimaces before drinking half her own glass. "Oh, it tastes horrible!" She crosses the length of the dining room in two strides, enters the small space which serves as a kitchen, and pours the remaining liquid in the sink. Violette watches with concentration but without apparent anxiety. Then she stands and yawns while her mother mutters over her shoulder, "I'll fetch the roast. It's overcooked."

Père Nozière rises shakily and tries to tell his daughter to go take a nap, but he cannot fully form the words. "My Vio.. My Viole..." he coughs, clutches the table and then falls backwards onto the floor, wheezing for breath. "What's the matter?" his wife shrieks, rushing towards him. She simultaneously stoops down and turns back towards her daughter. "Violette, stand up, your father is sick!" But almost immediately her own body begins to contort. She groans, exhales hoarsely, tries to pull herself up off the floor and then looks in horror at her daughter before gasping and falling between the table and the wall.

Violette waits for silence before kneeling beside her father to see if he is still breathing. She retches and rushes towards the bathroom to vomit, then stumbles back into the dining room, crouches over her mother's inert body and searches her pockets for the keys to the bureau in which her parents have hidden their savings. She finds it, walks with purpose to her parents' bedroom, unlocks the bureau and rummages through its contents. She finds the money, which she balls up in her fist. Then she walks back into the dining room, sits at the table set for three, pulls the baking pan with the overcooked roast towards herself, hacks off a large piece, and eats it with her fingers.

From *L'Avenir* (directed by Mia Hansen-Løve, 2016):
"*Salut!*" Nathalie calls to her husband while tossing her keys and her bag on the console near the front door. "Oof!" She walks swiftly to the couch, throws herself down, and swings her feet up onto the coffee table and her head back into the pillow. She has walked to and from work in heels. The walls and the upholstery of the small apartment are white, and the sun shines through the glass double doors which open onto the balcony and reflects gently off the lacquered wooden table. Husband and wife are both professors and their walls are lined with tightly packed books whose spines provide most of the color in the room. "I'm exhausted. Aren't you?" Her husband walks gingerly towards her from the kitchen, his face strangely grim.

"What is it? Why so down?" she asks him, still slumped against the cushions.

"Nathalie, I must tell you. I met someone."

"What do you mean?" she says, pulling her legs down and leaning towards him. Without changing her tone or expression, she asks, "And why tell me? Couldn't keep it a secret?"

"I'm moving in with her."

"What?" Her voice rises very slightly, and her eyes widen

but do not glimmer. He sits down across from her and looks at his feet and then over at his wife's face. "Are you sure?" she asks him, quietly but firmly.

"Yes, I'm sure."

"Has it been going on for a long time?"

"A while."

"A student?"

"Of course not."

"Who then?"

"You don't know her."

She pauses, looks away, and then mutters to herself, "I thought you'd love me forever... How stupid!" She stands and walks past him towards the kitchen.

"I'll always love you, Nathalie. You know it."

"Oh, stop it," she murmurs.

She spends the next morning grading papers on the balcony, but caps her pen and stands when she hears her husband come home. "Lunch is ready, just warm it up," she tells him. "You're not eating?" "Not here." Nathalie walks past him and out the door.

From *Elle* (directed by Paul Verhoeven, 2016):

A man in a black ski mask forced his way into Michèle's spacious high-ceilinged living room, threw her to the ground, ripped open her shirt, and raped her. He left his victim on the floor. A streak of blood covers the length of her left thigh. Fragments of glass and china are littered around her head, as she had pulled the tablecloth on which she had been eating to the floor while flailing to escape. A black and blue mark is rapidly materializing over her left eye. She sits up slowly, blank-faced, and dimly notices the debris beside her. She retrieves a broom and dustpan and sweeps the clanking shards up and into the trash. She strips, throws out the dress she had been wearing, and draws a bubble bath. In the tub blood rises to the surface and stains the bubbles above her groin.

She dries off and dresses, then orders sushi on the phone. "Some hamachi. Two pieces. What is a 'holiday roll'? ... Okay... Thank you."

Her son rings the doorbell and apologizes for being late. "How are you?" he asks.

"I'm ok."

"What's that?" He gestures towards the bruise above her eye.

"I fell riding my bike."

"That thing?" He nods at the bicycle.

"Yes."

"Looks like you never rode it."

"And you can see why," She replies, walking past him and into the dining room. "So, you've carefully avoided saying what this job is."

He admits he has just started an entry level job at McDonalds. "Mmm." She grunts, displeased but not surprised.

"I bought you a present," he tells her while rooting around in his bag. He hands her a framed photograph of himself with his arms around a very pregnant young woman. "It was all Josie's idea, really." Michèle tells him he looks very handsome and then hands back the frame. He places it on the end table. "Josie has all kinds of ideas about decorating."

"How much money do you want for the apartment?" she asks, abruptly.

"I didn't ask for money."

"Noooo, it was just me hearing voices."

"I planned to ask you for collateral, not money."

"And Josie's boyfriends? Any of them moving in, too?"

Startled, he drops the bit of sushi clenched between his

chopsticks onto his pants. "Shit! These were just cleaned!"

When she stands to retrieve a napkin from the cupboard, she moves the framed photograph that he has just given her behind a pair of candlesticks.

"That girl is clearly dysfunctional. You know nothing about her, except that she was raised in a commune of idiots who never bathe."

"An arts collective!"

"Why you? What's she after?"

"What could she be after? I have no money."

"I do!"

"What's with you today?"

She looks glumly at him while chewing. After he leaves she rifles through a drawer of tools and finds a small hammer. That night she holds it beside her on the pillow while she sleeps.

For the entirety of their respective films, each of these women torment viewers with their perplexing behavior. In *Violette Nozière*, after it has been discovered that she poisoned both her parents, a judge says to her, "I am trying to understand." And Violette replies, "There is nothing to understand." Neither Michèle nor Nathalie do anything like poison their parents, but both respond unpredictably, maddeningly, to the things that happen to them. And if similarly probed, both Michèle and Nathalie would have responded just as Violette did: "there's nothing to understand." Understanding is emphatically not the point.

Interviewers — who, like most of us, abhor ambiguity — routinely ask Huppert why her characters make the choices they make, assuming that an actor's job is to furnish her characters with motivations. If pressed, Huppert insists that bafflement was precisely her objective. She is not being coy. Her acting is devoid of psychological causation. She doesn't know why Violette poisoned her father and mother, or why Nathalie didn't scream at her husband when he announced that he was leaving her for another woman, or why Michèle pursues a sexual relationship with her rapist. And Violette, Nathalie, and Michèle do not understand themselves any better than Huppert does. They are in this way exactly like ordinary human beings.

Another subject about which Huppert is regularly asked is her "process," since it is assumed that playing complex, emotionally taxing parts requires research, or preparatory rituals, or a litany of exercises. "Did you study the character's profession?" "Did you read scholarly historical works about the period?" "Did you talk to the director about your character and did you together decide *why* she behaves as she does?" Huppert has been peppered with these and analogous questions in virtually every interview she has done since *Violette Noziere*. She has been explaining for just as long that these questions evince a total misunderstanding of how she approaches film. For one thing, her relationship with a director is the most essential element of every movie she makes: she picks her movies on the basis of who is directing them, and she never talks to the directors about her character. In fact, the two directors with whom she has enjoyed working most, Claude Chabrol and Paul Verhoeven, said nothing to her while she was in front of the camera. Their communication was all non-verbal:

> [Verhoeven and Chabrol] never said anything verbally. But there are different ways to communicate between

a director and an actress. Cinema is a language in itself and it is certainly more powerful than anything that can be communicated verbally. I think there was direction but it was all about the *mise en scène* and the camera movements and camera frames and that language was strong enough and eloquent enough that we didn't have to go through the usual explanations. I think that all questions are indiscreet for a director and I expect a different kind of answer so it doesn't bother me if Paul [or Claude] didn't ever say a word to me.

Enveloping herself in the *mise-en-scéne* of the role is entirely how she readies for it. "I don't do any research." "There is no preparation." "When you decide to do a role, something starts to grow within you."

Once she has committed to do a part, Huppert's process is "very technical," by which she means it is tactile. Among the most important elements are wardrobe and hair and make-up. Costume envelopes her in this new person's weather. They help Huppert to decide "how she's going to move, how she's going to walk," and facilitate a kind of chemical reaction. She "clicks chemically," and she does "it more by intuition than reflection." This strange alchemy creates a new person, an admixture of Huppert and her character, which is among the reasons that Huppert always feels so startlingly present, so immediate, on screen. "[This is] the only way to make [the character] live, which is the ultimate goal. To make it close to life, to the truth, and the only way to be close to life is to impose yourself." There is no mediation between her and the roles that she plays. No inner program, no "method," comes between Huppert and her character.

It was determined at some moment in recent history that the swiftest way of communicating Isabelle Huppert's prestige to American audiences was to christen her "the French Meryl Streep." Insofar as both women command, in their respective countries, an almost religious reverence, the analogy is useful. It is also misleading: Streep's and Huppert's conceptions of acting are diametrically opposed. There is no more fruitful exercise for grasping the demands that Huppert makes of her audiences than to compare her approach to film acting with Streep's.

In a documentary about the production of *Kramer vs. Kramer* that was released in 2001, twenty-two years after the movie it considers, Streep commented that "if there's anything that runs through all my work, all my characters, it's that I have a relationship with them where I feel I have to defend them." (Is there a less Huppertian sentiment?) Joanna Kramer, the part which won Streep her first Oscar, was Streep's personal cause from the moment that she auditioned for the role. She had read the novel on which the film was based to prepare for her audition — research! — and believed that in the book Joanna was presented as "an ogre, a princess, an ass." When Dustin Hoffman asked Streep at her audition what she thought of the story, she hectored that they had gotten the character all wrong: "Her reasons for leaving Ted are too hazy. We should understand why she comes back for custody. When she gives up Billy in the final scene, it should be for the boy's sake, not hers. Joanna isn't a villain; she's a reflection of a real struggle that women are going through across the country and the audiences should feel sympathy for her." Huppert, of course, is totally uninterested in garnering sympathy from her audiences. She scoffs: "I don't really bother with the idea that a character should be 'sympathetic'; you know it's not really my problem... It's true that I believe in the power of cinema to make a character attractive [but] without being sentimental or without being too much explained." *Kramer vs. Kramer* could not sustain such a character. It belongs to a different genre of film.

The movie is based on a book whose author, Avery Corman, had written it for the stated purpose of rebutting the "toxic rhetoric" that feminists had been unleashing on men, whom he felt were collectively painted as "a whole bunch of bad guys." Streep considered it her responsibility to give feminists a voice in a movie-length anti-feminist diatribe. She got her chance. During shooting one day, the director pulled her aside and asked if she would rewrite the speech that Joanna gives in the final court scene. This was the opportunity Streep had been hoping for: "I thought [Joanna] was a rat in a maze, you know she had no choice, sick people often don't have a choice, and I thought she was mentally ill, depressed, out of control... I knew I had the chance at the end to come back and explain who this terribly imploded person was." Without that speech, the whole movie would have been a meditation on Ted Kramer's admirable development as a father. Joanna would barely have been in the movie at all, and viewers would have seen nothing of her as a mother. Feminism was on trial, and Streep took the stand to fight for it. This was acting as apologia, acting as politics.

Huppert would never have done that. She would never have auditioned for the part in the first place. An anti-feminist diatribe is not a movie in the shape of a question, it is a movie in the shape of an exclamation point, and it belongs on a protest sign at a rally, not on a screen in a movie theater. *Kramer vs. Kramer* takes place in a universe in which every

The Shape of a Question

character is campaigning to be the good guy. Huppert could never vivify a character like that:

> I never try to idealize a story or people. I like to show there is no clear border between the good and the bad… It's by instinct it's not a crusade. I'm not trying to defend anybody. It's just that I like to see myself as the audience by which I mean I don't like to be told lies. I never thought good feelings made good films, I can't act any other way. It's like a scorpion. A scorpion can do nothing but sting, and I can't act any differently than I do it.

It would be wrong to deduce that Huppert gives less of herself to her characters than Streep does. On the contrary, Huppert throws herself entirely into every breath that her characters take. Every gesture and every sigh is charged, but none are justified. If you grabbed her character by the shoulders in the middle of the movie, shook her and demanded that she explain herself, she would not be able to oblige with explanations. She would not understand herself well enough to do so.

And isn't that how life is actually lived? "There is nothing to understand." Logic is not an operating principle for the vast majority of the significant actions that human beings take. We have compulsions, and shames, and furies, and appetites, and we act on these things or we resist them. Those acts of surrender or resistance make up who we are. We are the records of what we do. Most of what is significant in human life is not intelligible, cannot be articulated through language or conceived of accurately in our own minds, and so cannot be lucidly grasped and then lucidly communicated. Actions can be accepted or reckoned with, or rejected, condemned, or argued with, but they cannot be thoroughly and satisfactorily understood.

Liberties

This incomprehensibility is a deeply troubling aspect of human existence, and one that we arrange to ignore because to recognize it would be paralyzing. We will never give up the delicious delusion of our own transparency. We constantly ask ourselves why the people we love or the people in power or the people across the street do the things they do. We must believe that they have a reason, and we must believe that we can grasp it. We ask ourselves this question so often that it requires no articulation — and the cleverer we are, the better we get at formulating answers which provide us with partial comprehension. This can be more dangerous than total confusion, since it blocks from view the parts of life that defy reason. There is always more to a person than can be rationally grasped. Huppert knows this, she regularly demonstrates it, and she forces audiences to reckon with it. This is why she is terrifying, and why we are drawn to her and repulsed by her. It is this quality which makes our skin crawl.

Trying to convey the fullness of life through language is like kissing instead of loving — something is exchanged but not remotely the desired good. Belief in the incommunicability of certain kinds of knowledge, belief in the existence of knowledge that cannot be commensurate with language, and comfort with those beliefs — all this carries us to the edge of mysticism. Bertrand Russell claimed that Wittgenstein was a mystic because he was happy to discover that there was knowledge that fell outside of language's purview. In his later introduction to the English translation of Wittgenstein's *Tractatus*, Russell wrote of its author: "totalities concerning which [he] holds that it is impossible to speak logically are nevertheless thought by him to exist, and are the subject-matter of his mysticism." Among those totalities are good and evil, which in Wittgenstein's view subsisted outside the realm of language. "If good or bad willing changes the world, it can only change the limits of the world, not the facts; not the things that can be expressed in language."

Suspicion of the power of language is destabilizing, and Huppert is destabilizing in precisely this way. Society, and all the artifices and etiquettes which regulate it, cannot survive this suspicion. A white-knuckled faith in the capacity to express all essential thoughts out loud in words is predicated on the belief that there is no essential knowledge which defies the capability of words. I do not see how such a faith can survive even a little experience in the world. Yet without it we are crippled by fear. This fear propels us to construct fictional universes in which everything of any importance can be verbalized. But "good" and "evil," squeezed into those four-letter words and safely separated by a coordinating conjunction, are not like this. Most treatments of those concepts defang rather than reckon with them. Huppert has those fangs, and she bites us with them. Look her dead in the eyes and invite her violence.

LEON WIESELTIER

The Rise of Narrative and The Fall of Persuasion

I

"We tell ourselves stories in order to live." This must be the most overly admired sentence by the most overly admired writer of our time. It is the renowned opening of Joan Didion's essay "The White Album," a canonical document of high-end alienation, and it long ago achieved fortune-cookie status. Didion was making the unsophisticated point that we abhor incoherence and so we attempt to defeat it by ordering it with interpretation. "We interpret what we see." Yes, yes. "We live entirely, especially if we are writers, by the imposition of a narrative line upon disparate images, by the 'ideas' with which we have learned to freeze the shifting phantasmagoria which is our actual experience." We certainly do, though this is still a long way from an interesting view of knowledge.

The problem, of course, is that the phantasmagoria keeps shifting. No sooner has Didion stabilized the mental situation than incoherence again rears its ugly head. It turns out that stories may not settle the matter. "I am talking here about a time when I began to doubt the premises of all the stories I had ever told myself, a common condition but one I found troubling. I suppose this period began around 1966 and ended around 1971." There follows her account, so adamantly cool as to be overheated, of the grand convulsions of the 1960s, which in her telling turns out to have been a lot of fun: she is in a recording studio with the Doors ("Manzarek ate a hard-boiled egg"), she hangs out with Eldridge Cleaver, she shops at I. Magnin for the dress ("Size 9 Petite") that Linda Kasabian will wear at her trial for the murder of Sharon Tate and the others at the house on Cielo Drive owned by Roman Polanski ("[he] and I are godparents to the same child"). She also goes to Hawaii a lot. Didion finds no meaning in any of this, only a vast disorientation, a senseless crack-up. "I believe this to be an authentically senseless chain of correspondences, but in the jingle-jangle morning of that summer it made as much sense as anything else did." Her are stories unlike other stories, because they are "stories without narrative."

But of course there is a narrative — "a script" — in Didion's annals of her adventures, which she, like all narrators, has composed according to a principle of selection, a criterion of significance, from among all the incidents of her life in that period. It is the conventional narrative, of which she was one of the primary authors, that the 1960s were history's epic pivot, that nothing since has ever been the same or will ever again be what it seems to be, that there never were phantasmagoria like those phantasmagoria, that the participants in those convulsions (and certainly their chroniclers) were aristocrats of consciousness, that the highest status is insiderhood and the chief arena of significance is the scene, that Dionysus is an American, that reason is for squares, that it is too late for liberalism, that the entertainment industry stands in some relationship to questions of ultimate importance, that we are living in (and driving through, with the wind in our hair) the ruins of our civilization — the whole helter-skelter-gimme-shelter narrative of the second half of the twentieth century in America. This, too, is a story, an invented version, a constructed tale; it is the tale of breakdown and privilege that Didion peddled, with epicene austerity, in all her writing. She made incoherence chic. Her contribution to the culture of her time was not to warn it about the seductions of story — as per her famous adage, if indeed it is a warning — but to invent a new story for it, a story of storylessness. She was not alone in this enterprise, obviously: her story is an old story. The fracture and fragmentation of experience is one of the cliches of modern culture, the failure of traditional narrative to capture a reality that has allegedly outstripped our powers of understanding and representation. She, too, told herself a story, a calming and fortifying story, in order to live. She, too, could not suffice with what a Muslim thinker once called the incoherence of the incoherence. Maybe nobody can.

"We tell ourselves stories in order to live." This is a practical view of narrative. We tell stories because we need them. We tell the ones that meet the need. Without them we could not stir, or in any way advance; we would be stranded in the inundation of random occurrences, in confusion and fear. And the stories that we tell about ourselves are ourselves; they create us, which is to say, we create us. The striking thing about this utilitarian view of narrative — and about the larger belief in the supremacy of narrative — is its indifference to the question of truth. Compare Didion's sentence with another famous one: "We possess art lest we perish of the truth." Nietzsche made that observation in 1888. It, too, is a practical recommendation, concerned more with the wounding psychological consequences of a perfect lucidity than with the actual substance of what we cannot bear to know. It is odd to hear Nietzsche speak of the truth, when it was he who gave the world "perspectivism" and degraded truth into an expression of power; but at least his formulation comes with the implication that it is indeed truth that may be too much for us, that truth is what we are evading when we accept the embroideries of narrative. We tell ourselves *lies* in order to live. Yet the alternative to truth that Nietzsche contemplates, the preference for a more pleasing and elevating standpoint, is not merely what used to be called, in Didion's California, a "coping mechanism." It is not a shelter for the weak but a value for the strong. He precedes his comment with this: "For a philosopher to say, 'the good and the beautiful are one,' is infamy; if he goes on to add, 'also the true,' one ought to thrash him. Truth is ugly." This enlarges and ennobles Nietzsche's point about the role of illusion in life. The mind in flight from truth is not seeking only to get by, to muddle through, to locate a haven, to get hip; it is ambitiously searching for a place in the heights — in beauty, which philosophically may be no less exalted than truth. As always, Nietzsche's subject is how to live. But who can live merely to tell stories in order to live?

    The narrativization of reality, the takeover of public and private discourse by story, hardly needs to be demonstrated. Storytelling is now itself a flourishing profession, a respectable career, a revered occupation. Organizations and institutes have vice-presidents for storytelling; the Ancient Mariner is a consultant. The narratorial imperative reaches to the highest levels of power: one commentator on contemporary politics has called this "the Scheherazade strategy." Reflecting on his first term in office, Barack Obama once remarked that "my biggest failure was not to tell a story," adding that "the nature of this office is to tell a story to the American people that gives them a sense of unity and purpose and optimism." In 2017, the *People's Daily* in Beijing, praising Xi Jinping as "the master storyteller," instructed its captive readers that "telling stories has been a common characteristic of celebrated statesmen and thinkers in China and beyond since ancient times, and it is a clear characteristic of General Secretary Xi Jinping's leadership style." (He hides his vivacity well.) Emmanuel Macron, who never tires of vividly recounting the past glories of France, was Paul Ricoeur's assistant at Nanterre when the philosopher was writing *Memory, History, Forgetting*, one of his grand defenses of narrative.

It is story time in the gardens of the West. What these days is not a story? We translate everything into narrative. I once heard a lecturer in philosophy teach his students "the story that Kant tells about reason." (Once upon a time, there was a manifold of perception...) I have my story, you have your story, we have our story — which is to say, we now regard the entirety of a life and the entirety of a society as a tale, though we may differ about the plot. In politics, a candidate must have a story; in business, a company and a product must have a story; in law, a lawyer and a client and a judge must have a story, until the "narrative turn" in the legal academy became so overwhelming that the study of law and literature became the study of law as literature. Perhaps as a recoil from quantitative social-scientific historiography, from the "cliometricians," or perhaps out of a more fundamental sense of inadequacy owed to what Henry James described in *The Sense of the Past*, his last and unfinished novel, as a desire for "evidence of a sort for which there had never been documents enough or for which documents mainly, however multiplied, would never be enough," the writing of history in our time has become increasingly a summons to the campfire, stories about the powerful and stories about the powerless, riots of color and charm, lively yarns about exemplary lives to serve as prooftexts for sermons about the way we live now, so that the satisfactions of reading history approach the satisfactions of reading fiction or journalism. (If journalism is the first draft of history, history sometimes seems like the second or third draft of journalism.) In journalism, the warm anecdote has replaced the cold fact in setting the tone for reportage, as even breaking news opens in the style that used to be called "feature writing." ("Jesus, 31, a wandering Galilean with soft eyes and a hard sense of purpose, could no longer stand the incessant clanging of the coins. He had walked this street many times before, but this time the large polished stones that formed the avenue outside the Temple felt different. He was a long way from the verdant banks of the harp-shaped lake in the north on whose peaceful waters he had recently strolled. Romans were everywhere.") War reporting has yielded substantially to war stories, which have the laudable effect of humanizing the faraway ordeals but do not leave the reader with a strategic or historical grasp of the conflicts. In medicine, cancer now has a "biography" and the gene has an "intimate history" and the cell has a "song"; all of these informative entertainments are the result of the enormous influence of the twinkling Oliver Sacks, who turned case studies into bewitching fables and made medicine safe for Robin Williams. How many readers of these romps through science can judge the methods and the findings that they deftly relate? But the American public likes to be put to bed with a story.

Twenty years ago Jerome Bruner, who had previously written an influential essay on "the narrative construction of reality," began a book called *Making Stories* this way: "Do we need another book about narrative, about stories, what they are and how they are used? We are so adept at narrative that it seems almost as natural as language itself. Our lives with stories start early and go on ceaselessly: no wonder we know how to deal with them. Do we really need a book about as anything as obvious as narrative?" And then he proceeded to deliver a thoughtful one. But the obvious, of course, can be the most recondite subject of all. Whether or not storytelling, or some kind of *fonction fabulatrice*, is one of our evolutionary traits, whether or not we are in our essence what has been called *homo narrans*, it is past time to point out that there are many ways to organize knowledge and to describe feelings, and that narrative is only one of them. However natural the impulse to narration seems, it needs to be de-naturalized, so that we may discover the particular distortions that it, like all arrangements of human experience, manifestly or latently conveys. What follows is a brief catalog of those distortions, or some of them, so as to suggest what may be the highest price that we are now paying for our addiction to stories.

The great challenge of the rush of experience is to make order out of it, to find some way to bring its endless welter under mental control by giving it form. Our lives are shapeless until we decide to do something about it. The most common method of unifying the bedlam of sensations and relations and occasions is to translate it into narrative. For every life many narratives are possible — many lines can be run through it, and many threads; we choose the one that we prefer, usually on unexamined grounds, and we give it our names. Some professors call this "self-fashioning." The stories that we choose need not be simple, but they must be intelligible. They need not be linear, but they must show a pattern, and the pattern must show movement. The storification of a life, or of anything, is an account of how it went from here to there. Storytelling, by means of memory or imagination, is a shaping exercise. For this reason it leaves us confident and even consoled. (The wise Frank Kermode used to speak of "the consoling plot.")

But how many years does one have to live before one recognizes the specious nature of this confidence, and of the clarity upon which it purports to be based? Every shaping exercise is an editing exercise; stories are created by what they leave out as much as by what they leave in. (In some instances the omissions can be responsible for cruelty, symbolic or real, toward the excluded.) There is no such thing as the whole story, or the story of the whole; there are only the products of selectivity. The transparency about experience to which stories aspire is a deceiving ideal. Unlike stories, experience does not possess a beginning, a middle, and end, except of course the end that abruptly terminates it all; and many religious traditions have been spun to make the end of endings, the final ending, itself into an episode in a narrative, posthumously within reach of coherence and continuity. The notion of the immortality of the soul represents a spectacularly stubborn commitment to narrative form.

Moreover, the temporal structure that a story imposes upon experience can interfere with, well, the experience of experience. The forward propulsion of narrative, its controlling structure, does not adequately capture the way moments and hours and days are actually lived. If verisimilitude of some kind is the aim of narrative representation, we should beware the total erasure of the commonplace chaos. A story is an exchange of the here and the now with the there and the then. It is a displacement, a means of transport; it abolishes time and place to create another time and another place; and it traps the present between the past and the future, and encourages us to regard the present developmentally, historically, as a stage and a station. In this way it flattens and diminishes the present even as it sets it within a framework of meaning.

But historical meaning is hardly the only meaning there is. The present deserves to be protected against the hastenings of narrativity. It may be ephemeral, but it may be beautiful. Precisely because it will soon slip away and become the past, the present should be lingered in, prepared for, relished, cultivated. It is the most vulnerable temporal mode of all, not least to contemporary busyness, to the frantic blur of our efficient existences, which were conceived in part to save us from the sensual and spiritual challenges of a particular moment in a particular setting, of finding what we seek where we happen to be found. Pleasure, for instance, happens only in the present. For the way we live now, however, there may be nothing more impossible than a non-utilitarian and non-historical understanding of the immediate.

And who believes, really, that we heroically fashion ourselves? Indeed, there is something positively unheroic about identity. Surely it is more plausible to think of the self as an inflection of its givens, a revision of its inheritances. The inflection may be radical and the revision may be heterodox;

but much can be accomplished without the silly conceit of self-creation. We do not begin in emptiness, though if we are not careful we may end in it. The eighteenth-century English poet erred: we are never, at any moment in our lives, wholly originals or wholly copies. I am always more than the story I tell about myself, and always less. The story that I tell you about me may be a fabrication; I may be posing as me, not least for the rewards of the tale. No man is the final authority on himself. And no man is an inevitability. The élan of narrative, the assurance of the storytelling spirit, confers an impression of inexorability upon what it recounts, which is one of the reasons that children like to hear the same story over and over. They enjoy the foreknowledge, the ceremonial disappearance of uncertainty. But adults, too, are not immune to the thrills of teleology. The appeal of both religion and science is owed in part to their power to make contingent lives feel like inevitable outcomes, and thereby liberate people from accountability for their fates; and both religion and science, which have ideas at their core, are received by most people as stories.

Storytelling is designed to inculcate certain responses, certain mental stances, in the listener. They are passivity, credulity, and wonder. All of them are stances of surrender. A storyteller desires nothing so much as a rapt audience upon whom a spell may be cast; there is an element of mesmerism at work in narrative. "You could hear a pin drop." I have always been partial to that impudent pin. Wonder is an easily cheapened emotion; it is often the consequence of manipulation. In our time the greatest exponent of narrative and its magic is Salman Rushdie, whose novels have become so saturated in exotic conjurings that in other hands they would be decried as Orientalism. He refers to stories as "wonder tales." He sees in them nothing less than a mark of our species:

"We were born wanting food, shelter, love, song, and story." It is a somewhat arbitrary list, but his point is that "man alone is the storytelling animal." Never mind that there are also other pursuits and activities that are characteristic only of humans. About the universality of story there can be no doubt. Rushdie supplies a definition: "Story is the unnatural means [even if this is our very nature?] we use to talk about human life, our way of reaching the truth by making things up." I will return to the question of the relation of story to truth. Rushdie adds that "fantasy is not whimsy" and that "the fantastic is neither innocent nor escapist." But that is hardly the rule. Three cheers for whimsy! I am reminded of Walter Benjamin's remark that "anyone who has never been bored cannot be a storyteller."

Rushdie writes in praise of fairy tales and folk tales and myths, many of which certainly are repositories of wisdom and ingenious pedagogical tools, though this begs the question of how pertinent the message is to the form and its enjoyment. The justification of narrative should not be achieved by transforming stories into parables, by making them into allegories of "truth." Rushdie argues ardently for narrativity in part because it "is pretty much out of fashion these days," since "we live in an age of non-fiction." Clearly we see the cultural situation differently. He defends fabulism under the impact of his deep love for the stories of his childhood, which arouses in me an old suspicion that wonder tales are a technique of infantilization.

This set me to pondering the stories of my own childhood. I was not raised upon the infinite richness of the South Asian storybook, of course; nor did I grow up with Hans Christian Anderson or the Brothers Grimm. I never even read *The Phantom Tollbooth*. The wonder tales of my youth were the stories of the Hebrew Bible, except that we were emphatically discouraged from regarding them as stories. The record of God's words and the words of His prophets was not a storybook; it was a revelation of the truth. There was nothing playful about hearing it or reading it. Still, owing in large measure to the endless narratological imagination of the ancient rabbis, for whom the scriptural tales were exasperatingly elliptical and could not sate their appetite for the sacred past, we had many stories. I remember warmly, for example, the legend of Ashmedai. He was the lord of the demons. When King Solomon was building the Temple, he needed to find a rare insect (or bird) called the *shamir* in order to cut stones from the local quarry, since the Torah had explicitly prohibited the use of iron tools in the creation of the altar in the Tabernacle. The *shamir* had the strange power of splitting stone, and only Ashmedai knew where the *shamir* was. The king dispatched his chief warrior to capture the demon, and equipped him for the quest with a ring inscribed with God's true name. The warrior cleverly succeeded in his difficult mission and after a rather colorful journey brought Ashmedai to Solomon. Ashmedai divulged the location of the *shamir,* and it hewed and split the stones, and the Temple was built — but Solomon made the mistake of imprisoning the demon, who tricked him, the wisest king who ever lived, and contrived to take his place on the throne. Ashmedai sent Solomon into exile, where he wandered for three years in humble poverty and learned many lessons. (Those episodes now put me in mind of the *jataka* stories.) Eventually the king returned and routed the evil pretender, though the sight of the wrathful and defeated demon so terrified him that he never again slept a night without a company of guards.

 As a boy I kindled to all the extravagant details of the story. I even grasped the moral in some of its moments. When

I grew up, I learned that scholars call the demon Asmodeus, and that the main contours of the tale are in the apocrypha and the Babylonian Talmud, and that the tale was marvelously embellished in many ancient and medieval sources. (In kabbalistic legend, Ashmedai was the spawn of a night that King David spent with the roof-dancing she-demon daughter of Lilith!) I also discovered that the study of the tale pleased me more than the memory of the tale. I lost interest in child-like wonder because I am no longer a child. Adult wonder is another matter, to be sure, but it is as scarce as the *shamir*, and generally it has not been given to me, when it has been given to me, by stories. The ethos of storytelling prides itself on its primordiality: it harks back to earlier and therefore more authentic times — indeed, as Walter Benjamin put it in one of his many tributes to narrativity, it restores us to "the absolute power of the authentic." There is something brazenly anti-modern and pre-modern about the enterprise, a magical extension of the oral tradition, of the romance of the archaic. "Experience that is passed from one mouth to the next is the source from which all storytellers have drawn," Benjamin writes ruefully. I say ruefully, because he is certain that "the art of storytelling is dying out." It has been usurped by the novel — "the demise of storytelling in the rise of the novel" — in which narrative is mercilessly trapped inside a book.

Storytelling has also been overthrown by a "new form of communication," which Benjamin presciently calls "information." Information, he writes, "is valuable only for the moment in which it is new," whereas a story "does not use itself up." That is a very timely distinction. All this is in keeping with Benjamin's larger theory of the depletion of experience by modern capitalism, and also with the anti-bourgeois hunger of his Weimar generation for atavistic, non-rational, subterranean energies. A book, in his view, is not an experience, though he certainly lived as if it is. (His anger about the destruction of story leads him to cite Paul Valery's defense of patience and craft in his exquisite little essay "The Embroidery of Marie Monnier," a text that should be required reading now.) It is hard not to sympathize with Benjamin's scorn for the accelerations of modern life, even when it issues in philistine pronouncements such as this one: "We have even managed to abbreviate stories. We have witnessed the development of the 'short story,' which has withdrawn from the oral tradition and no longer allows for that slow accumulation of thin, translucent layers which offers the most fitting image of the process in which the perfect story is revealed through the stratification of numerous retellings."

There is, then, an anti-intellectual temper in the cult of story. Scheherazade is not particularly interested in explanation; credulity and wonder are not the states of mind most conducive to thought. The specificity of an event, which is the storyteller's strength, the savor of the particulars, defeats the generalizing impulse about human behavior that is the beginning of philosophical and historical reflection. A narrated sequence of events gives an impression of causality where causality has been invented, not confirmed: that is a part of its magic, of its storiness. The charm, or the fascination, or the horror, of a story lies in the subsequence and the succession of its incidents. Every story is definitive, but only for itself. Benjamin praises Leskov's stories for "the chaste brevity that eludes psychological analysis," so that even opacity of character counts as a virtue. The more folkloric, the better.

The advocates of storytelling always champion its relationship to wisdom, but wisdom is not the same as understanding, or explanation, or critical inquiry. Perhaps this is what

Benjamin inadvertently reveals when he writes, "we know only how to moan and complain, not how to tell stories." I am not suggesting, of course, that stories should be anything other than stories; only that their contribution to our comprehension of the world may be limited by their form. A story may be *a* world but it is never *the* world. And a story is not an analysis, just as you cannot tell a joke point by point. To be sure, the tyranny of analysis would be as partial and misleading as the tyranny of narrative, but we are not suffering from the tyranny of analysis. After all the paeans to the suspension of disbelief, it is time to say a few words on behalf of the suspension of belief.

II

The aesthetic and emotional satisfactions of narrativity should not delude us into accepting its techniques as the most useful or illuminating method for the exposition and the resolution of the problems that we face. If we tell ourselves stories in order to live, we also challenge stories in order to live. It is wonderful, therefore, to discover the beginnings of a backlash to what Peter Brooks has denounced as "the mindless valorization of storytelling." (His recent book, *Seduced by Story: The Use and Abuse of Narrative*, which meticulously exposes "the pervasive narrativism that dominates our culture," is the best backlash of all.) Some of the dissents are old, such as Lawrence Stone's castigation in 1979 of "the revival of narrative" in the writing of history. "The narration of a single incident or personality can make both good reading and good sense," he observed. "But this will be so only if the stories do not merely tell a striking but fundamentally irrelevant detail of some dramatic episode of riot or rape, or the life of some eccentric rogue or villain or mystic, but are selected for the light they can throw upon certain aspects of a past culture." There are realms, in other words, in which stories are not enough, in which they demand too little. There are questions that cannot be answered by a narrator, reliable or otherwise.

In legal discourse, it may be that narrativity is inalienable: aren't "fact patterns" stories? But in law, too, there have been dissenters. Martha Minow, who otherwise approves of narrativity as a method for advancing legal analysis, has some doubts. "Stories do not articulate principles likely to provide consistency in generalizations to guide future action," she warns, and her warning is good not only for law. She rightly adds that "stories on their own offer little guidance for evaluating competing stories." Should the criteria for such an evaluation be literary, then? But this is a narrative domain in which literary criteria are beside the point.

In law, the most formidable indictment of the limits of narrativity has been made, not surprisingly, by Catherine MacKinnon. Cautioning against the epistemological dead-end of *Rashomon* and its pile-up of versions, she asks: "Are all stories equal as long as they are stories?" She, too, is concerned about the deception that may be perpetrated by a calm recitation of a series of events: "Maybe only one thing *did* happen, just not the one we were told." MacKinnon recognizes what we might call the humanistic advantage of stories — "the breath of human life animates stories as it never did facts", and one of its effects is that "empathy is encouraged" — but there are inquiries (and not only legal ones) that require more than empathy, more than the sage recognition that everybody has their reasons.

Most importantly, MacKinnon makes the stark and unsentimental point that stories are inadequate as instruments of justice. "The form itself is certainly no guarantee of a view from the outside or the bottom." This goes against the grain of the present-day culture of justice-warrioring: a recent contribution to the progressive literature, for example, is entitled *We Need New Stories*. MacKinnon asserts that "storytelling as method originated in powerlessness and can bring a fear of power with it. Instead of telling power it is wrong, tell it a story." More, "storytelling can be a strategy for survival when one dare not argue." Anyway, "how do you counter the appeal of a story that power wants to believe? A story on the other side, of which there are many, has not been enough."

It may be that MacKinnon is too dismissive of the cultural basis for political change, but she is right that a story about politics or for politics must not be mistaken for politics itself. For MacKinnon, and here we come to the heart of the matter, the fatal weakness of narrative in the context of society and politics is that it may be false. "Lies are the ultimate risk of storytelling as method." Such a worry is undergirded by MacKinnon's splendid and militant belief in what has become perhaps the most contested idea of our time: that politics must be based on truth. Stories may have many winning qualities and still be rankly untrue. "Stories can be powerful, evocative, resonant, death-defyingly influential, yet cover up the most relevant possible facts." (Consider this dictum from the unlamented Sean Spicer in the White House press room: "I think we can sometimes disagree with the facts but our intention is never to lie to you.") The imagination may be necessary for a vision of justice, but there is nothing imaginary about injustice; and a vision of justice, which may be communicated unforgettably by stories, is not a remedy for injustice.

Rhetorically and methodologically, the antithesis of narrative is argument. I propose that the popularity of story in American life has something to do with the fact that we are living in a society that is beyond argument. I would even suggest that as the fortunes of narrative rise, the fortunes of argument fall. A society in flight from evidence and logic does well to seek shelter in the telling of tales. The proper methods of persuasion — reason and a skeptical examination of emotions — are too onerous for Americans now. An empiricist readiness for discovery, even the most rudimentary sort, is a bridge too far. The democratic torment that we commonly decry as "polarization" comes down to this: What do you do in a political order designed for persuasion when persuasion is no longer possible?

An open society is based upon the malleability of opinion, so that its members, when presented in good faith with information and argumentation that contradict what they believe, will change their beliefs; but behold, beliefs in America do not change. We are a republic of the unrevised and the unreconstructed. In the practice of politics, this petrification of belief has led to a conceptual innovation: the "persuadable," the coveted voter whose mind is not yet made up or whose made-up mind is still hospitable to new "input." There was a time, not too long ago, when the burning question for political strategists was whether to win with the base or the independents, whether to hunker down or reach out. But the prospects of reaching out are no longer very promising, and so the hunt is on for the unicorns that graze between the elephants and the donkeys, for the rare citizens in an environment of fevered partisanship who can still be convinced. Indeed, they may hold the honor of democracy in their hands.

But how to persuade the persuadable? Dare we reason? I

fear not. I will give an example. At a pastoral summertime gathering of people with ideas and people with money to pay to hear the ideas, there recently appeared a representative of an admirable national organization that was created in the belief that "growing partisan animosity is the crisis of our time" and therefore convenes meetings of people who disagree with each other for the purpose of recovering a common sense of humanity. It is an unimpeachable objective; when people have asked me what to do about polarization, I have always advised them to go out and make a friend of someone whose views they despise. But I have a nagging feeling that these breakthroughs in goodwill will not solve the problem but only dodge it, and also abrade some of the toughness that is required for serious politics. When the representative of this organization addressed the gathering, she said: "If you actively want to get to truth, the thing you have to build is trust, and the way you build trust is not by getting stuck on the conversation about what's true, but by making progress on the conversation about what's meaningful." I heard in her words a melancholy acknowledgement of the difficulty, and even the futility, of engaging in discussions about true and false and right and wrong.

As a practical matter, trust will certainly help, especially when it is founded on the realization that the apotheosis of trust occurs between people who are significantly different from one another. And yet I wondered whether this trust is not just a way of softening the blow of a contradiction that cannot be eliminated. One of the oldest techniques for treating the pain of contradiction is to stay away from the question of truth. And the preference for meaning over truth is really just the postponement of a reckoning, of the dreaded hour of verification. Listening to the good woman offer her approach to social harmony, and nodding in agreement that we should indeed wish "to get to truth," I pondered whether you can fight the contempt for truth with the suspension of truth, however temporary and tactical. My hunch is that those eclectic and compassionate conversations will never get to the work of argument, that the friendships sweetly coaxed out of the reds and the blues will be based on the avoidance of the substance of genuinely momentous disagreements. (As Lyle Lovett sang, "Baby, I just judge the distance, not the words I hear.") I was not surprised to learn, when I went to her group's website, that the first rule of its convenings is to "emphasize storytelling."

In politics, and in business too, the tension between story and belief goes almost unrecognized, and instead narrative is cheerfully included among the tools of persuasion. Here is a typical passage from one of the many books addressed to executives who are confronted with the problem of "convincing others when facts don't seem to matter": "All success, in life and in business, is based on the skill of persuasion. Put simply, you can have the best product, the best plan, the best policy, but if you're not telling your story in a way that connects and resonates with your audience, none of that matters. You will not persuade people to choose your company or follow your lead." It is all a question of narrative skill — an affair of rhetoric and theater. "What is more important," our executive coach asks, "having a good story to tell or telling your story well?" She does not deny that quality is an important factor in making the sale, but she grimly points out that "the best product [does] not always win in the marketplace." And so we must avail ourselves of the black arts of non-rational and not-factual influence.

But what kind of persuasion is accomplished by

Liberties

storytelling? I fear that many people confuse being moved with being convinced, and mistake susceptibility for a fair mind. Being moved, even by tragedy, is always welcome, especially by people who like to exercise their inwardness; but fictions, and tendentious depictions of human experience, can also be profoundly moving. The sophistry of emotional athleticism is no better than the sophistry of intellectual athleticism. I hope that you are shaken to your core by a visit to the Holocaust Museum, but I will not expect your visit to persuade you of my views about the Israeli-Palestinian conflict. The National Museum of African American History and Culture rattled me deeply, but I still do not concur that this country was founded in 1619. The stories in those institutions are overwhelming, but they are not the final word on their respective subjects or a sufficient foundation for political opinion and political consensus. Tears are not proofs. In the difficult task of distinguishing the true from the false, emotions should have no place, even if they will never be completely banished. One of the conditions of the mind's work is that it resist the heart, at least if it seeks a conclusion that will be acceptable to people with different minds and different hearts.

The problem of other hearts is just as decisive for the achievement of social agreement as the problem of other minds. I cannot expect you to agree with me because of what is in my heart. If you do not feel what I feel, there is nothing I can do about it — and there is nothing you can do about it either, which is why, in a dialogue in which it is my intention to convert you to my opinion, I will not offer my emotions as a reason for you to accept my thoughts. And if your refusal to accept my opinion is based on your feelings, then I must lower my expectations of our encounter: my feelings cannot

The Rise of Narrative and The Fall of Persuasion

refute your feelings, just as my story cannot refute your story, and at some point the discussion of our difference of opinion must arrive at the harsh business of refutation, especially if our difference is a contradiction and both of us cannot be right. Attempting to change somebody's mind by changing somebody's heart is the definition of demagoguery.

The most urgent question for our riven politics is how to proceed from contradiction — more specifically, whether compromise can be extracted from contradiction without a loss of intellectual integrity or a betrayal of group solidarity. The road from contradiction to compromise is Madison's road, the high road, the American road, and it is premised on the possibility of partial agreement, which is to say, on the possibility of mental flexibility. And here the problem becomes thornier. After all, "uncompromising" is also a term of praise. Compromise can denote weakness and infirmity. We sometimes admire mental inflexibility, since it signifies genuine conviction and strong belief. Shouldn't we hold strong beliefs? They are certainly preferable to drifting between worldviews as between brands, and to acquiescing to ideas that are in vogue. There is dignity in partisanship. The real task, then, is to hold strong beliefs undogmatically.

But how? Psychologists have for a long time recognized that — in the words of Lee Ross, Mark H. Hepper, and Michael Hubbard in 1975 — personal impressions and beliefs "become relatively autonomous from the evidence that created them." They call this problem "impression perseverance" or "belief perseverance" — perseverance beyond the reach of reasons, which is one of the symptoms of the death of persuasion. More recently the taxonomy of bias developed by Daniel Kahneman and Amos Tversky addressed the same perplexity. The classic study of this phenomenon appeared in 1956 in *When Prophecy*

Fails, an almost cinematically riveting account by Leon Festinger, Henry W. Riecken, and Stanley Schachter of a small community of millenarians in the American Midwest whose expectation that the world would end on December 21, 1954 did not come to pass, but whose disappointment did not damage or alter their orientation. Their experience of "disconfirmation" had the opposite effect: they simply chose another eschaton. Their mental framework was irrefutable. They stuck to the story.

The phenomenon of "disconfirmation" and the strategies of recovery from it is familiar to historians of religious and political messianism. One cannot base a faith on circumstances and keep it for long, since circumstances change. But one can keep a faith forever by insulating it from circumstances. There is nothing so wonderful as unfalsifiable encouragement. Like all victims of eschatological disappointment, the dejected adventists in Festinger's, Riecken's, and Schachter's account resolved to secure against history their belief about history. These are the opening words of the book:

> A man with a conviction is a hard man to change. Tell him you disagree and he turns away. Show him facts or figures and he questions your sources. Appeal to logic and he fails to see your point.

> We have all experienced the futility of trying to change a strong conviction, especially if the convinced person has some investment in his belief. We are familiar with the variety of ingenious defenses with which people protect their convictions, managing to keep them unscathed through the most devastating attacks.

But man's resourcefulness goes beyond simply protecting a belief. Suppose an individual believes something with his whole heart; suppose further that he has a commitment to this belief, that he has taken irrevocable actions because of it; finally, suppose that he is presented with evidence, unequivocal and undeniable, that his belief is wrong: what will happen? The individual will frequently emerge, not only unshaken, but even more convinced of the truth of his beliefs than ever before.

Out of this mental predicament, this refusal to be permanently disconfirmed, Festinger developed the concept of cognitive dissonance, which he introduced a year later. Cognitive dissonance is the mental pressure caused by a discrepancy between one's view of a situation and the situation itself. Insofar as this inner stress represents, at least in part, a concern for validation by the world beyond oneself, cognitive dissonance is a kind of tribute to the tenacity of the empirical attitude. It signifies that one has not been completely swallowed up by subjectivity, and that subjectivity has not been deemed to be adequate for establishing a sense of reality.

Cognitive dissonance, in other words, is the distressed state of awareness that precedes relief and reconciliation. What America needs now is a pandemic of cognitive dissonance. Everybody's story is too satisfying; everybody's view is too invulnerable. We need a season of wavering and wobbling, if we are to enjoy the rewards, and not just the costs, of strong conviction. As J.B.S. Haldane once said, "a little more thought and a little less belief."

There is a certain irony to the process of persuasion: one goes from being persuadable to being persuaded, and then from being persuaded to being unpersuadable. Once one is satisfied that something has been properly verified, one becomes mentally unavailable to further contributions to the subject. Out of the working of an open mind comes a closed mind. When one has been persuaded by evidence and by argument, dogmatism can seem rational. Yet we cannot be content with such a conclusion, and not only because dogmatism is the problem and not the solution. The process of persuasion does not usually work, alas, in a rational manner, as I have just described it. The unconvinced mind is not a vacant mind; it is already stocked with opinions which it asserts firmly even though it may not have justifications for them. The reasons for an opinion generally do not precede it. Contrary to rational procedure, they follow it. The American sense of reality is now marred by an overwhelming preponderance of opinions that are held in the absence of reasons.

Are we, then, to give up on reasons? Is narrative our best bet? I hope not, though there are grounds for gloom: the psychology of opinion-formation is not truth's most reliable ally. Instead we should take a closer look at what it means to hold strong beliefs undogmatically. We might begin, for example, by adjusting our standards for certainty. They should be higher than doubt but lower than dogma. The purpose of such a mitigation is not only to avoid the intellectual and political pitfalls of the absolutist mentality; it is also to acknowledge that the supply of evidence and argument never dries up, so that perfect certainty is never warranted. As long as there is life, there is surprise. The quest for inductive knowledge, for learning from the phenomenal world, is never over, because conditions change and there are new things under the sun; and rational discussion is never over, because in such a discussion a rigorous and well-wrought intervention is forever welcome. (That is why we still debate with Aristotle but not with Ptolemy.) In the sealed world of perfect certainty there are always the escape hatches of empiricism and reason, however small or hard to locate they are.

Intellectual honesty demands not only intellectual open-mindedness but also intellectual open-endedness, even when we are properly satisfied that we are on terrain sufficiently solid to allow us to proceed. Any belief that is thrown into crisis by the possibility that one day it may have to be revised is an overweening belief. This is true even of religious faith, if one cares about its intellectual integrity. Our politics, which is now a war between perfect certainties, must become a war between sufficient certainties; between strong believers, not true believers; and certainly not between reeds in the wind and the wind.

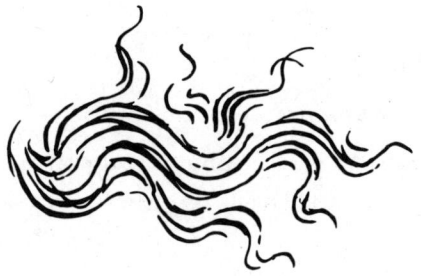

CONTRIBUTORS

ANITA SHAPIRA is an Israeli historian. She is the author, among other books, of *Ben Gurion: Father of Modern Israel* and *Israel: A History*.

OKSANA FOROSTYNA is a Ukrainian writer and Europe's Futures Fellow at the Institute for Human Sciences in Vienna.

CHRISTIAN LORENTZEN is a writer and critic based in Brooklyn.

ROBERT B. PIPPIN is the Evelyn Stefansson Nef Distinguished Service Professor for the Committee on Social Thought at the University of Chicago, and the author of *Filmed Thought: Cinema as Reflective Form*.

ALAN JENKINS' most recent book of poetry is *White Nights*.

JAMES MCAULEY is a contributor to the *Washington Post* and the author of the *House of Fragile Things: Jewish Art Collectors and The Fall of France*.

KENDA MUTONGI is a professor of history at MIT. She is the author, among other books, of *Matatu: A History of Popular Transportation in Nairobi*.

JACK GOLDSMITH teaches law at Harvard University.

MORTEN HØI JENSEN is the author of *A Difficult Death: The Life and Work of Jens Peter Jacobsen*.

CHAIM NACHMAN BIALIK (1873-1934) was one of the founders of modern Hebrew poetry.

WILLIAM DERESIEWICZ is a writer and critic, and the author most recently of *The End of Solitude: Selected Essays on Culture and Society*.

ADRIAN NATHAN WEST is a translator and the author of, among other books, *The Aesthetics of Degradation*.

ANNA BALLAN is a writer based in New York.

MIRON BIAŁOSZEWSKI was a Polish poet who died in 1983. These poems were translated by Clare Cavanagh and Michal Rusinek.

HELEN VENDLER's many books on poetry include *The Poetry of George Herbert, The Odes of John Keats,* and *Wallace Stevens: Words Chosen Out of Desire*.

CELESTE MARCUS is the managing editor of *Liberties*.

LEON WIESELTIER is the editor of *Liberties*.

Liberties — A Journal of Culture and Politics is available by annual subscription and by individual purchase from bookstores and online booksellers.

Annual subscriptions provide a discount from the individual cover price and include complete digital access to current and previous issues along with the printed version. Subscriptions can be ordered from libertiesjournal.com. Professional discounts for active military; faculty, students, and education administrators; government employees; those working in the not-for-profit sector. Gift subscriptions are also available at libertiesjournal.com.

Liberties Journal supports copyright. Copyright is a necessary engine of creativity, free speech, and culture. In honoring copyrights and buying this book, you support our writers and poets and allow us to continue to publish in print and online.

Liberties

As a matter of principle, *Liberties Journal* does not accept advertising or other funding sources that might influence our independence.

We look to our readers and those individuals and institutions that believe in our mission for contributions — large and small — to support this not-for-profit publication.

If you are interested in making a donation to *Liberties*, please contact Bill Reichblum, publisher, by email at bill@libertiesjournal.com or by phone: 202-891-7159.

Liberties — A Journal of Culture and Politics is distributed to booksellers in the United States by Publishers Group West; in Canada by Publishers Group Canada; and, internationally by Ingram Publisher Services International.

LIBERTIES, LIBERTIES: A JOURNAL OF CULTURE AND POLITICS, is published quarterly in Fall, Winter, Spring, and Summer by Liberties Journal Foundation.

ISBN ISBN 979-8-9854302-2-6
ISSN 2692-3904

Copyright 2023 by Liberties Journal Foundation

No part of this journal may be reproduced in any form or by any means without prior written consent of Liberties Journal Foundation.

ALL RIGHTS RESERVED

LIBERTIES, LIBERTIES: A JOURNAL OF CULTURE AND POLITICS and our Logo are trademarks and service marks of Liberties Journal Foundation.

Printed in Canada.

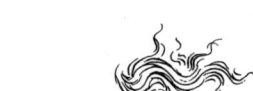

The insignia that appears throughout *Liberties* is derived from details in Botticelli's drawings for Dante's *Divine Comedy*, which were executed between 1480 and 1495.

Liberties